Gaming as Culture

Gaming as Culture

*Essays on Reality, Identity and
Experience in Fantasy Games*

Edited by J. Patrick Williams,
Sean Q. Hendricks *and*
W. Keith Winkler

McFarland & Company, Inc., Publishers
Jefferson, North Carolina, and London

LIBRARY OF CONGRESS CATALOGUING-IN-PUBLICATION DATA

Gaming as culture : essays on reality, identity, and experience in
  fantasy games / edited by J. Patrick Williams, Sean Q.
  Hendricks and W. Keith Winkler.
     p.   cm.
  Includes bibliographical references and index.

  ISBN-13: 978-0-7864-2436-8
  ISBN-10: 0-7864-2436-2
  (softcover : 50# alkaline paper) ∞

  1. Fantasy games — Social aspects.   2. Role playing — Social
aspects.   3. Leisure — Social aspects.   4. Popular culture.
I. Williams, J. Patrick, 1970–   II. Hendricks, Sean Q.
III. Winkler, W. Keith. IV. Title.
GV1469.6.G36   2006
793.93 — dc22   2006001521

British Library cataloguing data are available

Cover photograph ©2006 Brand X Pictures

Manufactured in the United States of America

McFarland & Company, Inc., Publishers
  Box 611, Jefferson, North Carolina 28640
    www.mcfarlandpub.com

ACKNOWLEDGMENTS

The idea for this book had been brewing in our individual minds for a long time, but was sparked to life by chance meetings at a series of Linguistics Program faculty and graduate student parties at the University of Georgia in the fall of 2003. There, we first met each other and began an on-going conversation about fantasy gaming and game studies. Over the course of only six months, we collectively turned our conversation into a book proposal and call for contributions. Bypassing all the drama associated with actually getting our ideas into print, the rest is history.

As with any book, many people are responsible for *Gaming as Culture*'s creation and evolution. As the editors of this collaborative project, we would like to collectively acknowledge and thank all the gamers— amateurs, professional, industry insiders, and anyone in between — who worked with us on this project or who served as the empirical ground upon which the research rests. We would like to also thank the contributors for their supportive spirits and their help in getting each chapter just right. Finally, we would like to extend special thanks to B. J. Ard for his dedicated work during the editing and proofreading stages, and to Ed Kick for his analytical help when the project first began.

TABLE OF CONTENTS

Introduction: Fantasy Games, Gaming Cultures, and Social Life

J. Patrick Williams, Sean Q. Hendricks, W. Keith Winkler

"Gamers ... don't play alone."
— King and Borland 2003:6

Approaching fantasy gaming as a cultural phenomenon is not a new idea. On the contrary, fantasy gaming has been understood primarily in cultural terms since table-top fantasy role-playing games emerged in the 1970s. Unfortunately, much of the attention fantasy gaming has received is one-sided: fantasy gamers have been characterized and caricatured in popular media as socially inept, psychologically unstable, or occultist. At the same time, however, there has been a steady growth of fantasy gamers over the last quarter century and a growing awareness and appreciation of fantasy in mainstream popular culture. Likewise, there is an emerging field of game studies called *ludology*, "the study of play" (Wolf and Perron 2003:11), from the Latin word *ludus*: play, game, sport or pastime. According to Frasca (Gamespot, N.d.), "A ludologist is somebody who wants to have a better understanding of games." Many researchers, however have limited their application of the term to a specific perspective within *video*game studies (e.g., Frasca 1999). In this book, we offer a corrective to this relatively narrow trajectory and offer insights into a wider range of studies on contemporary games and gaming culture.

Three changes in material culture over the past thirty years help explain the explosion of popular and academic interest in fantasy games. First are the new game genres, such as role-playing, collectible, and online video and computer games, whose markets have steadily grown in the past decade. Second, advances in information and communication technologies have facilitated the expansion of advertising about games as well as fostering communities in and around virtual game worlds. Third, the growth of fantasy gaming is witnessed and supported by the success of television programs and films based on fantasy and sci-fi (such as *Harry Potter*, *Star Wars*, and *The Lord of the Rings*). In short, what once could be strongly characterized as fantasy gaming subculture is now becoming distinctively less *sub*cultural, as the fields of role-playing games, fantasy and sci-fi literature and film, and video and computer games continue to dialectically shape one another (Mackay 2001).

In spite of the growth of fantasy games and gaming culture, there has been little systematic investigation of fantasy games in contemporary social life that attends to the cultural and constructionist dimensions of fantasy gaming as a leisure activity. This has remained true despite the assertion that fantasy "games provide a unique form of entertainment that novels, comic books, sports, movies, television or theater cannot replace or substitute for [and they] deserve further study in determining their unique place in our culture" (Lancaster 1994:78). Further, there are no research volumes that take the breadth of ludology into account. As an important step toward mapping out the boundaries of both fantasy games and ludology as they exist at the beginning of the 21st century, as well as moving beyond pejorative journalistic work on the topic, this book offers a collection of original research that investigates the relationship between fantasy games, players, and larger social processes from various social constructionist perspectives.[1]

Brief Descriptions and Histories of Fantasy Game Genres

So far, we have alluded to fantasy gaming as a relatively homogenous category without staking any specific claims to its boundaries. In fact, we see fantasy gaming as a fluid, unstable category that is somewhat difficult to map — it is made up of multiple genres of games and gaming subcultures that overlap in some ways, yet differ in others. We need to say something less ambiguous than this, however. Broadly speaking, fantasy gaming is grounded in shared worldviews, lifestyles, tastes, and affinities, as well as collectively-imagined selves/identities. That is, fantasy game players feel that they have something in common with other fantasy gamers. Fantasy gaming also involves the creation of virtual identities through which players interact with games and other players. These "virtual identities" (Gee

2003) can be realized through randomly generated sets of numbers, special decks of cards, or even three-dimensional digital avatars. Gaming in this sense does not include traditional mainstream games such as chess, bridge or rook, nor any type of gambling (e.g., poker). In this book, we conceive fantasy gaming in terms of three broad genres: role-playing games, collectible strategy games, and online video or computer games. These genres overlap and are characterized by a continuum, from unstructured dramatic play to structured combative play.[2] Recognizing these three genres of fantasy gaming provides us with useful windows into the distinct cultures of fantasy gaming. Here, we will briefly describe each genre.

Role-Playing Games

A role-playing game (RPG), or more specifically a tabletop fantasy role-playing game (TFRPG), has its historical basis in miniature war-gaming — historical or hypothetical battles waged using tokens or miniature figures to represent armies (Holmes 1981; Paxson 1971). War-gaming has existed since at least the early 1800s, but war-gamers in the 1960s and 1970s became increasingly interested in taking on the role of specific heroes in battle — to get inside their heads, so to speak — rather than manipulating entire armies (Fine 1983, Mackay 2001). In 1974, Gary Gygax's company Tactical Studies Rules (TSR) released the first edition of *Dungeons & Dragons (D&D)*, which is commonly considered to be the first contemporary fantasy RPG. *D&D* was set in a medieval fantasy world and allowed players to take on the roles of warriors, elves, wizards, and other stock fantasy characters and interact with other characters. Since then, *D&D* has evolved, with the third edition recently released, socializing new generations of players to the genre. During the last thirty years, many other companies have developed many different games, set in a bewildering array of fantasy worlds, from western to pulp adventure, horror to steam-punk, cyberpunk to superhero.

A basic RPG, such as *D&D*, is one where several people (two or more) come together, usually for several hours over the course of an evening. Most RPGs consist of a *setting*[3] and a *system*.[4] One person is designated to be in charge of the story and is typically given a specific title depending on the RPG in question (e.g., the Storyteller, Dungeon Master, or Referee). This person is responsible for all aspects of the game (setting and system) except the actions of the *players*.[5] The players create fictional personas called *characters*,[6] within the rules and genre specified by the game, and then collectively engage in protracted storytelling. Any challenges or obstacles that arise are resolved according to the system, either referencing a number on a character sheet (which details the strengths and weaknesses of the character), by rolling a die, or by some combination of the two. Once the outcome is known, for good or ill, the story continues. In this way there are never really "winners" or "endings" in RPGs. Rather, the players are interested in experiencing a good story, but also improving their characters' strengths and diminishing their weaknesses, thereby allowing them to experience grander and more epic stories.

As an example, suppose we have a new RPG called *Academia: The Overeducated*. Players assume the roles of first-year college students that want to make it to graduation. The players create characters according to the system outlined in the rulebook, and the setting will be a modern-day university town. Each player creates a unique character based on the game's structure, for example a party-oriented fraternity guy, an older non-traditional student in her thirties, an introverted female art-student, and a brilliant but unmotivated musician. The characters' actions are monitored and constrained by the Referee (which in our fictional game is called the UP, for University President). The UP will have written and developed the overall story outline, or purchased a prepared module from the manufacturer, and will hopefully have some plot hook to get the characters involved. As the evening progresses, the players get more comfortable with their characters, perhaps even adopting relevant speech patterns or mannerisms. Throughout the course of the campaign (i.e., getting to graduation day) this group may play once a week for four years, or they may narrate two years of college in one night and finish over a weekend. Most likely, the manufacturer will have support products in the works so that the group of players does not run out of ideas or setting material, such as special campaigns to rescue the university mascot or to complete an impossible senior Advertising project.

Some examples of current, popular RPGs are: *D&D* (Wizards of the Coast), *HERO* (Hero Games; see Hendricks, this volume), *Vampire: The Requiem* (White Wolf), *Fading Suns* (Holistic Design), and *Ars Magica* (Atlas Games).

Collectible Strategy Games

A collectible strategy game[7] (CSG) is usually played between two players, but most have multi-player variations. Like an RPG, a CSG has a setting and a system, but the setting resides in the background, while the system is integrally tied to some set of collectible material artifacts, such as cards, miniature figures, paper dice, pre-formed plastic constructibles and even pinback buttons. The collectible card game (CCG) was the first form of CSG, and so we use it as an exemplar. In a CCG, a player assumes the identity of a wizard or fighter who engages in combat with other wizards or generals; the deck of cards that each player brings to the table may represent a wizard's mental repertoire of spells or a fighter's weapons and skills. The cards may be divided into attack or defense cards, or some other tactical division relevant to the CCG in question. Whereas RPGs use dice to bring an element of chance to the game, CCGs take advantage of the fact that the card decks are shuffled, thus limiting a players' ability to bring cards into play in a specific order. This ensures that two people with the same decks will not play the same game twice. The "collectible" aspect of the genre refers to the fact that not all cards are equally common. Players typically buy randomly assorted packs of cards and then assemble a deck of cards to play. Packs each have mix of mostly common, a few uncommon and one rare card. Manufacturers regularly offer limited edition, ultra-rare or foil-laminated cards and so on, in order to generate additional revenue. The more cards a player buys, the greater the likelihood s/he has of getting a really rare (i.e., powerful) card to include in a deck. Since most decks can be built according to a variety of strategies, it also encourages players to trade cards amongst themselves, since a rare card that does not fit one's strategy is of no strategic value and essentially worthless for play, yet valuable for trade.

As its premise, our fictional CSG *Academia: The Overeducated,* supposes that each player possesses her/his Ph.D. and both are applying for the same tenure track job at a prestigious university. Each player assembles a set of cards that will help her/him get the job first. For example, a card might give a player one publication in a top academic journal or reduce the number of classes s/he has to teach one semester. The players alternate drawing a card from their decks and laying it in front of them; each is trying to develop a strategy that will win, but is hindered by not knowing which card will be drawn next and not knowing what cards her/his opponent holds. Let us assume that the first player to accumulate one hundred points gets the job and wins. So, the first player lays out his "two published articles" card, and it is worth eight points. His opponent counters with "one published book, with award" and it is worth fifteen points. The first player draws, and gets lucky. He lays down his "any publication on the table has factual errors and will require a revised edition" card, which is minus five points to the target of the player's choice — naturally he chooses the opponent. Now it is eight points to ten. The game continues until one of the players "gets the job."

Some examples of current popular CSGs are: *Magic: The Gathering* (Wizards of the Coast; see Weninger, this volume; Williams, this volume), *.hack//ENEMY* (Decipher), *Legend of the Five Rings* (Alderac Entertainment Group), *Mage Knight* (WizKids; see Williams, this volume) and *Vampire: The Eternal Struggle* (White Wolf).

Online Video and Computer Games

Video and computer games emerged around the same time as role-playing games—during the 1970s—and there has always been a certain overlap between video and computer games and larger fantasy and sci-fi communities (King and Borland 2003). Many early games were solitary endeavors, but the past decade has witnessed a massive explosion in the popularity of networked games, with titles such as *Doom* and *Quake* standing out as early exemplars. In the mid 1990s, online video and computer games (OVCGs), which could be played through servers that connect hundreds of thousands of computers together, began to appear across the US, Europe and Asia. OVCGs do not require that players be physically co-present; rather, players gather in virtual game worlds where they play avatars—computer-mediated fantasy characters. OVCGs differ from RPGs and CSGs in that they require either a personal computer or a gaming console in addition to game software, rather than source books, cards, or dice. In addition, many online games, such as *EverQuest* (Sony) and *World of Warcraft* (Blizzard), have a monthly subscription fee. Similar to RPGs and CSGs, but different from many non-networked video and computer games, OVCGs are specifically designed to offer hundreds of hours of highly interactive gameplay and for the development of characters' identities (Schubert 2003). OVCGs have *settings* and *systems*, just like RPGs, but the computer controls both, which simplifies the games in some important ways.

OVCGs involve multiplayer game worlds and allow for instant peer-to-peer communication, either through typed conversation or through voice-over chat. As players cooperate with one another on multiple occasions and for multiple purposes, they develop the same sense of shared community, and become known to one another through their specific style of play and their characters' names. Perhaps the biggest draw of on-line gaming, however, is the visual effects, which can be highly detailed with a sense of three-dimensional space. The ability to play at any time one desires, for as long or as short a time as desired, is also an advantage since a player can find others online at any hour of the day or night. Many online games today allow for a high degree of character customization and allow various paths towards success, so it is possible to create an interesting, original character that is not only present in one's head, or on a piece of paper, but which is walking, jumping, fighting, or flying on the screen in front of the player. As OVCGs become more akin to "movies that I can control" their attractiveness increases. Unfortunately, OVCGs require a substantial monetary investment and a degree of technical proficiency. Additionally, OVCGs are still less portable RPGs and CSGs.[8] Despite these problems, OVCGs are the fastest growing segment of the fantasy game industry and have gained more widespread acceptability than either tabletop RPGs or CSGs.[9]

To continue our fictional example of *Academia: The Overeducated*, the online version immerses players in a virtual university and the opening shot on the computer screen is that of the Registrar's Office. There, the player selects her/his character's name, age, sex, height, weight, race, and other physical characteristics, and also signs up for first-year classes. This would generate a graphical representation of the player's character that one could then watch, control, and manipulate through the virtual world. The character would be given a campus map and directions to a dorm room, as well as a key to the room. From that point on, the player would navigate through the halls of the Administration Building, on his or her way to the dorm, realizing that every person walking through the hall is also a player; a real person, somewhere in the world, sitting in front of a computer. The player could have the character stop and ask people about classes, inquire if a teacher was strict with attendance or not, and learn other useful bits of information that would help the character succeed in whatever tasks were encountered during game play.

Many role-playing and collectible strategy gamers are also computer gamers (Williams, this volume), and those that are not are typically at least familiar with online computer gaming and likely know some of the more popular game titles. In the gaming industry, several of the larger RPG and CSG publishers have produced computer games based on their projects, or else have licensed their products to computer game manufacturers. While each type of game has its distinct advantages and disadvantages, an increasingly internet-connected world and today's fast-paced life make OVCGs very attractive to gamers generally.

Some current online, multiplayer video and/or computer games include: *Halo 2* (Bungie Studios); *City of Heroes* (Cryptic Studios/NC Soft); *EverQuest 2* (Sony Online Entertainment), and *Dark Age of Camelot* (Mythic Entertainment).

Fantasy Gaming: From Moral Panic to Pedagogy

Fantasy gaming has been, almost from the beginning, constructed as a type of "moral panic" from structural positions within mainstream culture. Cohen (2002:1) characterizes a moral panic as:

> A condition, episode, person or group of persons [which] emerges to become defined as a threat to societal value and interests; its nature is presented in a stylized and stereotypical fashion by the mass media; the moral barricades are manned by editors, bishops, politicians and other right-thinking people; socially accredited experts pronounce their diagnoses and solutions; ways of coping are evolved or (more often) resorted to; the condition then disappears, submerges or deteriorates and becomes less visible.

Cohen was writing about the moral panic surrounding battles among members of two youth subcultures in England in the mid–1960s—Mods and Rockers—yet his definition works surprisingly well as a characterization of fantasy gaming. Following his outline, it is not at all difficult to find examples of each analytical phase of the panic.

We can see this panic most clearly with *Dungeons and Dragons* (*D&D*), the role-playing game that revolutionized contemporary fantasy gameplay and is widely recognized as a motivational force behind many subsequent fantasy games (King and Borland 2003; Mackay 2001). *D&D* was defined as a threat to societal values and interests soon after it emerged on the American mainstream cultural radar in the late 1970s. The threat was manifested primarily in fears of occult worship (Martin and Fine 1991) and negative psychological conditions including suicide, all of which the mass media presented in a stylized and stereotypical fashion (Adler and Doherty 1985; Brooke 1985; Dear 1984; Elshop 1981; Weathers and Foote 1979). In these and many other popular culture sources,[10] staff writers, apparently unfamiliar with fantasy games, reported the concerns of adults—parents, politicians, police, and religious leaders—over fantasy games as a source of child corruption.

Following the lead of pop culture critics, "socially accredited experts" (Cohen 2002:1), mainly psychologists, began survey research to diagnose the problems associated with fantasy gaming. Such work was typically carried out under a deductive, positivist paradigm by researchers who were not necessarily gamers and who applied "established" psychological tests and questionnaires to fantasy gamers without considering the cultural uniqueness of specific fantasy games. Some of this research left the question of fantasy-gaming "effects" ambiguously answered or negatively biased. For example, Douse and McManus (1993:508) found through survey research that role-playing gamers "show clear personality differences from controls"—they were "significantly more introverted, [...] showed less empathic concern," and were more likely to treat people as objects than members of a control group. DeRenard and Kline (1990) found that more players of *D&D* expressed feelings of cultural estrangement than controls, but fewer players expressed feelings of meaninglessness in their lives.

Such findings occupy a minority position within the larger psychological literature, however. In fact, much of the psychological findings during the 1980s and 1990s suggested that there were no significant correlations between fantasy gameplay and psycho-social problems. Abyeta and Forest (1991) investigated the links between role-playing and deviant (criminal) behavior and found that *non*-players in their sample were more likely to report engaging in criminal behavior than role-players. Rosenthal, Soper, Folse and Whipple (1998) found no significant differences between role-players and National Guardsmen—a social role that is generally respected in mainstream American culture. Carroll and Carolin (1989), Carter and Lester (1998) and Simón (1998) all studied role-players in contrast to non-gamers and found no significant differences on measures of antisocial behavior, affect by emotions, depression, suicidal ideation, psychoticism, or neuroticism.

While psychological research has focused on the self-reported psychological and mental states of *individual players*, more recent work on fantasy gaming has shed light on the *culture* of fantasy gaming. Unfortunately, there still appears to be mainstream suspicion about fantasy games and gaming culture despite the many studies that challenged or disproved simple correlations between fantasy gaming and psychopathology or sociopathology. In the early 1990s, Abyeta and and Forest (1991) questioned why a persistent negative view of fantasy games continued to persist. Martin and Fine (1991), Lancaster (1994) and others since have suggested that religious and political members of mainstream society, "moral entrepreneurs" (Becker 1963), continue to stereotype fantasy games in narrow ways to help achieve particular goals.[11] To some extent, the moral panic around fantasy games has decreased during the 21st century, due in no small part to the growth of what Mackay (2001:29) calls "imaginary-entertainment environments"—fantasy universes that are discursively built and spread through multiple communication media. George Lucas's *Star Wars* universe and J.R.R. Tolkien's *Middle-Earth* are perhaps the two best-known imaginary-entertainment environments today: these universes are spread through novels, films, television and cyberspace, as well as role-playing, collectible and video games. These and other fantasy/sci-fi universes are continually becoming more a part of everyday life, yet this does not mean that all members of mainstream culture are equally willing to accept fantasy images as normal. The legacy of fantasy gaming — especially role-playing and computer gaming — is still regularly approached from a pathology perspective (Berger 2002; Griffiths 1998; Wallace 1999).

Researchers who have sought to construct a more reflexive, humanistic (but still empirically-grounded) image of fantasy gaming and gaming culture continue to meet resistance. Aarseth (2002) identifies, with a wry sense of humor, some of the sources of this resistance: "the Public, the University Board of Directors, the Funding organizations, your department colleagues, Politicians, your computer lab admins, and one or two alien monster races." In spite of these sources, however, a growing minority of researchers have taken more nuanced, inductive approaches to studying fantasy gaming. This is perhaps best seen in the field of educational studies.

Role-playing has been researched as a useful pedagogical tool since the 1970s. Various handbooks have been produced for elementary to high school teachers (Taylor & Walford 1972; Furness 1976; van Ments 1983, 1999) with justifications for using games, simulations, and role-playing in the classroom, as well as providing examples for use in practice. Taylor & Walford (1972) discussed the concept of using computers for educational simulations, well before the explosion in popularity of video games in the late seventies. In more recent years, the idea of contextualized learning practice was reflected in the concepts underlying theories of situated learning (Lave and Wenger 1991), situated cognition (Brown, Collins & Duguid 1989), project-based learning (Blumenfeld et al 1991, Krajcik, Czerniak & Berger 1999), and goal-based scenarios (Schank et al. 1993; Kantor, Waddington & Osgood 2000).

The usefulness of fantasy games and simulations is not relegated only to simple educationally-driven paper or computer materials. Gee (2003) examined the role of popular video games in the processes of learning by investigating how video games are designed to allow players to engage in both active and what he terms "critical learning." By critical learning, Gee refers to not only engaging in the internal and external resources in a particular semiotic domain, but being able to reflect upon those resources in order to engage in transforming that domain to apply to future similar contexts within a related domain. From this perspective, video games are more able to engage participants in active and critical learning than current traditional educational structures.

Simulations and role-playing activities have become one of the most popular ways to effect situated learning environments in various educational activities.[12] Role-playing games and simulations, and specifically fictional simulations, bring at least three benefits to classroom experience: motivation, a safe fictional context, and fun. Research such as Druckman's (1995) confirms that simulation "games seem to be effective in enhancing motivation and increasing student interest in subject matter." The level of student motivation has been shown to have a link to the cognitive engagement with learning goals (Nolen 1988; Pintrich and DeGroot 1990), so if the students have sufficient motivation, they will more actively engage with the material. The benefits of role-playing and storytelling have also been discussed with respect to memory (Schank and Abelson 1994) and hypothesis-testing (Bruner 1986). There is also research to support the idea that a fantasy-based simulation, that is, one that is based on social situations that do not actually exist, can lead to positive learning outcomes (Parker & Lepper 1992, Cordova & Lepper 1996). These simulations, which offer analogies and metaphors for real-world issues, can provide a way for students to discuss issues in a safe environment, where there are no real-world consequences to their actions, a fact about simulations noted by Thomas & Macredie (1994) and Malone & Lepper (1987). Finally, students using fantasy simulation games are able to have fun with the material that they are learning. During the simulations, they are able to role-play and use their imagination towards actual problem-solving in a variety of subjects, from history to mathematics to science.

A Broader Ludology: Current Research on Fantasy Gaming

Ludology is still an emerging field of study. As such, focusing on the cultural aspects of fantasy gaming is an important task. The chapters in this book represent some of the current research trends on fantasy games. Each chapter investigates some social or behavioral aspect of fantasy gaming and provides into the cultural, linguistic, sociological, and psychological impact of games on social behavior. More broadly, the chapters illuminate the role of fantasy gaming in contemporary western societies through an admixture of different perspectives that can be broadly delineated into three overlapping categories: social reality, identity, and experience.

Social Reality

Fantasy gaming involves the creation of and interaction with and in social realities, composed of either computer pixels, miniatures, or on paper. Thus, gamers locate themselves and others within two social realities: the fantasy reality of the game itself — for example, navigating a dungeon with a group of fellow dwarves— and the "real world," where players act toward other players and game-related objects such as dice, character sheets, or computer screens. On one hand, in-game social realities appear static and constraining: rulebooks make allowances but prohibit certain actions; dice rolls have only so many potential outcomes; computer programming language determines what avatars can and cannot do. These realities do not typically change during gameplay (unless for example someone cheats). On the other hand, both fantasy and "real world" realities are emergent structures that evolve and change through players' interactions. The three chapters in Section 1 investigate both sides of reality in gaming — the face-to-face or out-of-game world and the fantasy in-game world. Each study provides insight into fantasy realities, "real world" realities, and the intersections and overlaps of the two.

In Chapter 1, *The Role-Playing Game and the Game of Role-Playing: The Ludic Self and Everyday Life*, Dennis Waskul explores the construction of reality and identity within the table-top fantasy role-playing genre. Through participant observation and interviews with gamers, he highlights how the construction of a fantasy world is dialectically related to the construction of the social reality of gamers. In Chapter 2, *Incorporative Discourse Strategies in Tabletop Fantasy Role-Playing Gaming*, Sean Q. Hendricks discusses how players use language to create fictional reality within a fantasy role-playing game, paying special attention to the discourse strategies participants employ. Through language, the participants traverse the boundaries between out-of-game and in-game realities, providing indices that allow other players to travel with them. In Chapter 3, *Social Events and Roles in* Magic: *A Semiotic Analysis*, Csilla Weninger analytically distinguishes among a host of events that together construct the social reality of two players of different experience levels in a game of *Magic: The Gathering*. Weninger shows how each participant uses various semiotic resources to index events, thereby exposing the inevitable overlap between in-game and out-of-game realities. These multiple events represent different aspects of the out-of-game and in-game realities that, in a similar fashion to the gamers in Hendricks's chapter, are navigated fluidly by each of the participants.

Identity

Just as social realities are dynamic phenomena, so are the identities of participants in those social realities. Human selves are layered with multiple identities that shift, emerge and recede as individuals interact toward their immediate reality. Identities may be complementary or may overlap extensively and it is the negotiation of these identities that allows us to interact in many different social contexts. For fantasy gamers, there is another side to this conception of identity as well: the basic premise of fantasy gaming is to take on virtual identities that exist within the context of the game. These virtual identities emerge within the social reality of the game, although like fantasy and "real world" realities, the border between in-game and out-of-game identities is permeable and fuzzy. The chapters in Section 2 look at the relationship between gaming and various aspects of identity, whether a player's situated self is some combination of the many personal and social identities that s/he presents in the out-of-game world, or a virtual identity that s/he constructs within the game frame.

In Chapter 4, *Consumption and Authenticity in the Collectible Strategy Games Subculture*, J. Patrick Williams explores how players construct game-related identities by analytically distinguishing between two dimensions of culture: the organizational and the expressive dimensions. Using participant observation and interview data with players of two collectible games—*Mage Knight* and *Magic: The Gathering*—Williams analyzes how each cultural dimension highlights a distinct frame through which CSG players construct "authentic" identities. Kevin Schut, in Chapter 5, *Desktop Conquistadors: Negotiating American Manhood in the Digital Fantasy Role-Playing Game*, discusses how modern American culture has presented multiple and often-conflicting notions of masculinity. Schut analyzes how video games provide a social space for men to negotiate and mitigate these masculinities. Looking at three aspects of video games: computer culture, idealized images of masculinity, and the Fantasy genre, Schut shows how fantasy video games provide a stage for the construction of specific masculine identities. In Chapter 6, *Playing with Identity: Unconscious Desire and Role-Playing Games*, Michelle Nephew examines the intersection of dreams, wish-fulfillment, gender stereotypes, and objectification from the perspective of psychology and culture studies. She argues that identity in role-playing, like dreams, taps into desires for power and wish-fulfillment, but that cultural influences and gender stereotypes impact the representation of players' characters in role-playing games. In Chapter 7, *The Business and the Culture of Gaming*, W. Keith Winkler describes the interrelationship between the culture of gaming and the business necessities of the gaming industry. He argues that the presence of a gamer subculture in all levels of the industry creates a unique business environment when compared to mainstream, corporate American industries.

Experience

From a social constructionist perspective, social realities and identities are socially experienced phenomena. Some researchers are particularly interested in how people construct social reality and focus more on the experiences of individuals and less on larger structures of society. In the third and final section on experience, we bring together three studies about gamers' experiences within and outside of gaming worlds. Because gamers' social worlds are co-constructed by numerous players who are working together within the technical boundaries of the medium, exploring how gamers visualize these worlds, and how they make sense and meaning within them, heightens our understandings of how humans experience reality itself.

In Chapter 8, *Online Gaming and the Interactional Self: Identity Interplay in Situated Practice*, three writers, Florence Chee, Marcelo Vieta, and Richard Smith investigate the massively multiplayer online game *EverQuest*. Using a phenomenological perspective and methods employed by ethnographers, they provide evidence that playing such online games is not a dysfunctional social activity, as some writers still suggest. Instead, such games represent a rich extension of personal and community relationships, wherein players value reciprocity, a consideration for others, and collaboration with others who share similar interests. In Chapter 9, *Invoking the Avatar: Gaming Skills as Cultural and Out-of-Game Capital*, Heather L. Mello discusses the skills that gamers develop and value within games and how those skills are transferred to out-of-game experiences in gamers' daily lives. This research contributes to the body of work on games and situated cognition, aligning itself to the work of Gee (2003) on video games and learning. In Chapter 10, *Vicarious Experience: Staying There Connected With and Through Our Own and Other Characters*, Tim Marsh explores how researchers might better measure vicarious experience by studying children at play in a virtual game world. Using oppositional emotional attribute sets understood by video gamers about themselves and other players, Marsh opens a line of inquiry into how video gamers locate themselves and others and experience in the game they are playing.

The chapters in this volume represent some of the most recent research in fantasy gaming. As a whole, they also highlight the power of a social constructionist approach to ludology. We hope that these chapters simultaneously enlighten readers and motivate researchers to further develop the emerging field of game studies.

References

Aarseth, Espen. 2002. *"The Dungeon and the Ivory Tower: Vive La Difference ou Liaison Dengereuse?"* Game Studies 2(1). Retrieved May 2005 (*http://www.gamestudies. org/0102/editorial.html*).

Abyeta, Suzanne, and James Forest. 1991. "Relationship of Role-Playing Games to Self-Reported Criminal Behavior." *Psychological Reports* 69: 1187–1192.

Adler, Jerry, and Shawn Doherty. 1985. "Kids: The Deadliest Game?" *Newsweek*, September 9, 1985, p. 93.

Becker, Howard. 1963. *Outsiders: Studies in the Sociology of Deviance.* New York: Free Press.

Berger, Arthur Asa. 2002. *Video Games: A Popular Culture Phenomenon.* London: Transaction Publishers.

Berger, Peter, and Thomas Luckmann. 1966. *The Social Construction of Reality: A Treatise on the Sociology of Knowledge.* New York: Doubleday.

Bernstein, Jeffrey L., and Deborah S. Meizlish. 2003. "Becoming Congress: A Longitudinal Study of the Civic Engagement Implications of a Classroom Simulation." *Simulation and Gaming* 34: 198–219.

Blumenfeld, Phyllis C., Elliot Soloway, Ronald W. Marx, Joseph S. Krajcik, Mark Guzdial and Annemarie Palinscar. 1991. "Motivating Project-Based Learning: Sustaining the Doing, Supporting the Learning." Educational Psychologist 26:369–398.

Brooke, James. 1985. "A Suicide Spurs Town to Debate Nature of a Game." *New York Times*, August 22, 1985, p. B1

Brown, John, Allan Collins and Paul Duguid. 1989. "Situated Cognition and the Culture of Learning." *Educational Researcher* 18: 32–42.

Bruner, Jerome S. 1986. *Actual Minds, Possible Worlds.* Cambridge, Mass. : Harvard University Press.

Carroll, James L., and Paul M. Carolin. "Relationship between Fantasy Games Playing and Personality." *Psychological Reports* 64:705–706

Carter, Robert, and David Lester. 1998. "Personalities of Players of Dungeons and Dragons." *Psychological Reports* 82:182.

Cohen, Stanley. 2002. *Folk Devils and Moral Panics* (3rd ed.). London: Routledge.

Cordova, Diana I. and Mark R. Lepper. 1996. "Intrinsic Motivation and the Process of Learning: Beneficial Effects of Contextualization, Personalization, and Choice." *Journal of Educational Psychology* 88 4: 715–730.

Dear, William. 1984. *The Dungeon Master.* Boston: Houghton-Mifflin.

DeRenard, Lisa A., and Linda Mannik Kline. 1990. "Alienation and the Game Dungeons and Dragons." *Psychological Reports* 66:1219–1222.

Douse, Neil A., and I. C. McManus. 1993. "The Personality of Fantasy Game Players." *British Journal of Psychology* 84:505–509.

Druckman, Daniel. 1995. "The Educational Effectiveness of Interactive Games." In David Crookall, Kiyoshi Arai, (Eds.), *Simulation and Gaming Across Disciplines and Cultures: ISAGA at a Watershed.* Thousand Oaks: Sage.

Elshop, Phyllis Ten. 1981. "D&D: A Fantasy Fad or Dabbling in the Demonic?" *Christianity Today*, September 4, 1981, p. 56.

Fine, Gary Alan. 1983. *Shared Fantasy: Role-Playing Games as Social Worlds.* Chicago: University of Chicago Press.

Frasca, Gonzalo. 1999. "Ludology Meets Narratology: Similitude and Differences between (Video)Games and Narrative." Retrieved May 4th, 2005 (*http://www.ludology.org/articles/ludology.htm*)

Furness, Pauline. 1976. *Role Play in the Elementary School.* New York, NY: Hart Publishing Company, Inc.

Gamespot. N.d. "Ludologists Unite." Retrieved May 3rd, 2005 (*http://www.gamespot.com/features/6106009/p-8.html*)

Gee, James. 2003. *What Video Games Have to Teach Us About Learning and Literacy.* New York, NY: Palgrave MacMillan.

Griffiths, Mark. 1998. "Internet Addiction: Does It Really Exist?" In Jayne Gackenbach (Ed.). *Psychology of the Internet: Intrapersonal, Interpersonal, and Transpersonal Implications.* San Diego: Academic Press.

Holmes, John Eric. 1981. *Fantasy Role-Playing Games.* New York: Hippocrene Books.

Kantor, Ronald J., Tad Waddington, and Richard E. Osgood. 2000. "Fostering the Suspension of Disbelief: The Role of Authenticity in Goal-Based Scenarios." *Interactive Learning Environments* 8:211–227.

Kashibuchi, Megumi, and Akira Sakamoto. 2003. "The Educational Effectiveness of a Simulation/Game in Sex Education." *Simulation and Gaming* 32: 331–343.

King, Brad, and John Borland. 2003. *Dungeons and Dreamers: The Rise of Computer Game Culture from Geek to Chic.* New York: McGraw-Hill.

Kovalik, Doina L., and Ludovic M. Kovalik. 2002. "Language Learning Simulations: A Piagetian Perspective." *Simulation and Gaming* 33: 345–352.

Krajcik, Joseph S., Charlene M. Czerniak, and Carl Berger. 1999. *Teaching Children Science : A Project-Based Approach.* Boston : McGraw-Hill.

Kushner, David. 2003. *Masters of Doom: How Two Guys Created an Empire and Transformed Pop Culture.* New York: Random House.

Lainema, Timo, and Pekka Makkonen. 2003. "Applying Constructivist Approach to Educational Business Games: Case REALGAME." *Simulation and Gaming* 34: 131–149.

Lancaster, Kurt. 1994. "Do Role-Playing Games Promote Crime, Satanism and Suicide among Players as Critics Claim?" *Journal of Popular Culture* 28(2):67–79.

Lave, Jean and Etienne Wenger. 1991. *Situated Learning : Legitimate Peripheral Participation.* New York : Cambridge University Press

Mackay, Daniel. 2001. *The Fantasy Role-Playing Game: A New Performing Art.* Jefferson, NC: McFarland.

Malone, Thomas W. and Mark R. Lepper. 1987. "Intrinsic Motivation and Instructional Effectiveness in Computer-Based Education," pp. 255–286 in Richard E. Snow and Marshall J. Farr (Eds) *Aptitude, Learning and Instruction. Volume 3: Conative and affective process analyses.* Hillsdale, NJ: Lawrence Erlbaum Associates.

Martin, Daniel, and Gary Alan Fine. 1991. "Satanic Cults, Satanic Play: Is "Dungeons & Dragons" a Breeding Ground for the Devil?" in James T. Richardson, Joel Best, and David G. Bromley (Eds.), *The Satanism Scare.* New York: de Gruyter.

Mercado, Simon A. 2000. "Pre-managerial Business Education: A Role for Role-Plays?" *Journal of Further and Higher Education* 24: 117–126

Nolen, Susan B. 1988. "Reasons for Studying: Motivational Orientations and Study Strategies." *Cognition and Instruction* 5: 269–287.

Parker, Louise E., and Mark R. Lepper. 1992. "Effects of Fantasy Contexts on Children's Learning and Motivation: Making Learning More Fun." *Journal of Personality and Social Psychology* 62 4: 625–633.

Paxson, E. W. 1971. "War Gaming." Pp. 278–301 in Elliott M. Avedon and Brian Sutton-Smith (Eds.) *The Study of Games.* New York: Wiley.

Pintrich, Paul R., and Elizabeth V. DeGroot. 1990. "Motivational and Self-regulated Learning Components of Classroom Academic Performance." *Journal of Educational Psychology* 82: 33–40.

Reilly, David A. 2003. "The POWER POLITICS GAME: Offensive Realism in Theory and Practice." *Simulation and Gaming* 34: 298–305.

Rosenthal, Gary T., Barlow Soper, Earl J. Folse, and Gary J. Whipple. 1998. "Role-Play Gamers and National Guardsmen Compared." *Psychological Reports* 82:169–170.

Schank, Robert C., Andrew Fano, Benjamin Bell and Menachem Jona. 1993. "The Design of Goal-Based Scenarios." *The Journal of the Learning Sciences* 3 4: 305–345.

_____ and Robert P. Abelson. 1995. "Knowledge and Memory: The Real Story." In R.

S. Wyer (Ed.), *Knowledge and Memory: The Real Story*. Hillsdale, NJ: Lawrence Erlbaum Associate.

Schubert, Damion. 2003. "Fighting Player Burnout in Massively Multiplayer Games." Pp. 333–338 in Jessica Mulligan and Bridgette Patrovsky (Eds.) *Developing Online Games: An Insider's Guide*. Boston: New Riders.

Simón, Armando. 1998. "Emotional Stability Pertaining to the Game *Vampire: The Masquerade*." *Psychological Reports* 83:732–734.

Spindler, Laraine, and Elyssebeth Leigh. 2003. "Reconciling Design Issues and Values in Simulations." *Simulation and Gaming* 34: 447–456.

Taylor, John, and Rex Walford. 1972. *Simulation in the Classroom: An Introduction to Role-Play, Games and Simulation in Education, with Six Established Games Described in Detail and a Directory of Published Material*. Middlesex, England: Penguin Books, Ltd.

Thomas, Peter, and Robert Macredie. 1994. "Games and the Design of Human-Computer Interfaces." *Educational Technology* 31: 134–142.

van Ments, Morry. 1983, 1999. *The Effective Use of Role-play: Practical Techniques for Improving Learning*. London: Kogan Page.

Wallace, Patricia. 1999. *The Psychology of the Internet*. Cambridge: Cambridge University Press.

Weathers, Diane, and Donna M. Foote. 1979. "Beware the Harpies!" *Newsweek*, September 24, 1979, p. 109.

Wolf, Mark J. P., and Bernard Perron. 2003. "Introduction." Pp. 1–24 in Mark J. P. Wolf and Bernard Perron (Eds.) *The Video Game Theory Reader*. New York: Routledge.

Notes

1. By "social constructionist perspectives," we are referring to an epistemological and ontological paradigm that has arisen in the social sciences — anthropology, communication, cultural studies, geography, linguistics, media studies, psychology, and sociology — over the past forty years. This paradigm can be traced to Berger and Luckmann's (1966) book, *The Social Construction of Reality*. In that book, the authors questioned the assumption that objects in the social world exist separate from human beings. Berger and Luckmann argued that, in fact, no aspect of obdurate reality — that is, the "real world" — could be understood without taking into account the meanings that people attribute to them. Over the last four decades, more and more scholars have come to accept the idea that, in order to understand social phenomena, they would do well to find out what those phenomena mean to people; how they guide people's lives, shape their values and beliefs, and influence their behaviors. Each chapter in this book is concerned in one way or another with the social construction of fantasy gaming and gaming culture.

2. These are analytical distinctions that many other gamers identify in their everyday talk about games. They are not "real distinctions," however, and other gamers or researchers may make other distinctions, for example distinguishing between table-top role-playing and live-action role-playing, or lumping all forms of role-playing (table-top, live-action, online, and so on) together as one genre.

3. The setting can be general, such as fantasy or science-fiction, or specific like Victorian London or Camelot.

4. The system is the mechanic for generating game-relevant values, such as a character's strength or agility rating, or for determining whether an action was successful. Most RPG systems involve the rolling of dice and the comparison of that number to a target number.

5. The players are the actual people controlling the characters; the people actually sitting around the table.

6. The characters are the fictional personas created by the players. They are often called Player Characters or PCs.

7. The term "collectible strategy game" has been used by Jordan Weisman, co-founder and CEO of WizKids, in reference a line of WizKids games, including *Mage Knight* and *Heroclix*. While Weisman used the term specifically to refer to his company's products,

we appropriate the term here analytically to refer to a broader range of games that are simultaneously collectible and strategy-based.

8. The newest generation of wireless networked game platforms is emerging, but they remain relatively expensive and are not heavily used.

9. In 2003, fantasy game industries combined generated nearly 8 billion dollars in annual retail sales in the US and more than 17 billion dollars globally. According to ICv2 (http://www.icv2.com/articles/home/4478.html), the collectible card game market in the US grew to approximately $850 million in retail sales in 2003, while table-top fantasy games (including role-playing and miniatures games) retailed approximately $230 million in the US.

10. For a comprehensive, though not exhaustive, list of popular and academic literature sources about role-playing games, go to: http://www.rpgstudies.net/.

11. "Moral entrepreneur" refers to an individual or group that tries to influence social policy from a particular moral standpoint. Moral entrepreneurs arise within moral panics and work to rationalize specific social policy agendas that "solve" the social problem (e.g., adolescent deviant behavior).

12. They have been used effectively in business training (Mercado 2000, Leinema & Makonnen 2003), language learning (Kovalik & Kovalik 2002) , political science (Bernstein & Meizlish 2003, Reilly 2003), intercultural awareness (Spindler & Leigh 2003), and sex education (Kashibuchi & Sakamoto 2001).

1. THE ROLE-PLAYING GAME AND THE GAME OF ROLE-PLAYING

The Ludic Self and Everyday Life

Dennis D. Waskul

Life, identity, and meaning are all understood as consisting of nothing more than language games, exercises in role-playing. Social reality is experienced through the performance of life, the performance of the everyday. The only difference between the entertainment form known as the role-playing game and the role-playing game of real life is that, for some reason, a great deal of seriousness and levity is handed to each person in tandem with the role they choose or are given [Mackay 2001: 154].

"Games," as Goffman (1961) wrote, "are world-building activities" (p. 27). Fine (1983) further notes that "By simplifying and exaggerating, games tell us about what is 'real'" (p. 7). For these reasons, among a host of others, games present an ideal context for examining a wide range of social and cultural dynamics. In this chapter I examine how players in fantasy role-playing games[1] negotiate themselves in the precarious margins between reality, imagination, and fantasy. I investigate this dynamic in the context of traditional dice-based role-playing games—overwhelmingly, *Dungeons & Dragons (D&D)*. Similar to Fine's (1983) landmark ethnography, this study examines roles, role-playing, and personhood in a circumstance where fantasy, imagination, and reality intersect in the confines of a complex game and oblige participants to occupy the role of a player-character (PC)—a marginal and hyphenated role that is situated in the liminal boundaries of more than one frame of reality. I conclude with commentary on what these simplified and exaggerated "world-building activities" reveal about how we all manage these kinds of distinctions in more normative experiences of everyday life.

D&D, as it is often called by gamers, is a dice-based role-playing game structured by guidelines specified in "core rulebooks." By using dice and gaming rules, participants play to create fantasy personas in fantastic universes of imagination. Dice are important in these role-playing games; they are the principal means of simulating chance and probability — maintaining an element of tension and uncertainty, a key characteristic of play (Huizinga 1950:47). However, in the final analysis, role-playing is only incidentally related to dice — more like games of mimicry than either chance or competition (see Caillois 1958).[2] By use of rules, dice rolls, and a hearty imagination players collectively generate what *is* most central to the game: "a habitable universe for those who can follow it, a plane of being, a cast of characters with a seemingly unlimited number of different situations and acts through which to realize their natures and destinies" (Goffman 1974:5). In short, role-playing games are largely about dramatic fantasy in which action occurs in make-believe scenarios aptly described by Goffman (1974:46, 48) as engrossing "realms."

The fantastic "realms" of fantasy role-play are not only generated from players, rulebooks, and dice roles, but also by a "Dungeon Master" (DM) who occupies the most important role in fantasy role-playing games. Often described by players as "God-like,"[3] the DM occupies a supreme status: he or she creates the worlds, plots, and scripts that become a make-believe setting for the game itself, plays the roles of "non-player-characters," orchestrates encounters with hostile creatures (e.g., what kind of hostile creatures they are, how they are armed, how they engage in combat, and what other actions they might take), and so on. In this way, a role-playing game is akin to a complex form of collaborative improvisational theater: fantasy action collectively sustains the dramatic narrative of a co-authored Goffmanian "realm" that is imaginatively fashioned by DMs *and* players, by use of dice *and* gaming rules, in a circumstance that is a game *and* drama.

Fantasy role-playing games are leisure activities that entail a unique form of play. The game is not competitive, has no time limits, has no scorekeeping, and, aside from the death of a player's persona, has no finite definitions of winning or losing. Unlike card games, board games, games of chance, or organized sports, the point of fantasy role-playing games is not merely for players to play well nor to "win." Instead, the goals are survival and character development: participants create and play fantasy personas that, if kept "alive," increase and advance skills and abilities over the course of many, often lengthy, gaming sessions. Most importantly, participants *play* fantasy personas, and in more than one frame of reality; participants bestow their characters with symbolic personas that are fashioned in the liminal boundaries between fantasy action in a fantastic world of dragons, goblins, valiant swordsmen, sagely wizards, and epic medieval warfare *and* interaction with other players. Although the thematic setting will vary from one game system to the next, this liminal condition is generic to all fantasy role-playing games and obligates participants to actively negotiate distinctions between persona, player, and person.[4]

In role-playing games each participant is the fantasy *persona* he or she plays — a brutal barbarian, a mystical illusionist, a sly gnome. "For the game to work as an aesthetic experience players must be willing to 'bracket' their 'natural' selves and enact a fantasy self. They must lose themselves to the game" (Fine 1983:4). The role-playing game is "not 'ordinary' or 'real' life. It is rather a stepping out of 'real' life into a temporary sphere of activity with a disposition all of its own" (Huizinga 1950:8). However, since fantasy personas are played — not merely generated by rules and dice — make-believe remains influenced by the same symbolic processes that mediate non-fantasy public personas: role-playing games are played with others who come to know fantasy personas (their own and others) on the basis of a collective history of real and fictitious action and interaction.

Participants in role-playing games are also *players*; they are the gamers who play the imaginary personas. As players, each participant must know and understand the rules of the game. Players must know which dice to roll in what situations, which rulebooks to consult in what circumstances, and how to manipulate a vast system of practical gaming knowledge that specifies what a fantasy persona can and cannot do. Successful and satisfying games involve players who are not only skilled in role-playing, but also are proficient with the complex rules by which role-playing is structured. A participant must play not only the role of a fantasy persona, but also of the player.

Finally, and most remotely in these gaming sessions, each PC is also a *person*. Participants in fantasy role-playing games are not only personas and players; they are also called students, employees, adolescents, adults, spouses, parents, and other terms describing who they are in everyday life. As Fine (1983) has detailed, sometimes these other roles can interfere with role-playing games and vice versa. However, for the most part, role-playing games are fantasy adventures (Simmel 1911/1971) or activity enclaves (Cohen and Taylor 1992): they are hobbies — a form of recreational leisure — a distinct sphere of activity that is segregated from the normal strictures of life. These are activities most people do when not preoccu-

pied with routine involvements, activities "outside and above the necessities and seriousness of everyday life" (Huizinga 1950:26). Like any hobby
or leisure activity, fantasy role-playing "is essentially a separate occupation, carefully isolated from the rest of life, and generally is engaged in
with precise limits of time and place" (Caillois 1958:6).

Role-playing games can be described, explained, and understood as
activities that exist in the unique interstices between persona, player, and
person. How do participants in fantasy role-playing games negotiate these
liminal symbolic boundaries? To what extent do these kinds of decidedly
playful negotiations illuminate the ways we all actively fashion the precarious distinctions between person and public persona? Since we all necessarily juggle a multiplicity of roles—sometimes shifting from one to the
next with remarkable fluidity — might we *all* be players of fantasy role-
playing games?

Precarious Boundaries and Fantasy Role-Play

> The mental sphere from which the drama springs knows no dis-
> tinction between play and seriousness.
> -Johan Huizinga. *Homo Ludens*

Because fantasy role-playing is structured by complex rules, I begin
by discussing the general nature of these games. My intent is to provide
enough detail to clarify gameplay while also identifying unique characteristics salient to how gamers create and play fantasy personas. The balance of analysis focuses on how participants in role-playing games
negotiate a person-player-persona symbolic boundary, and the extents to
which role-players are able to maintain these distinctions.[5]

The Social Structure of Fantasy
Role-Playing Games and Gamesmanship

Players use a complex system of rules to craft a fantastic universe for
fantasy action.[6] In practice, however, rules are less regulatory and more a
set of conventions and guidelines that provide a structure for exquisite
detail. In other words, rules are used as gaming resources rather than gaming limitations, and most experienced players fully understand that "there
are no rules that require us to obey the rules" (Carse 1986:10). Instead of
being bound by rules, role-playing games are structured by conventions

that loosely define basic persona traits and qualities of a make-believe world that participants play *at* and game *with* — which is exactly what one role-player said:

> Role-playing is enjoyable because I'm no longer bound by the rules, so to speak. In role-playing games I can be a wizard, a fighter, [or] a cleric while being a dwarf, human, elf, or half-orc. Because we don't live in the world that we role-play, we are able to bend the rules to fit how we want to play. But, in reality, you can't bend the rules. You can't hover, or throw fireballs, or take a hit from a giant or an ogre — but in role-playing games you can. That's what makes them fun.

Participants create fantasy personas from basic attributes generated by random dice rolls. From these dice rolls, players assign their persona varying levels of strength, intelligence, wisdom, dexterity, constitution, and charisma — creating imaginary personal characteristics that are best suited for the specific kinds of fantasy personas they would like to play. A player who intends to develop a wizard or illusionist needs a persona with great intelligence and wisdom, while the persona of a thief or assassin needs dexterity and charisma; each fantasy persona has prerequisite attributes:

> I usually construct characters according to how I hope to play them. If I think I'm going to play a strong fighter I'm going to give him a lot of strength and constitution points, but not a lot of intelligence or wisdom. These aren't important to a fighter.

Once created, participants role-play the words and actions of their personas. Akin to discursive impromptu acting, role-playing is generally unlimited — constrained only by an unspecified, yet shared, sense of presumed realism. That is, fantasy personas may say and do whatever they please, so long as other players and the DM agree that such actions are "reasonable." For example, if a player-character is told that he[7] notices a bright, shiny ring at the bottom of a pool of water, he merely needs to announce that he will dive into the pool, swim to the bottom, and retrieve the ring. The same player-character could not walk on imaginary water (without magical aid, which is possible in these games), but could go for a swim at any time — the latter action is perfectly "reasonable"; it adheres to a basic sense of presumed realism and is accordingly considered appropriate role-playing.

However, the game becomes much more complicated. As in real life, actions have consequences, and most significant actions (such as combat moves, spell casting, the use of specialized skills, and so on) depend on conditions that do not guarantee success. Dice rolls largely determine these variable outcomes and consequences. For example, the player-character who dove into a pool to retrieve a glimmering ring may have failed to announce that he would remove his armor before jumping into the pool — an oversight that could have serious consequences. Presumed realism suggests that it is difficult to swim while suited in battle armor. Thus, the DM would instruct the player to roll dice to determine if the fantasy persona would recover from his blunder or sink to the bottom of the pool. Even if the player remembered to remove his armor, he might swim to the bottom, grab the ring, and suddenly discover that it was a decoy placed by some mischievous agent of evil — the ring could be a trap that will be unwittingly sprung by his touch. Once again, the player would be instructed to roll dice to determine if he would be able to escape the trap or ensnared in a watery grave. These kinds of circumstances, along with their parameters, the situational rules for dice rolling, and the interpretations of potential outcomes, are detailed in core rulebooks.

For all practical purposes, this is how the game is played: Players describe what their fantasy personas say and do, and in the case of a significant action the rolling of dice determines an outcome which then compels further action contingent on the results of an ongoing chain of imaginary action, outcome, and reaction. Players' basic objective is to keep fantasy personas alive through numerous challenging and often violent encounters — doing so requires intelligence, skill, knowledge of gaming rules, and creative problem solving.

My description of game-play is grossly simplified and does considerable injustice to the actual complexities of the game. For example, in these games, a PC who becomes ensnared in a trap is rarely declared instantly "dead"; these circumstances only spring to action the other PCs who will quickly attempt to rescue their companion. In other words, "the game" is an ongoing co-authored narrative that is fashioned out of the enormous possibilities for dramatic imaginary action, consequence, and reaction that are mediated by probabilities determined by the roll of dice. *This* is what the game is all about; teamwork, cooperation, and survival are the organizing themes.

Although simplified, this brief description adequately highlights two critical characteristics of game-play: these games involve role-play in the form of discursive impromptu acting — players describe what their fantasy personas say and do in the various situations encountered and how they respond to the myriad of ongoing consequences that result from those actions. These games also involve rules and guidelines for dealing with chance, probability, and random outcomes. Infinite possibilities for imagined action intersect with finite yet indeterminate probabilities and random chance; finite guidelines are a structure for infinite play, "an open-ended game that any number can play forever" (Goffman 1974:6). Thus, neither can two players play the same fantasy persona in an identical fashion, nor can two identical situations result in precisely the same outcome. For this reason, these games are exceptionally "life-like,"[8] "more like life, and less like games" (Fine 1983:8). As two role-players said:

> I enjoy rolling the dice because I like the fact that I can't control everything.... chance is so important, because it is the only way to really simulate reality in the game setting. I mean, life doesn't really happen according to how we really want it to, so chance helps to keep things pretty real.

> Just like in life, quite often the unexpected can really change things that you never expected to change, and change them in ways that you never could have expected. This is what makes role-playing such a really wonderful time — you never know what's going to happen next.

All a player can know are the rules of the game, which detail probabilities for various actions characters might take. The development of a fantasy persona depends on how a player handles the outcomes of these probabilities, which always entail uncertainty and chance. Consequently, the fantasy personas of role-playing games are not unlike people in everyday life, chiefly influenced not by the basic traits they start out with, but the choices they make, the outcome of those decisions, chance, and the ongoing dialectical relationship between consequences and personal adjustments. As role-players said:

> When you roll a character, it's just paper, but what happens shapes what the character ends up being.

> I usually just play the character how he's rolled, and after a few hours I'll start evolving according to how he's been going. I adjust to how he's been reacting to others and how others have been adjusting to him.

Like the development of persons in everyday life, the development of fantasy personas in role-playing games is emergent from the innumerable possibilities that culminate over a history of choices, decisions, and consequences that are patterned and structured, yet also unavoidably unpredictable and indeterminate. Another role-player emphasized this point when he said:

> Simply because you roll up a character and put his or her stats down on paper doesn't mean he or she has any kind of personality yet. You have to play the character in order to develop a character's *real* personality [emphasis added].

The Persona, Player, and Person:
Negotiating Borders and Boundaries

[A good role-player is] someone who plays in character and doesn't let player knowledge interfere with character knowledge — doesn't let what happens in the game interfere with playing the game on a player level. He plays the game in the game and doesn't bring personal problems into the game. It's no fun when someone does that, because it plays the game out of characteristics.
— Dan, *Dungeons & Dragons* Player

In fantasy role-playing games, participants must actively establish symbolic boundaries between player, persona, and person and assume the right role in each situation. Some circumstances require the participant to act as a persona while others require a player. As a person, the participant must control non-game related elements so that they do not interfere with gameplay. Of the three, non-game related aspects of the person are the most potentially disruptive. This is not surprising. These are role-playing *games*; by design and intent participants are expected to be players or the personas they are playing. Or, as one role-player said, "You're not yourself, you're playing someone new.... That's the whole thing about role-playing; you're not there to play yourself, you're there to play someone else."

It is understandable why non-game aspects of the person are irrelevant, distracting, and extraneous; therefore, as still another player said, a good role-player is "someone who doesn't let personal feelings interfere with the game. I leave work at work and home at home — same principle in gaming." Indeed, many participants in this study used the same analogy of "leaving work at work" as part of their descriptions of what defines a "good" role-player or a "good" gaming session. Thus, participants in role-playing games may fluidly move between player and persona, but are careful about what aspects of personhood they bring into the game.

For the most part, this bracketing of the person is accomplished with relative ease; it is implicit in the social structure of the gaming sessions themselves. As noted in my field notes from one of our first gaming sessions, role-players are often a motley crew of dissimilar people who are otherwise separated by significant social, cultural, and institutional barriers:

It is an unlikely mix of people who have somehow come together to play this game ... a university professor, a few university students, a few high school students, and others whom I could not place. Ages seem to range somewhere between an approximate 16–early 30s. The Dungeon Master shows up still wearing his McDonald's work uniform, a couple players are wearing unremarkable t-shirts and jeans, one player sports a derby hat and long black trench coat, while another wears shaggy hair (partially colored and partially braided), overly baggy clothes, and hemp jewelry.... On the surface they appear to have nothing in common, aside from the fact that they all carry *Dungeons & Dragons* paraphernalia (books, gaming dice, character sheets, and miniature figurines).

By all indication, these people are quite different from each other; their interest in *Dungeons & Dragons* appears the only commonality. Yet, instead of hindering social interaction and group formation, these differences prove instrumental — even crucial — if for no other reason than players come to know one another in the course of game play, leaving little else to otherwise bind them in what becomes an unambiguously utilitarian relationship. As I further noted:

> At no point did anyone discuss issues of relevance to their work, family, school, or anything else that pertains to their life outside of this game. Indeed, in spite of the fact that there were new players present, no introductions were made, real names were not shared, and nothing was mentioned about players as people.... Since informal "get to know you" chitchat seems to be either unimportant or irrelevant, I decided not to ask. But, even more, normal conversation based on interactive cues seems strangely uncouth. It does not seem appropriate to actually ask the Dungeon Master if he does, in fact, work at McDonald's. It doesn't even seem appropriate to introduce myself to these players, nor does it seem unusual that they have not introduced themselves to me. Instead, players introduce themselves as the *character* they play during the course of gaming. I only know these people by the character they are playing, and they only know me as Cantrall — a rather standoffish fighter who, although brutish in appearance, [is] reliable in combat, and generally cooperative, [and] does not get involved in the "party politics."[9]

Not only did players come to know each other during the course of game-play but also, like the "friendly poker game" (Zurcher 1983), during role-playing sessions "it was understood that there were to be no 'outside' interruptions. There were no radios or televisions playing, no wives serving beverages, no children looking over shoulders" (p. 138). In fact, for one of the role-playing groups included in this study, it was necessary to repeatedly move the location of gaming sessions for no other reason than the struggle to find a setting free of these distractions — a context insulated from "outside" interruptions that not only interfere with gaming, but might also evoke roles from participants that are superfluous to the game. As Huizinga (1950) noted, "The play-mood is *labile* in its very nature. At any moment 'ordinary life' may reassert its rights ... which interrupts the game ... by a collapse of the play spirit, a sobering, a disenchantment" (p. 21, emphasis in original).

To guard against these potential interruptions, role-playing sessions are ephemeral situations encased not only by a "spatial separation from ordinary life" (Huizinga 1950:19), but also by symbolic boundaries that "declare as irrelevant [the] norms and roles that society at large deems mandatory in favor of idiosyncratic group norms and roles" (Zurcher 1983:154). However, in role-playing games, the bracketed irrelevance of the person is much more exaggerated than what Zurcher observed in the friendly poker game: it is rare for new players to introduce themselves to others; it is common for participants to come to know each other only as the fantasy personas they play — a dynamic also noted in Fine's (1983:55) study of fantasy role-playing games:

> As a new player I was struck by how little I learned about the private lives of others— even others to whom I felt close. One didn't talk about occupations, marital status, residence, or ethnic heritage. In some cases it was months before I learned a player's surname. Others confirmed this observation, and suggested that it represented a need to establish a distance from one's real self.

The bracketing of the person from both player and persona is implicit in the activity itself. Whether playing a game (such as poker or *Dungeons & Dragons*), or occupying more serious roles within institutions or occupations, part of what is implied in playing one role is that we are not playing others. The fact that non-game related aspects of a person are effectively bracketed or otherwise ignored in role-playing games should not be any more surprising than the fact that marital roles are often suspended when people are at work, work roles are often suspended when people are at home, and so on.

Even so, role-playing games become much more complicated because the activity necessarily involves two distinct, yet simultaneous roles during the same activity; participants are fantasy personas *and* the players who enact the personas. "There are two performances occurring in a role-playing game: a collectively imagined theater of characters and events shared among the players and the gamemaster, and the set of actual audio visual events that transpires among the players and the gamemaster" (Mackay 2001:89–90). This fine distinction proves salient among fantasy role-playing gamers:

> I try to separate myself from my character. When something happens ... instantly you, as a player, will react. [But] you [the player] need to be careful how you [the character] react and distinguish between the two.

Note the words that this role-player uses to describe the distinction between player and persona — also note how it is necessary to clarify what this role-player means by adding more specific information in brackets. In everyday life words like "you" and "me" are sufficiently precise indicators of self. When "you" ask "me" a question it is clear who is inquiring of whom, and it would be unusual for "me" to wonder which "you" is asking the question or which "me" ought to respond. However, as the previous quote illustrates, in fantasy role-playing these words can be ambiguous in a peculiar kind of way. Because participants are simultaneously both players and the fantasy personas they play, there exists a multiplicity of "you's" and "me's." It is not always clear which "you" or what "me" is being evoked. Even the authors of *Dungeons & Dragons Players Handbook* (Cook, Tweet, and Williams 2000) recognize this ambiguity and seek to distinguish player from persona:

> The action of a *Dungeons & Dragons* game takes place in the imaginations of players. Like actors in a movie, players sometimes speak as if they were their characters or as if their fellow players were their characters. These rules even adopt that casual approach, using "you" to refer to and to mean "your character." In reality, however, you are no more your character than you are the king when you play chess. Likewise, the world implied by these rules is an imaginary one [6].

The precarious distinction between player and persona is crucial to role-playing games. "The *character* identity is separate from the *player* identity. In this, fantasy gaming is distinct from other games" (Fine 1983:186, emphasis in original). As one role-player stated, "I separate myself from my character. Some of the things I may consider logical, my character may not. Sometimes they do coincide. But I can't play me and my character [at the same time]." Another role-player adds to this by saying:

> I try to think within the game as much [like] my character as I can, because there are certain things [that], as a player, I wouldn't do — but my character would do. I have to be careful in distinguishing between the two, or the game probably wouldn't be fun.

On the surface, this may appear to be a restatement of ways that role-players bracket non-game related aspects of personhood during the course of game play. However, the situation is more knotty: role-players must distinguish between the knowledge they have as a *player* and knowledge they presume their fantasy *persona* has. Distinguishing between "player-knowledge" and "persona-knowledge" is necessary in order for a player, as one gamer said, to "play their character *as* their character." In fact, this especially perceptive role-player went so far as to define this quality as "metagaming." He defines a lack of metagaming as a circumstance where "you use player-knowledge instead of character-knowledge," resulting in "bad role-playing ... that will ruin the game." He provides an example:

> A player may know the hit points of an ogre because you as a player just read the *Monster's Manual* and are transferring that knowledge to your character ... the Dungeon Master plans a game based on what the characters know. So it can ruin the game. If a character doesn't know a monster has invulnerability against fire he might just bring fire-based weapons instead of something else. But, if he does know that strength, he will prepare against it.

This poses a moral dilemma for role-players: in crucial gaming moments, will *players* use information they know, but their fantasy *personas* would not? The participants in this study consistently cited this moral dilemma as the key to good role-play. In the words of one role-player, when players do not separate player-knowledge from persona-knowledge — when they do not "metagame" appropriately — "it turns the game into dice rolling instead of role-playing." Another role-player described a situation where failure to segregate player-knowledge from persona-knowledge spoiled an otherwise good time:

> Once, when we were fighting an army of goblins— well, maybe an army is over exaggerated, but anyway — because one of the players knew the average hit points of a goblin and knew the average damage of his fireball spell, he knew exactly how many times he would have to cast the spell. While it could be seen that the player would know this, it seems that the player took the role-playing out and turned it into a numbers game — which, in my opinion, takes the fun out of the game!

Porous Borders and Erupting Boundaries

> *I think that player-knowledge and character-knowledge should be kept very separate, but it's impossible, no matter how hard I try. And, it's really important that I keep them separate, because a game can be ruined by too much player knowledge seeping in.*
> -Trent, *Dungeons & Dragons* player

The authors of *Dungeons & Dragons Players Handbook* (Cook, Tweet, and Williams 2000) provide a neat and tight analogy; "you are no more your character than you are the king when you play chess" (p. 6). Conceptually, this analogy holds; in practice, it fails wretchedly. Role-playing games are not board games; they differ in important ways (see Fine 1983:184). Although the game is purely fantasy, players *must* act, interact, and react by imagining how they would handle the same circumstances if they were their fantasy personas and the situations they encountered were genuine — by definition, that is what is implied by a *role-playing* game. As one role-player stated, "I try to be the character as much as possible. But, in absence of a reference point for the character's thoughts, it'd be my own thoughts and reactions that come into play." Another role-player reiterated the same idea when he said, "as I play the character, I think what I would do in this situation." Consequently, neat distinctions between person, player, and persona become messy; they erode into utterly permeable and interlocking moments of experience. Rigid distinctions between fantasy, imagination, and reality — between person, player, and persona — prove untenable. Instead, role-playing games necessarily involve, to borrow from Mead (1934), "taking the role of the other" — but in this case the "other" is not another person; the "other" is a fantasy character who is, in fact, the player and person himself. This peculiar dynamic does not escape the attention of role-playing gamers:

> You can't say that your PC will never be an extension of yourself because you are playing your character. If you think your character is supposed to act that way or this way it's still just your perception because no one else can take that same character and play it totally the same.... You can never think like the character because the character is you. Whatever the character thinks is coming from you so it is inherently a mixture. I could play a direct opposite from me — for example, a female, evil priestess — and play it well in character, and still the actions would be coming from me.... No matter what you do, it is tied with you. It's kind of difficult to separate sometimes.

> The reactions that my character takes I think or agree with, but the actions and actual role-playing are my character.

> In terms of character development I've never really regulated it. Some Dungeon Masters require 1–2 pages of character history. [However,] between creation and personality development, I try to find my characters in the playing of them and I try to think to myself when making a decision: "So if I do this now, is this what I will always do, sometimes do, [or] never do again? How will the actions I am about to take [apply to my character], does it fit with what I've done in the past?"

Even more, participants in role-playing games often find it difficult to play a fantasy persona that is *purely* fictional. One player said, "I'm not very good at making characters radically different than me.... Role-playing games are a fantasy projection of myself — me having adventures I wouldn't normally have." In fact, many role-players claim that effective play presumes gamers who identify with and otherwise apprehend their fantasy personas as extensions of themselves. "If a player doesn't care about his character then the game is meaningless" (Fine 1983:185). One gamer not only said, "I find it funner to play characters I understand," but also went on to describe other consequences of playing a persona that he did not identify with. He illustrated by telling about a time when he played a paladin, but found it difficult because "law and order are beyond me to understand." Further describing the situation, this role-player said, "when we started he wasn't like me, but as time went on he became more and more like me. He began as a defender of justice, but ended up a guy with a guilt complex." In short, he told about how he created a do-gooder fantasy persona but found it difficult to actually defend goodness and justice in the course of the game. Because he ended up role-playing in ways that were out of moral alignment for his persona, "he" felt guilty. The irony is that fantasy personas are purely fictional and thus cannot "feel" any more guilt than the player who plays them. Does the persona have a "guilt complex" or is the player merely guilty about how he has played him? Clearly, the answer is an ambiguous both but neither; his persona has a "guilt complex" *and* the player feels guilty about how he has played him — the guilt is real and exists in two simultaneous frames of reality.

As this evocative situation illustrates, participants in role-playing games are located at intersections between person, player, and persona in a manner that fundamentally blurs the distinctions between them. Another gamer gave an anecdote that further illustrates the curious ironies of role-playing:

> In Charlie's *Spycraft* campaign I play a face man character, which requires that I develop multiple personas to use at various times. What I usually do is choose a name like Jeremiah Bell, for example. Then I create a personality, well more of a persona, for this name from asking myself as a player but also as a character, "Is he rich? Is he poor? Is he smart? Is he backwoods?" These are all questions that, I as a player and as a character, have to answer to develop my character fully.

In this case we have a player who plays a "face man"— a fictional persona who is made up of other fictional personas. Yet even in this complicated situation of receding layers of fantasy, the role-player cannot create fictions of pure fiction. Instead, the player draws upon his knowledge both as a player and person to assist in the process of creating the personas of his persona. As these evocative examples illustrate, at a conceptual level role-players may be able to draw fine distinctions between persona, player, and person, but at a pragmatic level these distinctions ultimately erode. In the end, as one role-player said, "I try to make everyone a little different. I don't want to play a clone of the same character every time, though I do have personality traits that creep in anyway."

Discussion

> ... roles may not only be played but also played at, as when chil-
> dren, stage actors, and other kinds of cutups mimic a role for the
> avowed purpose of make-believe; here, surely, doing is not being.
> But this is easy to deal with. A movie star who plays at being a
> doctor is not in the role of doctor but in the role of actor; and this
> latter role, we are told, he is likely to take quite seriously. The
> work of his role is to portray a doctor, but the work is only inci-
> dental; his actual role is no more make-believe than that of a real
> doctor — merely better paid ... These desperate performers are
> caught exactly between illusion and reality, and must lead one
> audience to accept the role portrait as real, even while assuring
> another audience that the actor in no way is convincing himself.
> — Erving Goffman. Encounters

While role-playing games may be seen as unique social activities, at another level both role-playing and games are anything but distinct. All people play and play with roles; we take up, define, and negotiate a wide array of social roles that, though often structured in meaningful and consistent ways, are enacted uniquely from one person to the next. People play roles and roles play a significant part in defining self; just as we actively and fluidly construct the roles we play, these roles also define and structure self in broad social, cultural, and temporal frameworks of meaning.

From this perspective, play and games are discrete forms of role-playing activity that present a distilled lens for better understanding the relationships between fantasy, imagination, and reality. This is part of what is implied in Mead's (1934) articulation of role-playing, as well as play and game[10] — and certainly what Goffman (1961) meant when he wrote:

> It is only around a small table that one can show coolness in poker or
> the capacity to be bluffed out of a pair of aces; but, similarly, it is only
> on the road that the roles of motorist and pedestrian take on full mean-
> ing, and it is only among persons avowedly joined in a state of talk that
> we can learn something of the meaning of half-concealed inattentive-
> ness or relative frequency of times each individual talks [27].

In this way, the presumably distinct categories of fantasy/persona, imagination/player, and reality/person can be shown as a subtle continuum of finely graded experience. More precisely, all selves and social reality can be understood as emergent from the interstices of these *interrelated* provinces of meaning; "Conceptions are thus born as acts of the imagination" (Huizinga 1950:136).

Human beings do not experience reality directly; reality is fashioned and mediated by symbols, language, social structure, and situated variables of social interaction. Consequently, realms of fantasy, imagination, and reality are notoriously porous; experience, knowledge, and understanding routinely slips from one to another. In the lived experience of everyday life — just as in play and games—fantasy, imagination, and reality are not so easily compartmentalized; they necessarily blend and blur to such an extent they are often difficult to convincingly separate into mutually distinct categories. For example, Rosanna Hertz (2002) details how families created by anonymous sperm donors actively construct imaginary fathers out of the most minuscule scraps of information. Mothers, and eventually children, craft stories about these "ghost fathers" and, in the process, "the anonymous donor takes on a persona of his own — a person who may be more fiction than fact" (Hertz 2002:6). Hertz's analysis hinges on a powerful insight: fatherhood is an idea that exists independent of a father, and the idea of fatherhood is just as important — if not more so— than fathers themselves. The absence of an "actual" father makes the "looking-glass" (Cooley 1902) of fatherhood all the more apparent. "Actual" co-present fathers may be just as ghostly as the fathers of children conceived by anonymous sperm donors; in all cases, fatherhood is defined in a process that includes the fictions of looking-glass idealism. Given Hertz's analysis, it is easy to see how the symbolic role of father is not only distinct from men themselves, but also perhaps more important to the processes of pinning down a self. In noting the same dynamic for motherhood, Carse (1986) suggests this feature characterizes all social roles:

> It is in the nature of acting, Shaw said, that we are not to see this woman as Ophelia, but Ophelia as this woman.... To some extent the actress does not see herself performing but feels her performed emotion and actually says her memorized lines— and yet the very fact that they are performed means that the words and feelings belong to the role and not to the actress... So it is with all roles. Only freely can one step into the role of mother. Persons who assume this role, however, must suspend their freedom with a proper seriousness in order to act as the role requires. A mother's words, actions, and feelings belong to the role and not to the person — although some persons may veil themselves so assiduously that they make their performance believable even to themselves, overlooking any distinction between a mother's feelings and their own [15–16].

To some extent we are all participants in fantasy role-playing games. Father, mother, professor, student — all words to fashion symbolic self-claims in reference to social roles and statuses— uniquely situated provinces of meaning that, as Rosanna Hertz (2002:3) described, are often "more ghost like than real." I must be cautious; I do not want to push this conclusion too far. As Goffman (1974) once wrote, "social life is dubious enough and ludicrous enough without having to wish it further into unreality" (p. 2). Instead I suggest that paramount reality is not distinct from fantasy and imagination; fantasy and imagination are inseparable components of paramount reality, and among its most interesting and fluid dimensions.

In role-playing games, participants are uniquely situated in the loose boundaries of a person-player-persona trinity. The distinctions and permeable boundaries between person, player, and persona roughly adhere and are related to the more general trinity of reality, imagination, and fantasy. Participants in fantasy role-playing games literally and consciously play with this trinity of social reality; the significance of this research is that those same porous distinctions and active negotiations also occur in everyday life.

Conclusions

Participants in this study actively and playfully construct categorically unreal, fictitious personas that obligate participants to construct symbolic boundaries between person, player, and persona. Yet, in practice, these conceptual distinctions fail — boundaries inevitably implode as person, player, and persona blend and blur into an experience that necessarily involves all three. In this respect, as I have suggested, neither are fantasy role-playing games unlike experiences of everyday life, nor are fantasy role-players necessarily unique.

I don't mean to dismiss the uniqueness of fantasy role-playing games. It is obvious that, on one hand, role-playing games are whimsically distinct: it is reasonable to assume that only a minority of people can claim experience at playing the role of a dwarven barbarian. Yet, on the other hand, I have sought to magnify a character of role-playing games that is all *too* familiar: it is equally reasonable to assume that most people understand precisely what it means to occasionally play other kinds of roles— often of occupational or institutional origin — with a similar sense all is a ruse, charade, or game.

Carse's (1986) brilliant analysis of society and culture through the lens of finite and infinite games concludes with a chapter that contains a single sentence: "There is but one infinite game" (p. 177). This conclusion is the same that role-players in this study have illustrated. In spite of the heroic ways by which they distinguish between fantasy and reality, persona and person, player and persona, person and player, they inevitably find themselves a part of "but one infinite game." Finite boundaries and neatly crafted conceptual provinces of meaning ultimately blend and blur to such an extent that nothing remains except a player whose gaming activities include much more than the rolling of dice. In the final analysis, it is doubtful that any of us can honestly claim otherwise. We all find ourselves as players located at the liminal margins between the people we believe we are and the personas we play in various situated social encounters— between what we believe we are and what we aspire to become — between what we believe of ourselves and what we believe others believe of us.

Acknowledgments

Parts of this study were originally coauthored with Matt Lust ("Role-Playing and Playing Roles: The Person, Player, and Persona in Fantasy Role-Playing." *Symbolic Interaction* 2004. 27/3: 333–356). I would like to extend my gratitude to Matt Lust for his excellent assistance in crafting the original study.

References

Caillois, Roger. 1958 [2001]. *Man, Play and Games*. Chicago, IL: University of Chicago Press.
Carse, James. 1986. *Finite and Infinite Games*. New York, NY: Macmillan.
Cohen, Stanley and Laurie Taylor. 1992. *Escape Attempts: The Theory and Practice of Resistance to Everyday Life*. 2d ed. New York, NY: Routledge.
Cook, Monte, Jonathan Tweet, and Skip Williams. 2000. *Dungeons & Dragons Player's Handbook: Core Rulebook I*. Renton, WA: Wizards of the Coast, Inc.
Cooley, Charles Horton. 1964 [1902]. *Human Nature and Social Order*. New York, NY: Scribner's.
Fine, Gary Allen. 1983. *Shared Fantasy: Role-Playing Games as Social Worlds*. Chicago, IL: University of Chicago Press.
Goffman, Erving. 1961. *Encounters: Two Studies in the Sociology of Interaction*. Indianapolis, IN: Bobbs-Merrill.
___. 1974. *Frame Analysis*. Cambridge, MA: Harvard University Press.
Hertz, Rosanna. 2002. "The Father as an Idea: A Challenge to Kinship Boundaries by Single Mothers." *Symbolic Interaction*. 25 (1): 1–31.
Huizinga, Johan. 1950. *Homo Ludens: A Study of the Play Element in Culture*. Boston, MA: The Beacon Press.
Mackay, Daniel. 2001. *The Fantasy Role-Playing Game: A New Performing Art*. Jefferson, NC: McFarland.
Mead, George Herbert. 1934. *Mind, Self, and Society*, edited by C. Morris. Chicago, IL: University of Chicago Press.
Simmel, Georg. 1971 [1911]. "The Adventurer." Pp. 187–198. In *Georg Simmel: On Individuality and Social Forms*, edited by D. Levine. Chicago, IL: University of Chicago Press.

Stone, Gregory. 1970. "Appearance and the Self." Pp. 394–414. In *Social Psychology Through Symbolic Interaction*, edited by Gregory Stone and Harvey Farberman. Waltham, MA: Xerox College Publishing.

Zurcher, Louis. 1983. *Social Roles: Conformity Conflict and Creativity.* Beverly Hills, CA: Sage.

Notes

1. Fantasy role-playing games are best defined by Mackay (2001:4-5, emphasis in original): "an episodic and participatory story-creation system that includes a set of quantified rules that assist a group of players and a dungeon master in determining how their fictional characters' spontaneous interactions are resolved. These performed interactions between the players' and the dungeon master's characters take place during individual sessions that, together, form episodes or adventures in the lives of the fictional characters.... the episodes become part of a single grand story that I call the role-playing game narrative."

2. In role-playing games, dice rolls are used to simulate chance and probability. In this way, role-playing games share some similarities to games of alea — one of four main classifications of games identified by Roger Caillois (1958). However, role-playing games are, more often than not, the antithesis of roulette or other true games of alea where "The player is entirely passive; he does not deploy his resources, skill, muscles, or intelligence" (Caillois 1958: 17). Likewise, role-playing games involve elements of agon-like card games, the use of "knowledge and reasoning that constitute the player's defense, permitting him to play a better game" (Caillois 1958:18). Yet, neither Caillois's alea nor agon is adequate; role-playing games also involve significant mimicry, a "deploying [of] actions or submitting to one's fate in an imaginary milieu ... becoming an illusionary character oneself, and of so behaving" (Caillois 1958:19). At best, one must concede that role-playing games are a complex synthesis of these classic forms of play, if not something else altogether.

3. It is not quite accurate to call Dungeon Masters "God-like"; in gaming situations that involve deities the Dungeon Master plays these gods as well. In fantasy role-playing games, Dungeon Masters are above the gods—they create, organize, and operate these fantasy worlds and mediate the supernatural forces that dictate them. Within the frame of the game, it is not unfair to deem Dungeon Masters as holding ultra-supreme status.

4. The distinction between person, player, and persona adheres to what Fine (1983:194, 205) describes as the "three basic frames" that operate in fantasy gaming. As Fine wrote, each of these frames "has a world of knowledge associated with it — the world of common-sense knowledge grounded in one's primary framework, the world of game rules grounded in the game structure, and the knowledge of the fantasy world." Fine's investigation is solidly supported by his use and extension of Goffman's (1974) Frame Analysis. Indeed, Goffman (1974) also provides strong statements differentiating between person, player, and persona: "The difference between actual and scripted becomes confused with the difference between personal identity and specialized function, or (on stage) the difference between part and capacity. I shall use the term 'role' as an equivalent to specialized capacity or function, understanding this to occur both in offstage, real life and in its staged version; the term 'person' will refer to the subject of a biography, the term 'part' or 'character' to a staged version thereof" (p. 129).

5. I spent many of my adolescent years playing *Dungeons & Dragons*, continuing these games intermittently through my undergraduate college career. After a decade hiatus, I joined a role-playing group as a participant observer while teaching at Southern Utah University (Cedar City, UT). Original research was conducted with Matt Lust. Matt Lust has been role-playing since 1998 and is much more involved in a broader range of contemporary games. Matt extended observations and data collection to other role-playing games including *Mekton Zeta, Dragon Quest, Big Eyes Small Mouth, Spycraft,* and *Epic.* However, we collected the vast majority of data from groups playing *Dungeons & Dragons.* Between October 2002 and January 2003 we participated in approximately 90 hours of fantasy role-play gaming sessions. We actively maintained field notes with multiple gaming groups, but the primary source of data is derived from forty semi-structured qualitative interviews with thirty gamers. Although games were sometimes held in private loca-

tions, the principal setting was a local gaming store where we conducted fifteen to twenty-five minute interviews before or after game sessions.

6. In *Dungeons & Dragons* there are three core rulebooks (and a massive supply of other publications) that specify detailed guidelines for character classes, fantasy humanoid races, medieval weapons and armor, magical spells, skills, abilities, movement, mythical monsters, and supernatural forces that include powerful competing gods (to list a few major categories). From these guidelines players craft characters within a shared fantasy (Fine 1983): a vast cosmos of collectively constructed imaginary actions, interactions, reactions, and the myriad of consequences that result from fantasy events.

7. I use male pronouns because all the participants in our study are male. Fine (1983) also comments and discusses this gender bias in fantasy role-playing games—a bias that, in my unrepresentative and very localized sample, appears to remain unchanged in the two decades since Fine's ethnography was originally published. I admit the possibility that gender has influenced the dynamics explored in our research.

8. As Goffman (1974) notes, "with the possible exception of pure fantasy or thought, whatever an agent seeks to do will be continuously conditioned by natural constraints, and that effective doing will require the exploitation, not the neglect, of this condition.... the assumption is, then, that although natural events occur without intelligent intervention, intelligent doings cannot be accomplished effectively without entrance into the natural order" (p. 23). From this perspective, role-playing games also become "life-like" because the actions of PCs are always subject to the outcome of random dice rolls that mock natural constraints.

9. All participants knew I was conducting a study of fantasy role-playing games. However, some participants apparently overlooked the fact that I am a professor at the local university, and, since I do not look much different from a student, the occupational role seemed easy to forget or ignore. I did not conceal my intentions or identity, but without formal introductions the situation was sometimes ambiguous. During gaming sessions, I was a player; other players did not seem to care about these kinds of insignificant and distracting details. The full extent of the irrelevance of these occupational roles was illustrated after over a month of game-play. The Dungeon Master made a casual remark about me being a professor at the university. Somewhat surprised, a younger player asked what I teach. When I responded, "sociology," the player merely said, "Cool. I think I'll take that next year when I'm at the university." The subject of my occupation never came up before, or again. It simply did not matter.

10. Others have also noted how Mead's framework necessarily entails richly layered, interrelated, and thoroughly inseparable elements of both fantasy and reality. Gregory Stone (1970) provides one of the clearest articulations of these relationships in his discussion of "fantastic socialization." Stone identifies two kinds of socialization that can be found in Mead's "play." The first is widely noted by sociologists: genuine "anticipatory socialization." Here, realistic roles are acted according to expectations that one would reasonably expect to be adopted or encountered later in life. The second is often overlooked: in "fantastic socialization" one entertains roles that can seldom, if ever, be expected or adopted. Stone provides the example of children playing cowboy or Indian—we may add to this a long list of superheroes, dead historical figures, media produced characters, and others who clearly occupy a central role in the "fantastic socialization" of us all.

2. INCORPORATIVE DISCOURSE STRATEGIES IN TABLETOP FANTASY ROLE-PLAYING GAMING

Sean Q. Hendricks

One of the earliest attested forms of tabletop fantasy role-playing games (TFRPGs) is *Dungeons & Dragons*, which was introduced in the 1970s. Rather than the competitive game play characterized by traditional board games, many networked computer games (*Quake, Doom, Heretic,* etc.), and collectible card games, the game play of TFRPGs is primarily characterized by cooperation and storytelling. At the very least, such games include a number of players (often between three and ten), a referee (often called the Game Master (GM), or Dungeon Master), a set of standard rules (*D20, Hero, Storyteller*), and a random element (normally dice, although some games, such as *Deadlands* and *Castle Falkenstein* use playing cards). The goal of such games is the construction of a narrative that is the result of the interactions of the GM, the players, the rules, and the random element. There are no winners or losers among the players, but a game is considered successful if the resulting story is engaging and creative.

In order for such a narrative construction to be successful, it is necessary for the GM and the players to both visualize a shared world within which the narrative takes place and to extend themselves into this world. By extension, I mean that each player, who exists in the real world, must become more identified with the character he plays, who exists in the fantasy world, so that the boundary between the two worlds is more blended. Otherwise, the resulting narrative can be disjointed, with conflicting interpretations of how the world functions on a social, cultural, and even physical level. In this chapter, I will focus on the extension of the gamers into the fantasy realm that is created. Since these games often have very few, if any, physical representations to serve as reference points, incorporation into the fantasy world must be effected primarily through language, and it is this language that I investigate here.

The analysis in this chapter is informed by Critical Discourse Analysis (CDA) (Fairclough and Wodak 1997) and post-structuralist theory, influenced notably by the works of Bakhtin (1981), Foucault (1972, 1980) and Derrida (1987), among others. Both traditions take as axiomatic the assumption that elements of the social space, such as organizations, institutions, social categories, concepts, identities and relationships are determined by language use. Individual selves and identities are constantly restructured and repositioned through discourse, rather than being fixed roles or entities. It is through this discourse that gamers position and reposition themselves both outside the fantasy world of the constructed narrative and within it.

Background

Although there are games that are set in established worlds such as *Star Wars*, *Babylon 5*, and *Men in Black* that already have a visual element that players and GM have shared through motion pictures and television, this paper will be primarily focused on games that exist only "on paper," designed by the GM, either alone or by making use of published source material, such as the *World of Darkness*. These games vary in the amount of existing material from which players and GM can draw to co-create the world of the narrative, but they generally lack an active, immersive, visual three-dimensional element.

In this chapter, I analyze a one-day 12-hour gaming session among long-acquainted players in a world designed entirely by the GM. In the author's experience, gaming groups tend to be insular, where new players are invited by the established players, and where observers are not entirely welcome. Therefore, in order to more readily collect data on such games, it is useful for the researcher to be an established player in the group. I was the GM for the group being studied here, and acted as participant observer. I, as well as three of the other players, have played TFRPGs together as a group for nearly twenty years, while the other two players, Colin and Alex (pseudonyms), are approximately ten years younger than the others. The younger players have interacted with the older players socially for many years, but as of the time of this study, they have only interacted with the older players in a game setting for a brief time. The game session was recorded using a DAT recorder, using an omni directional pressure-zone boundary microphone designed to capture sound from large groups. The resulting digital files were then transcribed using Transcriber[1], a freely-available software tool.

The discourse strategies discussed in this chapter allow gamers to extend themselves into the world of the narrative, the unreal world. However, as stated above, the success of this extension relies upon the gamers' abilities to cooperatively understand how the world works. That is, in order for the GM and players to have their characters take world-appropriate actions and interact with other characters in the social context appropriate to the world, each player must share, to the extent possible, the vision of the GM and the other players. This vision often extends beyond the visual appearance of the world, including socio-cultural, historical and psychological characteristics of the world. This requirement for success in TFRPGs is shared with other similar activities, including MMORPGs (Massively Multiplayer Online Role-playing Games), such as *Dark Age of Camelot* and *City of Heroes*, as well as improvisational theater, such as the improv comedy troupes discussed by Sawyer (2003). TFRPGs differ from improvisational theater in that they have a much longer duration, out-of-game social interaction, and pre-game preparations (development of character, choice of rules, and so forth). They differ from MMORPGs in that computer games often include a visual 3D element within which characters interact across the internet. This visual element allows online players to all have a shared vision of what the world looks like, as defined by the game designer. In contrast, TFRPGs have only a few static artifacts, including perhaps maps, representative pictures of character types, and miniatures. But these artifacts are not always present, nor are they necessary.

The primary purpose of this chapter is to show that the GM and players do, indeed, incorporate themselves into the fantastic world of the game through the use of language. I accomplish this by investigating and illustrating some of the discourse strategies used by players and GM. By discourse, I refer to a broad range of verbal and non-verbal communicative devices used in language interchanges. One example of such a strategy is pronoun usage, discussed in the section Pronoun Usage. As discussed by Tea and Lee (2004), the ambiguous usage of "me" and "you" by players during game play indicates a blending of player and character that can signal a level of extension by the player into the game world. I also include the use of third person references, such as "he/she/it," names, or terms like "this guy" or "dude," by players during game play to refer to their characters. Different players move in and out of third person in their own fashion, shifting the blended entity along a continuum with a mental state closer to the player on one end, where third person is used, and a mental state incorporating the character on the other, where first person is used. I discuss these different modes, and how the strategies interact with other strategies as the game progresses. Other strategies I discuss are the use of popular culture references to draw other gamers into a closer rapport with the world using familiar analogies (discussed in Popular Culture References, and the use of world-specific languages and names to index a gamer's investment in the world (discussed in World-Specific Language Forms).

Throughout this chapter, I use specific terminology to refer to various elements of the TFRPG experience. I use the term "gamer" as a generic to refer to any participant in the game, such as a "player," a gamer who is playing a specific character in a world defined by the "game master," who is the gamer who acts as referee and plot development chairman. A "character" is the game-specific entity that is being controlled by a gamer. A "player character (PC)" is a character that is under the control of a player, while a "non-player character (NPC)" is a character that is under the control of a GM.

A Shared Vision

In order to attain extension into the fantasy world, there must be some sort of mental image, or "shared vision," that is commonly indexed by all the gamers. But what exactly is meant by a "shared vision"? Is it, as Fine (1983) suggests, some parallel to an instance of *folie à deux*, a condition in which similar delusions occur simultaneously in two individuals? I take a more moderate stance, by defining the shared vision of a TFRPG as a set of beliefs and understandings about a fantasy world that are shared among gamers during game play. These beliefs and understandings can refer to physical descriptions of objects and people, cultural norms, environmental effects, components of the fantasy.

This shared context can be categorized in a variety of ways, but I choose, following Fine (1983), to categorize this context in terms of the notion of the frame, introduced by Goffman (1974), and elaborated on by Moscovici (1984), van Dijk (1977, 1980), Lakoff and Johnson (1980), Fine (1983), Sawyer (2003), and others. Goffman (1974) presents the notion of natural and social frameworks created by cultures that create meaning out of otherwise meaningless reality. That is, based on real experiences, cultures create shared contexts, sometimes as rule systems, sometimes as shared epistemological knowledge, that provide a "conceptual structure, through which people can digest information" (Fisher 1997).

Layered over these primary frameworks are what Goffman calls "keyings" or "stagings," which simulate primary frameworks but differ in some fashion from the reality of the primary frameworks. Plays, games, and deceits are all examples of this "keying", i.e., a play is designed to simulate some event or set of events that do not exist in reality. For example, Shakespeare's *Romeo and Juliet* and the events delineating their tragic lives do not exist in the primary framework of reality, but the play *Romeo and Juliet* creates a frame wherein the characters exist and events take place. In the case of the role-playing game, as illustrated by Fine (1983), the act of cooperatively constructing a fantasy world can be considered a form of keying primary frameworks. Fine (1983) identifies three frames that are keyed into by gamers during a game. One is the primary framework, but the other two are the "game frame" and the "fantasy frame". The "game frame" is the frame in which players are constricted by the rules of a game, and is similar to the frame into which players of any game, such as bridge or checkers, might key. The "fantasy frame" is the frame in which the characters live, breathe, and act. In this paper, I focus primarily on the "fantasy frame," blending the distinctions between the "game frame" and the primary framework.

The keying of the primary framework will not be uniform across participants in the game. Each individual will have a slightly different mental picture of the fantasy world, and a different understanding of its social and historical contexts. In order for the shared vision to act as a focus for a gamer to extend into, each individual keying must have as much intersection with the others as possible. And it is that intersected frame, that shared vision, into which players incorporate themselves.

Linguistic anthropologists, such as Sherzer (1987) and Urban (1991), approach the development of culture through the idea that language, or discourse, is at its center. Under such theoretical structures, the evolution of cultures is the result of continuing language use by individual members of a cultural group. As individual members of a cultural group use language with each other, their sets of beliefs and understandings intersect, resulting in shared cultural behavior across the group. In a sense, this is what gamers are doing when involved in a TFRPG. They are using discourse to create a shared culture, or set of beliefs and understandings about the fantasy frame. The sets of beliefs and understandings that are included in each individual's frame are adjusted based on the discourse, and the intersection of the sets becomes closer to a single intersected fantasy frame that is shared by the participants. This emergent intersecting frame then impacts the actions taken by the gamers through the game, even as it is being developed by the gamers, a concept similar to that proffered by Sawyer (2003) in research on the emergence of creativity in improvisational theater.

Incorporative Discourse

Over the course of a game, gamers jump in and out of the fantasy frame and, in many cases, straddle both the fantasy frame and the game frame. The involvement in the fantasy frame can be reflected in the discourse used by the gamers, discourse that I term incorporative discourse. Most directly, the use of "in-character" speech (discussed in more detail below) indicates a high level of involvement in the fantasy frame, where the gamers are speaking as if they are the characters themselves. However, there are other, more indirect strategies used by the gamers that can result in a higher level of involvement in the fantasy frame, both while in character and out of character.

Players and GMs use different strategies with respect to incorporative discourse, because each type of gamer takes on different roles during the course of the game. For example, the game master is the referee, and plays a multitude of different characters (NPCs). As such, the GM is not associated with one particular character, and remains at a distance from the fantasy frame, by dint of his status as adjudicator and font-of-all-knowledge, that is, his "divine" status. Each player, on the other hand, is canonically associated with one character throughout the game. Thus, whether a pronoun refers to a gamer or a character is much more frequently ambiguous between player and character than between GM and NPC. In this chapter, I investigate three types of indirect strategies used by gamers that reflect the amount of involvement in the fantasy frame: first person pronoun usage, popular culture references, and world-specific language forms.

Pronoun Usage

When a player speaks during game play, these words reflect at least two voices, those of the player and the character. As such, one could describe these two voices in a Bakhtinian sense as *diglossia*, or dialogic speech (Bakhtin 1981). As Bakhtin notes, when one experiences a novel and reads the spoken utterances of a character within that novel, one is not only hearing the voice of the character, but also the voice of the author who wrote the work and put the words to paper. The utterance of a player speaking "in character" (and also, as I will show, "out of character") not only makes evident the voice of the character, but also of the player.

And there are more than merely these two voices. These many voices express different aspects of the interconnections between the fantasy frame, the character, and the player. Another helpful analogy to this type of discourse is the work of Goffman (1981), with respect to what he terms *foot-ing*. A speaker, under Goffman's framework, is not a singular unit, but can take on any of three roles: animator, author, and/or principal. A player often engages in these roles throughout the game, moving in and out of them very fluidly. When a player speaks "in character," one may say that she is acting as "animator" and "author" but not necessarily as "principal." That is, she is the voice box through which the words are spoken, the mechanism by which words are produced, hence the "animator." However, she is also the "author," in that she selects the "sentiments that are being expressed and the words in which they are encoded" (Goffman 1981). The "principal," however, is the entity for whom the words form a position-ing, or form a commitment, etc. In the case of the "principal," it is the character whose beliefs or positions are being brought forth, not the player.

For example, take the following "in-character" speech:

(1) In-Character Speech 1

>GM: Dinner? (.) First? or (.) sing first (.)
>MARK: I'll sing for it.
>GM: All right.

(2) In-Character Speech 2

>MARK: ()
>Zhasa, I have a suspicion that (.) if the men (.) those men from last
>night, they represent some sort of sect.
>U:m (.) some sort of organization
>Where it is we're going, we're probably going to find them, or allies of
>theirs (.) at that place
>I'm betting
>It's an educ- this is just a guess, but, uh (.) Dan steles?
>GM: Mmhmm
>MARK: I think I strongly suspect we're looking for (.) an ancient city.
>Dansteles was
>Dansteles invited me to this town so we could find this ancient city
>(.) and search it.
>COLIN: Beneath the mountains?
>MARK: Within or beneath, I'm not a hundred percent certain.
>Now, there are doors involved, but uh (.) I have a loose
>description ( ) to go by.
>But um (.) I strongly suspect that (.) Dansteles was kidnapped or (.)
>was kidnapped and captured by these men (and) is being coerced (.)
>to help them find this place also.
>And they've probably beaten us there.

In this instance, the words are formed by the player and the words are chosen by the player. However, the condition of finding a physical ancient city or singing for one's supper in a tavern is a property of the char-acter. It is not a property of the player, and indeed, could not be. Thus, one can think of in-character speech as an instance where the player is the "animating author," but the character is the principal.

The above characterization may not be satisfactory. The words are, indeed, animated by the player. However, the other two roles are arguably much more ambiguous. Are the words chosen by the player independent of the character? The player has created the character, the character's emotions, background, social relationships, and other attributes, and therefore one could say that the player determines the words being used, rather than the character, because the player is the one holding the strings, and thus the player could also be considered the principal, not just the animator. This complex layering and interdependence between the notions of "character" and "player" causes analyses based on a clearly defined set of roles (such as "animator," "author," and so forth) that can be uniquely attributed to one or the other to become quickly unsatisfactory.

Tea and Lee (2004) discuss how player and character entities within the context of a computer-mediated role-playing game can become blended, where knowledge, skills, emotional responses, and other resources are drawn from both entities as the game play takes place. Taking the theoretical background of mental spaces and conceptual integration (Fauconnier and Turner 2002), the authors argue that this blended entity can account for the referential ambiguity shown by participants in the computer role-playing environment. They take as their analytic focus the usage of the pronouns "me" and "you" in data collected from game sessions of a popular on-line computer role-playing game. The human player is one participant for study, and the computer designer (through the third-party mediation of an independent software package) is another participant.

This "blended entity," argued for by Tea and Lee, can be seen as one way to characterize an incorporation of the player into the fantasy frame. The "blended entity" is a conglomeration of multiple sets of semantic and cognitive relations, or mental states, representing player and character. For example, a character from the fantasy frame may be described as tall, pale, agile, trained in swordplay, curious, overconfident, and having other skills and characteristics inherent to having been raised and socialized within a tribal culture located in a sub arctic region. These traits constitute aspects of the mental state of the character. In contrast, the physical and mental state of the player may involve less athleticism, being shorter, skills in baking, training in mathematics, and other skills and characteristics inherent to having been raised and socialized within a rural culture located in the Southeastern United States. The "blended entity" is a psychological entity that combines aspects of both mental states, each mental state being grounded in either the fantasy or the game frame.

Taking a cue from the research ideas presented in Tea and Lee, I propose that the usage of first person referents is one strategy players use to incorporate themselves into the fantasy frame, by accessing the mental state of the blended entity. The character only exists within the fantasy frame, and thus, when the player uses a first person referent in reference to a character, she is blending her own player entity with the character entity, bringing the player entity more in contact with the world of the fantasy frame. This hypothesis can be supported by the following observations regarding pronoun usage throughout a single-episode role-playing game, wherein I focus on the use of "I" and "me" in comparison to the usage of third person referents, such as "he" or "dude" to refer to a character currently played by the speaker.

Beginning Versus Ending of Game

Sawyer (2003), in a thorough study of improvisational theater, discusses how the emergent frame created by the various offerings of each actor involved in the improvisation takes on a life of its own, after a fashion. Just as the actors create the emergent frame, the frame, in turn, limits and directs future offerings by actors. Through measurements of utterance length, targeted speech, and other types of speech, Sawyer shows that as the improvisation moves in time, the emergent frame is strengthened. The resultant discourse strategies used by the actors in their offerings and receipts change appropriately to match the consolidation of the frame, or shared vision. This can also be seen during the course of a TFRPG, particularly one in which the players begin the game with new characters and in a new world.

At the beginning of the first session of a game, whether it is the only one (one-shot), one episode (episodic), or one session of a longer game (campaign), players are becoming accustomed to their characters. While it is true that in many episodic and campaign adventures, players have been the primary creative influence on their characters, the first game provides the first opportunity for the player/character entities to engage with the world. The discourse of the game proceeds much as improvisational theater, as there is no script, but each player/character's actions and discourse can be seen as offerings and receipts that contribute to the emergent narrative. Just as offerings and receipts in improvisational theater are looser and less targeted at the outset of the improvisation, one should expect that the TFRPG players have not fully engaged with the world in such an introductory game, and as such, there is not as much incorporative discourse, particularly at the beginning of the session.

In the case of pronoun usage, one reflection of this can be the greater usage of third person pronouns by some players at the beginning in contrast to their usage in later times during the adventure. Although a fully quantitative study of pronoun usage across time during a TFRPG of this nature is yet to be done, observations of these data indicate that there is a much greater usage of first-person pronouns as the game progresses, even among players who use third person more often, such as Colin. Such observations are consistent with the use of first person pronouns as incorporative strategies, provided that the emergent fantasy frame comes to play a stronger role in the structuring of the shared vision of the world.

Action and Description

Two broad categories of interchanges commonly take place within the course of a TFRPG. One type of interchange is one in which the content of the interchange revolves around an action taken by a player/character, such as entering a room, making a combative maneuver, or exploring surrounding areas. The other type of interchange is one in which the content of the interchange revolves around a description of the fantasy environment (architecture, weather, objects, and so forth) or the character (what the character is wearing, the size of the character, the differences between the character and accepted societal norms, and so forth).

When a player/character is involved in an action interchange, there is arguably a more immediate incorporation between the character and player. Actions are often involved in the achievement of a goal, a goal which is shared by both player and character. For example, if a player/character is involved in a combat maneuver interchange, both the player and the character share the intent of defeating a combatant. Thus, the action can result in the achievement of a shared goal.

When a player/character is involved in a description interchange, there is a greater distance between the player and character references. While the goals of an action are highly intertwined between the two entities, characters often are very different from their players in physical appearance, emotional state, socialization, and even gender. The author, for example, who is a tall male, has played both a 3' 8" character and a woman during the course of different games. Because of the greater possible difference between the physical descriptions of characters and descriptions of their players, one should expect that descriptive interchanges will not be as incorporative as action interchanges.

Evidence from the data suggests that descriptive interchanges are not as incorporative. During the game, five of the players were each involved in introductory dialogue, in which they described their characters to other players whose characters were in the vicinity. Each of the five players used third person within these descriptive interchanges (even Alex, who normally uses only first person, both in and out of character) and, as shown in (3), gamers also used third person to refer to other person's' characters as separate from the players.

(3) Description Interchange 1

> CHAD: **He** doesn't really see how (.) **he** looks intimidating
> GM: Mm-hm
> CHAD: So
> GM: I mean but he's wearing sort of like the (.) sort of the (.) Ushadi dress? or is he (.) dressing more (.) like (.) everybody around here
> CHAD: **He** doesn't see why they would (.) why they would have an issue with **him** dressing normally [so.....
> MARK: [(is **he** a big dude?)
> CHAD: N-um: (.) not particularly *I mean*
> GM: Do **you** act **I** can't remember do **you** actually have a: a caste mark?
> CHAD: No, ah **he** chose no even though **he** [won the fight **he**

In this transcript, Chad maintains a third person reference to the character in terms of not only physical description, but description of emotions and inner thoughts ("He doesn't see why they would (.) why they would..."). He maintains this, even though the GM uses a non-third person to reference the player/character.

(4) Description Interchange 2

> MARK: As **I** enter?
> GM: Mm-hmm
> MARK: **I'll** look for ( ) first
> GM: Ok
> MARK: **He** sittin around in here anywhere?
> GM: **You** don't see him anywhere in there
> MARK: Just uh (.) to minimize you know to minimize the (.) impact of **my** entry to these places,
> MARK: **I** Figure (.) uh **dude** travels (.) with (.) some kind of lampblack (.) on **his** face like yo you know (?) smear

Once again, in this transcript, a player uses third person referents (dude, his) when involved in a descriptive interchange (the use of lampblack on the face). Contrast this with the rest of the transcript, where the player uses first person pronouns when describing actions such as entering the room and looking for a person. As expected, actions, which involve both the player and the character, use more incorporative discourse.

Knowledge Acquisition

Continuing the discussion of action interchanges, one may also note that the goals that the character and player share require acquiring knowledge about the environment in order to achieve these goals. This information might involve relative locations of potential achievement loci, names of places or people that are themselves achievement loci, relevant abilities and how they interact with the "realities" of the world of the fantasy frame, as well as other knowledge.

Since the characters and their players share similar goals, this knowledge can be seen as requested by both. There is therefore often an ambiguity when there is a use of first person pronouns in querying the GM. For example, Colin asks, at one point, "(o)kay, that brings **me** to **my** second question: would **I** have caught ANY part of that conversation?" in reference to his character's ability to hear in a crowded tavern. One could imagine the character musing to himself and drawing on his own knowledge to make that determination, if he had the relevant knowledge to do so. The player, on the other hand, is not necessarily musing to himself, but asking the GM, because the player lacks the relevant knowledge to make such a judgment. Both the player and the character are attempting to access relevant knowledge to judge their access to knowledge of the conversation.

Popular Culture References

Another incorporative discourse strategy used by gamers during a TFRPG is the use of shared popular culture references. GMs and players can both draw from a rich set of movies, books, songs and other media that can be used to draw the other gamers closer into intersection with the emergent narrative frame. As stated earlier, in most TFRPGs there is no multimedia component. Images and sounds pertaining to the game's fantasy environment exist primarily in the minds of the gamers themselves. Discourse that includes popular culture references is incorporative, as it strengthens the fantasy frame by creating an avenue by which a gamer can access the fantasy frame and allowing other players to elaborate on the fantasy frame so as to continue to narrow its possible variations.

In some cases, the gamer can reference a specific work, such as a movie:

(5) Popular Culture Reference 1

> Mark: What does this look like?
>   Just a (.) eldritch bolt of energy stuff?
> GM: Basic- actually- you w- it's it's sort of like a a just a (.) a shift in the air.

> Sort of like picture the **bullets in um** (.) **Matrix**
> Like just the the wind [(.) the rippling air currents behind it?

(6) Popular Culture Reference 2

> GM: Pretty (.) like I said it's (.) if y if you if you want sort of an analog,
> **Mos Eisley spaceport is kind of a good place to think about it.**
> CHAD: Oh, ok.
> ?: ((singing the Cantina Theme from *Star Wars*))

In these two cases, the movies *The Matrix* and *Star Wars: A New Hope* are being referenced by the GM to further define the fantasy frame.[2] This strategy has the effect of narrowing the set of possible interpretations within each gamer's internal frame, as well as creating intersecting lines between each gamer's frame and the emergent narrative frame. This intersection is not complete, however, as each player has different contexts within which the cinematic references are relevant to the instant at hand. However, any conclusions drawn about the shared vision are based on evidence from a narrower pool of possibilities.

Beyond narrowing the intersecting fantasy frame and thereby creating a stronger sense of commonality across the gamers' visions, the use of these references also serves to bring players into more contact with the fantasy frame. In this case, even if a player has not used other strategies, such as pronoun usage to bring himself into the fantasy frame, the player can indirectly gain higher involvement in the frame by recognizing the reference, by dint of sharing an understanding of an aspect of the frame through the reference. Once a gamer has visualized Mos Eisley spaceport, he is now, like it or not, seeing the world, at least from one dimension, and is therefore incorporated into it.

The reference itself need not be a specific film or book, but can be a genre of films or books. For example, in the following example, the GM is referencing the genre of film commonly known as "westerns":

(7) Popular Culture Reference 3

> GM: Yeah (.) basically it's sort of like (.) I mean (.) if you want to think
> about it picture (.) picture this place like an **old western town** in a lot
> of ways
> CHAD: [Oh
> GM: [You'll actually there's there's a sheriff's office and the sheriff is (usually) kind of sitting in there at his desk probably with (.) feet propped up
> CHAD: Ok. Ok.

In this case, the GM offers what could be construed as a historical analogy, namely a town found in the "Old West" period of American history. However, by continuing to paint a picture of a sheriff seated casually at his desk, the players can also reference a common image of this historical period used in film and television.

The success of this strategy can be noted in two ways. In (6) above, after the GM references a location from *Star Wars: A New Hope*, one of the players begins to sing a tune made popular by one of the scenes that took place the referenced location. If no player can recognize the reference being used as an analogy, then the analogy fails, and a new strategy or new reference must be brought into play. Therefore, the singing of the tune shows the recognition by at least one of the players, and thus, the success of the strategy.

Also, for the reference to be successful, it must be seen to narrow the possible set of interpretations by the players, further defining the intersecting frame. In the case of the reference to the western genre, later interchanges can be interpreted as picking up on this reference. For example, this interchange takes place upon the entrance of a character to a tavern:

(8) Narrowing of Frame by Pop-Culture Reference

>   GM: Now (.) so you you're watching around and people do have that sort
>   of guilt they look around at you kind of like (.) making sure that they
>   don't have anything around that would (.) like
>   CHAD: Kind of stop playing [cards
>   GM: [you know
>   No, they'll (.) they'll play cards but they're (.) you know
>   COLIN: So, they're playing Go Fish

Early on in the discussion of the game, previous to the actual game session, it had been established that the genre of the game would be medieval fantasy. In fact, the term "tavern" is commonly used in fantasy game genres and has been used up to and after this point to reference the location of a meeting-place. However, the activity of playing cards is arguably not a stereotypical activity found in medieval fantasy genres, at least not among the lower classes of society. Playing at dice, or even games such as chess, might be more stereotypical for a fantasy genre of this type. However, card-playing is very common as a western genre image.

French (1977: 128–130) speaks of poker as being "in some way central to the Western mystique" and goes so far as to theorize that poker itself is a microcosm of the quintessential western film style. Although the term "poker" is not used as such in the data shown above, Colin makes a reference to the game "Go Fish" as being the type of game one might play when a member of the clergy is present. Such a reference would only make sense in contrast to a game that might normally be played, something less stereotypically innocent, such as poker, which involves gambling. Thus, the use of card-playing by a player to negotiate the fantasy frame could indicate an uptake by the player of the western reference that was introduced earlier.

World-Specific Language Forms

Language is an important part of human experience, and, as Pinker (1994) puts it, it "is so tightly woven into human experience that it is scarcely possible to imagine life without it" (p. 17). Anthropological research as far back as Sapir (1929) and Whorf (1940) has postulated a connection between language and culture, wherein the language used by speakers reflects and is reflected by the culture of those speakers. As discussed earlier, researchers such as Sherzer (1987) and Urban (1991) have theorized that culture is shaped by the very language being used by members of a community. Humans use different language forms as indicators of group identity and solidarity, we use language to communicate and share cultural ideas, and we fight for the right to speak the languages we choose. In fact, this very chapter is about how gamers use language to incorporate themselves into a shared fantasy reality that does not provide a visual component as a reference point.

Arguably, then, for a world to seem "real," it must reflect this basic, yet pervasive, aspect of human experience. Thus, use of specialized language can be another strategy through which gamers draw themselves and each other into the shared vision of the game. Gamers can use language forms specific to the world of the fantasy frame or their characters' identities to become part of the shared vision. In the data from which this paper draws its conclusions, the fantasy world is a creation of the GM, and as such, does not transparently exist outside of the game sphere. This created world includes linguistic material that is specific to the world and its characters.

Normally, the game progresses through the use of a language common to all the players, in this case, English. This is a necessary convention; otherwise, the players would not be able to communicate with each other to engage in the narrative being constructed. Even when characters are speaking to other characters, the language being used by the players/characters is English, although the assumption is often that they are speaking a language common to the world in which the events of the constructed narrative take place.

If we take a more post-structuralist position, wherein all elements of a social space are determined by discourse, or even a more mitigated position, such as the discourse-centered view espoused by Urban (1991) and Sherzer (1987), then one must assume, if the societies within the fantasy world are "real," that the various societies within that world are the result of the language forms used by the members of those communities. Those language forms are not English, but languages of the fantasy world. Therefore, by using English language forms, the players/characters continue to align themselves more closely to the player aspects of the blended entity, and are thus less incorporated into the fantasy frame.

By using portions of the language resources provided by the GM, characters are able to create links between their fantasy frame and the fantasy frame of not only the GM, but also other characters. These world-specific language forms allow the blended entity to access linguistic and cultural resources of the character aspect. The players do, indeed, make use of these language forms in the context of the game, allowing them to reach into the world on a more cultural level. For example, Mark plays a magic-user, a character who manipulates magical energy. Mark has been given a list of possible magical actions ("spellbook") that his character can take, and he references them by name when using them:

(9) Magical Spell Terms

> MARK: it's **Eh thek el es** ((uncertain pronunciation))
> GM: **Ethelkeles**
> MARK: **Ethelkeles**Shove

In this example, Mark references a particular combat action by the name given in the spellbook, even though he is not in character. He is declaring his action to the group, and as such, can be said to be, at least partially, within the game frame, not the fantasy frame.[3] Since he is out of character, it is not strictly necessary that he use terms that his character would know. However, although there are other (perhaps less difficult to pronounce) options, such as using the description of the action based on the game's rule system (e.g., Energy Blast 2d6), he chooses to use the term that is specific to the world of the fantasy frame.

Repeating another example from earlier in this chapter, Mark also uses the term *Zhasa*, when referring to one of the other characters, while Mark is in character. This term is from a constructed language specific to the game, means something akin to "sibling of either gender," and is used to refer to members of a religious order, again specific to the world of the fantasy frame.

(10) Use of World-Specific Term

> Mark: **Zhasa**, I have a suspicion that (.) if the men (.) those men from last night, they represent some sort of sect.

In fact, when Mark asks the GM how to refer to the members of this order, he is given two options:

(11) Options for Reference

Mark: What do we call this dude?
     Do we call him father [or brother?
GM: [U:h the:
     Well, brother usually and the term is **zhasa**.
     If you if you actually use the Kalistan (.) phrasing, it would be **zhasa**,
     but (.) brother would work just fine.
Mark: **Zhasa**, do you need help? ((in character))

As can be seen from the above interchange, even though Mark is given the option of using an English term, he chooses the less-familiar, but more world-specific term. Thus, Mark indexes his incorporation into the fantasy frame by using language that is an aspect of the character entity, an entity who more fully interacts within the fantasy frame, and indexes, by transitivity, a world-specific culture through the use of the language forms.

Conclusion

In this paper, I have illustrated a few of the discourse strategies used by gamers in a TFRPG to incorporate themselves into the world of fantasy that they and other gamers are cooperatively constructing. Using first person pronouns, a player solidifies a blending of himself with his character, creating a mental state in which his abilities and goals intersect with those of the role he is playing. Using references from popular culture, gamers strengthen their shared vision of the world, allowing for greater incorporation of themselves and other gamers. Using language and names specific to the fantasy world, gamers are able to ratify their involvement in the world through claiming the language of the world as their own.

References

Bakhtin, Mikhail M. 1981. *The Dialogic Imagination.* M. Holquist (Ed.) (M. Holquist, and C. Emerson, Trans.). Austin, TX: University of Texas Press.

Derrida, Jacques. 1987. *A Derrida Reader: Between the Blinds.* Brighton: Harvester Wheatsheaf.

Fairclough, Norman and Wodak, Ruth. 1997. Critical Discourse Analysis. In *Discourse as Social Interaction,* edited by Teun van Dijk. London: Sage.

Fauconnier, Gilles, and Mark Turner. 2002. *The Way We Think: Conceptual Blending and the Mind's Hidden Complexities.* New York: Basic Books.

Fine, Gary A. 1983. *Shared Fantasy: Role-playing Games as Social Worlds.* Chicago, IL: University of Chicago Press.

Fisher, Kimberly. 1997. Locating Frames in the Discursive Universe. *Sociological Research Online,* 2(3) (*http://www.socresonline.org.uk/socresonline/2/3/4.html*).

Foucault, M. 1972. *The Archaeology of Knowledge and the Discourse of Language.* New York: Pantheon.

_____. 1980. *Power/Knowledge: Selected Interviews and Other Writings, 1972–1977*. New York: Pantheon.

French, Philip. 1977. *Westerns: Aspects of a Movie Genre*. New York: Oxford University Press.

Goffman, Erving. 1974. *Frame Analysis: An Essay on the Organization of Experience*. Cambridge, MA: Harvard University Press.

_____. 1981. *Forms of Talk*. Philadelphia, PA: University of Pennsylvania Press.

Lakoff, George, and Mark Johnson. 1980. *Metaphors We Live By*. Chicago, IL: University of Chicago Press.

Moscovici, Serge. 1984. The Phenomenon of Social Representations. In *Social Representations*, edited by S. Moscovici and R. M. Farr. London, UK: Cambridge University Press.

Pinker, Steven. 1994. *The Language Instinct*. New York: William Morrow and Company.

Sapir, E. 1929. The status of linguistics as a science. *Language* 5: 207–14.

Sawyer, R. K. 2003. *Improvised Dialogues: Emergence and Creativity in Conversation* Westport, CT: Ablex Publishing.

Sherzer, Joel. 1987. A Discourse-Centered Approach to Language and Culture. *American Anthropologist* 89(2): 295–309.

Tea, Alan J. H., and Benny P. H. Lee. 2004. Reference and blending in a computer role-playing game. *Journal of Pragmatics* 36(9):1609–1633.

Urban, Greg. P. 1991. *A Discourse-Centered Approach to Culture: Native South American Myths and Rituals* Austin, TX: University of Texas Press.

van Dijk, T. A. 1977. *Text and Context Explorations in the Semantics and Pragmatics of Discourse*. London, UK: Longman.

_____. 1980. *Macrostructures: An Interdisciplinary Study of Global Structures in Discourse, Interaction and Cognition*. Hillsdale, NJ: Lawrence Erlbaum.

Whorf, B. L. 1940. Science and Linguistics. *Technology Review* 42(6): 229–31, 247–8.

Notes

1. http://www.ldc.upenn.edu/mirror/Transcriber

2. It may be noted that both examples of popular culture references are initiated by the GM. This is a normal consequence of the fact that the GM is the creator of the world, and arbiter of its characteristics. Rarely do players initiate such references, although, as shown in excerpt (8), they may elaborate on the reference.

3. In this instance, since Mark is referencing an action taken by the player/character, it is arguably taking place in both the fantasy and the game frame simultaneously.

3. SOCIAL EVENTS AND ROLES IN *MAGIC*

A Semiotic Analysis

Csilla Weninger

Research on fantasy games has remained marginal within the social sciences. More specifically, there are virtually no sociological or linguistic studies focusing on the decade-old collectible strategy game (CSG) genre. The role that language plays in this social activity presents an important research point for discourse analysts interested in exploring issues of how social roles and relations are actualized through/in talk. Given the multiplicity of sign systems of which players make use during a game, CSGs as conversational encounters (Goffman 1983) provide an interesting ground for research into the semiotics of social action.

In this chapter, I examine the role of semiotic systems in playing the collectible card game *Magic: The Gathering* (*MTG*) on the basis of a videotaped game session between two people, one of whom was the researcher herself. My analysis involves two levels: First, I argue that what on the surface appears to be a unitary social event (or speech genre) actually comprises a number of distinct social events, each of which entails specific sets of social relations for the two participants as well as relevant semiotic systems. Second, I look at how shifts in the semiotic resources upon which players draw index shifts from one event to another. The semiotic resources I investigate include spoken language, material objects, gaze and paralinguistic features.

The perspective taken in this research can be broadly situated within studies of language as social action and semiotic analyses of human interaction. In the first section, I briefly review the origins and development of this research tradition within linguistics as well as recent interdisciplinary directions within multimodal analyses. In the remainder of the chapter I discuss the methods and data used for the study and present the results of my analysis.

Language as Social Action

Throughout much of the history of linguistics, language has been conceptualized as a self-contained system of elements, with a resulting focus on describing the relations that obtain between linguistic units at various levels. A turning point came with Speech Act Theory (Austin 1962; Searle 1969), which advocated a view of language as a type of social action and shifted the emphasis from a pre-occupation with sentence-level structures to studying situated language use. This move coincided with and was influenced by Goffman's work on the dramaturgical nature of social interaction in sociology and also resonated in the research tradition of what has become known as conversation analysis (Sacks, Schegloff and Jefferson 1974; Sacks 1992). Various functional accounts of linguistics (Givón 1979; Halliday 1985) opened up a new line of inquiry and have informed analyses of discourse from a primarily social-critical standpoint (Fairclough 1995, 2003; Gee 1996). Empirically, research has favored face-to-face talk (interactional studies) or texts (predominantly critical studies) to glimpse the role of language in actualizing social relations and cultural norms. In semiotic terms, these approaches involved a move away from Saussure's conception of signs as composed of a signifier and a signified and the arbitrary relation connecting the two. Meaning is considered motivated as it indexes cultural, social or ideological preferences, and emergent because of contingent effects of the context in which it is produced.

While this conceptual move has resulted in a wide range of studies and theories about the role of language (discourse) in the realization and maintenance of socio-culturally motivated meaning and in the organization of action, spoken and written language have been the main focus of much analysis, mostly at the exclusion of other modes of semiosis, such as material surroundings and other meta-linguistic features. While inquiry into alternative but equally important systems of signification has remained marginal (particularly within linguistics), there have been some major recent developments in this direction, most notably with a focus on multimodality and social semiotics (Kress and van Leeuwen 1996; 2001), embodied interaction (Coupland and Gwyn 2003; Goodwin and Goodwin 1986; Goodwin 2000, 2002) and geosemiotics (Scollon 2001; Scollon and Scollon 2003).

In his analyses of talk-in-interaction, Goodwin conceptualizes action as involving participants' continuous and sequential deployment of multiple semiotic resources that include talk, gesture, the body and material structures. First, in an effort to de-center language as the sole carrier of meaning in interaction, Goodwin proposes the concept of *contextual configuration*, a "locally relevant array of semiotic fields" that is particular to a certain context (2000:1490). Action unfolds as a result of ongoing changes in the contextual configuration; that is changes in semiotic fields that speakers deem as relevant to the achievement of their current action. A second crucial element for talk-in-interaction is speakers' mutual orientation to a certain *participation framework* within which interaction occurs (Goodwin 1981; 2000). This is achieved partly through a shared bodily focus (by way of gaze and posture) and serves as the basis for collaborative action. Third, the acceptance and maintenance of a shared participatory framework requires *reflexive awareness*: participants have to constantly monitor each other's response and action in order to make sure that they are in agreement about which semiotic fields are regarded relevant to a current action.

Other linguists have studied the intersection of action, semiotics and the material world in making meaning, building on Goffman's microsociology (1959; 1963; 1983). In their theory of *geosemiotics*, Scollon and Scollon (2003) are particularly concerned with four factors that contribute to human action: (1) the social actor with his/her "habitus"; (2) the interaction order as a relational framework for social interaction; (3) visual semiotics that involves representation through images; and (4) sets of semiotic systems (place semiotics) that shape the meaning of a given place. Their discussion of geosemiotics also relies on three principles that are fundamental to meaning-making and interpretation: *indexicality* (the context and place-dependency of signs); *dialogicality* (all discourse builds on previous discourses and projects future ones); and *selection* (in any action, actors will select a subset of signs for attention and disregard others).The meaning of an action arises out of interactions among the above four factors and indexes at least two things: the person (aspects of his/her persona that can be "read off") and the discourses that are in place at the moment. Scollon and Scollon's notion of a "semiotic aggregate" is similar to Goodwin's "contextual configuration," with the exception that the former includes all discourses that are present in a place (through diverse signs) regardless of which subset a person selects for the completion of an action.

Both Goodwin's and Scollon and Scollon's research provide a useful conceptual background as well as some analytical tools for the semiotic study of situated interaction. In my analysis, I incorporate much of this previous work while applying it to examine new aspects of the role of semiosis in social interaction. Goodwin looked at how speakers drew on different semiotic fields to accomplish a certain action and focused on the moment-by-moment changes in semiotic reference frames that propelled action. I will examine the larger organizational unit of social events (composed of multiple social acts) and explore how larger shifts in relevant semiotic systems can index changes in social events and with them changes in the interpersonal relationship between participants.[1] In line with Scollon and Scollon's work, I look at the discourses present in the particular place of the interaction and their contribution to the meanings that can be generated in this context. I also employ the notion of indexicality and selection by looking at how aspects of the interaction order provide semiotic resources upon which participants rely in accomplishing ongoing action.

Setting, Method and Design

My analysis relies on data collected by videotaping one gaming session (60 minutes) involving myself and my husband playing *MTG* in our home. In short, *Magic* is played by two or more players with the main goal of eliminating co-players through successful manipulation of cards. The basic structure of *MTG* consists of players drawing cards from their decks, taking actions, and discarding cards. Unlike in regular card games, however, each player constructs his/her own deck from cards that can have very different appearances and functions. As a result, apart from knowledge of game rules, familiarity with *Magic* cards is necessary for a smooth game.[2]

During the period of the gameplay that I videotaped for research, we played two games. Although I had played *Magic* on a few previous occasions, my understanding of the game and my experience with *Magic* cards was rather superficial. Consequently, both my husband and I knew that questions and explanations would most likely abound during the game.

The close, qualitative linguistic/semiotic analysis that I undertake in this paper called for a focus on a relatively small corpus of data. It is quite common and often necessary in researching interaction and language use, particularly in a domain that has not been studied before, to concentrate on a limited number of conversations. After an initial understanding of the researched aspect has been reached, a larger and extended corpus may be used.[3] The videotape was transcribed in full and I made notes of the non-verbal aspects of the interaction as well (for transcription conventions, see the Appendix at the end of the chapter). During the analysis, I reviewed the video numerous times and relied on the text as well as my recollections of the event. Keeping with my general orientation towards a participant-inclusive analysis, I asked my husband to review my interpretation of his actions and suggest alternative explanations. In discussing the findings, I will refer to myself and my husband by our first initials, mainly in order to avoid an overuse of the first person singular that will be reserved for my voice as the author.

Analysis and Discussion

There are five social events that can be said to be present during the *MTG* gaming session. Importantly, it is only possible to analytically distinguish among these events and to characterize them in terms of a set of semiotic systems that are active during each event. Events overlap and are brought to "front stage" by way of diverse semiotic resources.

Event Structure

The event that is most obvious and prevalent throughout is *the game* with the participant positions of players. My choice of the game as the primary event is motivated by the fact that it provides the basic interactional framework, supported by the centrality of cards as semiotic elements. In other words, the game serves as the *matrix event*, within which other events are embedded. This is my adaptation of Myers-Scotton's (1993) term of a matrix language, the language within which other languages may be embedded through code-switching. Within the game we can distinguish between several sub-events. First, the *actual game*, involving the two player-wizards as they set out to battle each other with the help of creatures, enchantments and artifacts, represented in the cards. The *meta-game* as a second sub-event closely accompanies the actual game and represents an event of debate and analysis over what is taking place in the actual game. Here participants step outside of their battle to reflect and comment on the relative merits of certain moves undertaken by them. The third sub-event is also strongly related to the gaming event but characterizes another facet of it. One of the players (P) is an expert in *MTG* while the other (C) is a novice, although not a total beginner. As a result, there are frequent interactions about what is going on in the game that belong to neither the actual nor the meta-game but constitute a separate sub-event that I call the *teaching event*. Participants occupy the roles of the *expert/teacher* (P) and *novice/student* (C) and interactions focus on clarifying and explaining aspects of *MTG* in general; i.e. rules and effects of different cards. The fourth sub-event occurs as spouses engage in what may be called a *family leisure event*: husband and wife, in their home, are playing cards as a way to spend time together. Finally, this one hour of interaction can also be thought of as a *research event* where a *researcher-participant* and a *co-participant* are being video-taped for the purpose of a subsequent analysis of their interaction. In Figure 1, I offer a schematic representation of the events present during the session.

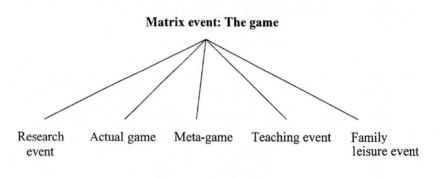

Matrix event: The game

Research   Actual game   Meta-game   Teaching event   Family
event   leisure event

Figure 1. Event Structure

Semiotic Resources in Events

In this section, I give an account of the key semiotic resources that participants draw on during each of the five events. This characterization may be considered as a gross analysis that condenses the intricate semiotic meaning-making into a series of snapshots, while acknowledging that what actually happens is far from static. Based on this description, however, I will be able to point out how divergence from the contextual configuration typical of (but not exclusive to) an event indexes the emergence and foregrounding of a different event. First, however, I want to briefly describe the physical place in which events took place, as the discourses afforded by it as well as its specific spatial arrangements represent potential semiotic resources.

Setting

The matrix event took place in our home one weekend evening.

The camera and microphone were positioned so as to include both participants, although during the session P's body partially moves out of the frame as he sits back in the chair. This shot actually represents the main participant framework: throughout most of the game, participants remain in this position, with some changes in posture, gestures and gaze.

The table and the manipulation of cards, however, constitute for the most part the point of orientation for participants.

As for the venue as a semiotic aggregate (Scollon and Scollon 2003), the most prevalent discourses appear to be those connected to the home, although they can be quite diverse. Discourses of food or dining; discourse of/about academic matters (also present through objects such as books and notebooks as well as the camera and microphone); discourse of family relations and relationships (including the players' own), indexed by various photographs and sentimental objects; but also discourses of gaming (e.g. fair-play) made present through the cards, for instance. These co-present discourses serve as a pool of semiotic resources from which players select some and disregard others as they go about playing the game.

The Actual Game

The actual game, as the event in which the gameplay proceeds, entails verbal (linguistic), material (various physical objects) and embodied systems of semiotic resources. The most prominent linguistic marker of the actual game is what has been called *eventcast* in the context of sports broadcasts (Heath 1985): the on-spot reporting of what is happening in a situation (Excerpt 1). It also includes brief comments about what a card does in order to legitimize the player's action (Excerpt 2). In terms of grammatical structures, this is mainly realized by present-tense verb form as well as the use of the future tense. As indicated by the upward arrows in the excerpts below, a further characteristic of this event is a rising intonation at the end of each "action", indexing that an event is in progress and possibly that the player has not yet finished his/her turn. In fact, the turn-closing statement "I am done" is frequently uttered with a falling intonation.

(1) P: Uhm I'm gonna pay one two three↑ (2.0) four↑ (2.0) I'm gonna play a *Winter Orb* ↑ (2.0)

(2) P: Okay. (3.0) I've got four so I can't gain any life↑ (.) I play *Mishra's Workshop* ↑ (1.0) the workshop gives me three *mana* for casting artifacts↑ (2.0)

Cards and dice represent semiotic resources in that a focus on them can index the actual game. The positioning and manipulation of various cards index specific acts that occur during the actual game (e.g. drawing cards, tapping or untapping cards, placing cards into the "graveyard"). Manipulation of the positions of the cards by hand movements thus generally occurs only as part of the actual game. However, it may co-occur with talk that is launching another event into the front stage.

The cloth that covers the table constantly indexes the game by diverting attention from its regular function. A glass-top dining table that is otherwise never covered is turned into a surface that is suitable for playing the card game; the cloth reduces the reflection of the overhead light and allows for a smoother handling of cards across the table.

It is difficult to characterize the actual game in terms of gaze, as it is one of the semiotic resources that changes most rapidly, indexing a change in orientation. Nevertheless, during the actual game, more so than in the other events, participants' gaze is directed at the cards (downward onto the table or towards their hand) and is in sync with what the hand is doing; e.g. moving from the cards in front of a player to the dice on the side. The gaze and bodily orientation of the person out of turn may not be as closely directed towards the cards and the table when the person in turn is deliberating his/her move silently (e.g. s/he may lean back or gaze at the other player). The stability of players' physical positioning during gameplay thus allows for a relaxation of reflexive awareness (Goodwin 2000) during these periods.

The Meta-Game

The meta-game is characterized by language use that topically centers around game analysis: the out-loud deliberation about the co-participant's or one's own moves. It also includes talk about hypothetical courses of action, primarily in the form of players reflecting about what the outcomes of an alternative move might have been. Explaining the function of a card that a player is using but that may be unknown to others can also be considered as belonging to the meta-game, although there are instances in which it is integrated into the actual game (Excerpt 2 above). Finally, contestation of moves or of the legitimacy of certain acts may also occur as part of the game analysis. Linguistic indices include past and future conditionals (with or without modals) as well as past tense verb forms. The following excerpts illustrate some of these points:

(3) P: [That would have been very nice.
   C: [That would have been perfect. Yeah.
   P: Yeah.
   C: 'Cause I could have countered your little fireball right?
   P: Oh no you couldn't have that's right. (.) Uh (.) because it wasn't an enchantment it was a sorcery so you couldn't have stopped it.
   C: Oh.

(4) P: A::h bringing out the *Serra*. ((commenting on C's move))

(5) P: M-m ((negation)) you just brought it out last time.
   C: NO! ((shakes head))
   P: Yes. You attacked with these two ((pointing)) last time.
   C: Are you sure?
   P: Mm-hm. (.)

Players' gazes are still primarily focused on the cards and the table in general, but there is also some mutual orientation towards the other player. In Excerpt (3), for instance, during the overlapping first two lines P and C are looking at each other but then their gazes turn to the cards again as P reconsiders what a particular card of C's might have done; P then points to a card while giving the explanation. The meta-game is thus characterized by players' gazes shifting not only in a primarily horizontal mode as in the actual game (i.e. from object to object on the table or to cards in one's hand) but also in a vertical direction from cards (table) upwards to meet the other player's gaze.

There is a great deal of pointing through gesture in this event mainly because the meta-talk does not automatically make it clear which card is being referred to (as in the actual game where talk and gesture are mostly synchronous). It is here that the importance of symbiotic gestures (Goodwin 2003) comes into the foreground: players' pointing to a card is vital for the interaction to be fully meaningful. It directs others' gazes toward the object that is also the topic of the verbal comment. Unless talk, gesture and gaze are linked and attended to by both players, the interaction may not be successful.

The Teaching Event

The teaching event closely follows the game as it builds on (inter)action during the actual and meta-game. P as expert and C as novice engage in talk, the purpose of which is to clarify basic game-related issues that are unlikely to occur if two experts are playing. The turn-type that is indexical of this event involves the sequence Question-Answer-Elaboration, where the first element can take the form of a yes/no or an information question, as illustrated by Excerpts (6-7), respectively:

> (6) C: Okay do *sorceries* die? [**Question**]
>   P: Yes. [**Answer**] *Sorceries* are just like *instants* but they can only be played on your turn. ((pointing to C)) They do their thing one time and then they go away. (.) I mean they go to the graveyard. [**Elaboration**] ((pointing to C's graveyard))
> (7) C: ((audible exhale)) Okay. The X in the top right corner is that- what does that mean? [**Question**]
>   P: That means you can pay more and whatever however much you pay it does a certain action. [**Answer**]
>   C: Okay. Oh yeah I see.
>   (2.0)
>   P: So like if you pay two maybe it gives your character plus- your creature plus two. Or if you pay (.) five extra *mana* you get five of something. [**Elaboration**]

Speakers often resort to the use of modal verbs and C, as the novice, is generally the one seeking clarification about rules. The reader might have noticed that both excerpts for the actual game (Excerpts 1-2) came from P, the expert player. The reason lies in the fact that much of the interaction during the teaching event focuses on the socialization of C by P into the game as a semiotically complex genre. Only on a few occasions is C able to produce continuous eventcast, for example. Most of her contribution towards "doing the game" is either done silently (by utilizing semiotic resources at the exclusion of speech) or is interspersed with talk that is either part of the meta-game or orients towards the teaching event.

The gestural action during this event underscores P's explicit instructions about how cards should be laid or moved in order for the actual game to take place:

> (8) P: [so take it back↑ (Pull) your plains↑ (1.0) You need to tap it↑ (1.5) Okay↑
> C: [(xxx)
> P: Okay.
> C: Now I'm done.
> P: And then usually to help you remember the difference between the two usually play *land* on one row↑ ((drawing imaginary line in front of C on the table)) and your *creatures* on another row ((drawing another imaginary line above the first one on the table)) so that you remember what you've got. And then some people play like this ((moving two of C's cards on the table)) and then have their hand out ((taking C's left arm with the cards in hand and moving it towards the middle of the table)) so it's hard for people to remember what the other person's playing but you play however. (.) Are you done?

Here, P is teaching C about card positioning as a semiotic resource within the game and the importance of the symbiosis between cards, gestures and verbal comment as semiotic fields that together index certain types of action. P's pointing to individual cards or to the die that is used to determine who goes first involves gestural movements. Here, however, gesture serves the main purpose of elaborating on what is being said verbally. By drawing on gesture as a semiotic resource, P the teacher ensures that the student C understands for instance how to use a 10-sided die or how to position her cards on the table. Both types of gestures (symbiotic and elaborative) might occur during the actual game, yet their combination with other semiotic fields to complete a certain action is unique to the teaching event.

Similar to the meta-game, the gaze of players is not only downward focusing strictly on actions on the table but includes a visual orientation to the other player, although as with other events, it is hard to characterize the teaching situation as involving one type of gaze only. Gaze, throughout the session, is the semiotic resource of the body with the least temporal steadiness. While players' lower bodies remain mostly in the same position, their torso may lean forward or backward for periods of time, and their arms and hands also shift positions, though more slowly than the speed at which gazes may change. Rather than treating it as indexical of certain events, gaze thus appears to be a local resource whose orientation indexes specific actions within a given event (cf. Goodwin 2000).

The Family Leisure Event

It might be argued that because of the home setting and the spousal relationship, the family event should be regarded as the matrix within which others are embedded. If we look at the place as a semiotic aggregate, discourses of the home certainly abound. However, the matrix event is the one that lends the encounter its basic organizational character — both in terms of roles and interaction. The primary activity is still the card game, even though it is indeed difficult to keep embedded events apart as the game unfolds.

While their relationship as husband and wife obtains throughout the game, participants rarely index their relationship through verbal means, although some terms of endearment and reference to people or episodes in their shared past, present and future signal the close bond. The family event and the intimate relationship between P and C enter the interaction chiefly via *affect* as a semiotic resource, manifesting itself through facial expression as the predominant displayer of emotions (Martinec 2001) or through paralinguistic means. Consider for instance Excerpt (9):

(9) C: Mm-hm, nice.
    P: Thanks. ((in a soft voice, making a face))
    C: Are you done? ((in the same voice quality as P, making the same
        face))

This short excerpt was preceded by P's deployment of a very powerful card and his explanation of what it does, in response to which C offers a compliment, which in turn is acknowledged by P. With regard to the speech act, this short segment can be assigned to the meta-game as a commentary on a player's action. The peculiar voice quality in which P delivers his line and then C's spontaneous response in a matching tone and with the same facial expression represents an adjacency pair that is habitually employed in the couple's informal interactions outside the present context. Such dialogicality (Scollon and Scollon 2003) thus indexes the exchange as one between intimates.

A recurring interplay of verbal interaction and embodied affect is triggered by an ongoing but subtle competition between C and P. Competition is an aspect of the game as the categories of "winner" and "loser" are generated as outcomes of that event. However, the verbal achievement of competition (e.g. teasing or accusation) between P and C is infused with humor and playfulness or overt annoyance as embodied performance (Goodwin and Goodwin 2001). Thus while competition may index the game, it is verbalized and enacted in a manner that also marks C and P as intimates, making the family event salient. In Excerpt (10), P's first comment concerns a card he just brought into play. The function of this card is to restrict players to untapping only one *land* card (needed to use the rest of their deck) per turn.

> (10) P: Makes for a slow game after it comes out.
>   C: ((looking at P annoyed, making a face, irritated tone)) What do you mean slow game I mean basically I'm screwed cause all I can untap for one — I mean —

C's overt annoyance with P's move can occur from her role as his wife. Competition of course is not restricted to spouses, but the strong emotional stance conveyed by lexical means, facial expression, gaze and intonation of the utterance would be unlikely to accompany talk between mere acquaintances.

Such embodied markers of emotion appear to be present during the entire session, often coloring other events by actualizing the intimate relationship. It may be useful to think of the family event in terms of Fine and Kleinman's (1979) distinction between centrality and salience of identification. In subcultural membership, centrality expresses the degree to which members commit to their particular group while salience refers to their frequency of identification with the group. When applied to the present context, the married relationship between C and P assumes a central role, even if it is not always in the focus of attention. The family event, while central to both participants, becomes less salient as they index non-family events.

Participants' use of objects also indexes the family event as the current one. In the second half of the session, C gets up and comes back with a bowl of apple crisp that has been baking in the oven since they started to play. In fact, the smell of the baking apples had been fairly constant although it was not until C noticed it that it became relevant as a resource. This smell is part of an "olfactory sphere" (Scollon and Scollon 2003) that can be viewed as a semiotic system capable of generating meaning. For C, the smell is part of the family sphere and her eating of the apple crisp occurs within that event, which however may overlap with other events.

The Research Event

One of the most obvious reminders of the research event during the session is the presence of the video camera and the microphone, both well within the sight though not necessarily within the participation framework of participants. Just as with other objects in the material surroundings, the recording equipment represents a semiotic field that can be brought to the fore of the interaction and thus be meaningful.

There are few occasions when this occurs and in most it is P who "addresses" the camera. The conversation segment in Excerpt (11) is preceded by a disagreement between P and C concerning a card (part of which is seen in Excerpt 5 above) as part of the meta-game.

(11) C: Okay.
    P: Tru::st me. I <u>wouldn't</u> lie.
    C: I know you wouldn't but–
    P: Are you done?
    C: My memory tends to be better than yours.
    P: Hmm.
    C: Yes I'm done.
    P: ((laughingly)) Shall we ((looking at and pointing to the camera)) rephra —(.)
        rewind the tape?
    C: ((slightly annoyed)) Don't worry about the tape just ignore the tape.

In this excerpt we also see another example of the family event — C's reference to an issue that concerns their relationship ("My memory tends to be better than yours") but here is used to deal with the conflict that occurred as part of the game. The move relevant to the research event comes when P — recognizing that C's comment may be too personal for inclusion in a research report — offers (though jokingly) to rewind the tape. By pointing to the camera and moving it also verbally in the middle of the interaction, P also draws the research event "on stage" from the position of the husband. In turn, C as the researcher requests that P the research participant not pay attention to the camera.

There is no verbal discussion during the session of anything that relates to the research that C is conducting. The only times it is made salient is by way of gesture (e.g. when P on one occasion waves to the camera while C is looking at her cards) or when it is introduced first by gaze (Excerpt 11; also when later C looks at the camera to see if the tape had run out) that directs attention to the camera. In a sense, because the entire session is captured from the perspective of the camera, the research event may be thought of as the matrix that frames all other events and also unites them to build the object of the present analysis. However, as my analysis has illuminated, the key issue is how the research event and all other events are embedded and become actualized within the framework provided by the gameplay.

I have looked at five events that are not only afforded by the semiotic aggregate of the setting but are also made relevant by participants' foregrounding them during their conversational encounter. Further, I have argued that each of these events can be characterized by participants' use of certain linguistic features and other semiotic resources to carry out actions within each event while keeping in mind that most of the time these events do not occur in temporal blocks but either co-occur or flow into each other. Exactly how this happens and what the role of semiotic systems is in the process is the focus of the next section.

Transitions and Overlaps In-Between Events

Although looking at frames rather than events, Fine points to the phenomenon of *frame-switching* in role-playing games; that is to how certain frames (i.e. what the interaction is about) are "up-keyed" (centered) or "down-keyed" (de-centered) during the game (1983:185). While I prefer "event" to "frame" as a more stable analytical unit, the same phenomenon seems to be happening during *MTG* as well. The difference is that, with some exceptions, when only one single event appears to be happening at one time, most of the interaction between C and P represents events flowing into each other, achieved by a polyphonic play of semiotic systems that participants draw on. Sometimes it is the verbal component that weighs in most, accounting for a change in events while other semiotic resources provide support and reinforcement. On other occasions, despite no verbal activity, there is a re-orientation of participants' focus that leads to a shift (however short it may be) in the event that is most salient at that moment. Finally, due to the complex semiotic work that characterizes the game and to the relatively stable participation framework, participants may engage in multiple events at the same time or each of them may orient to a different event. In the following, I illustrate these points through two examples from the video.

The first excerpt represents the unfolding of events where participants' verbal repertoire seems to be the primary, but not necessarily the only, semiotic resource driving the shifts. In fact, most of the time the game event is in place, participants have to rely on the cards in order to make their interaction meaningful and this will be true for Excerpt (12) as well. What I would like to draw attention to is how in less than one minute (56 seconds), participants shift between all five events. Moreover, as C and P invoke different events, the transitions among them appear smooth and do not impede the interaction.

> (12) C: Hmm (.) okay. (8.0) ((chuckles)) <u>Off</u> they go. ((C pushes 3 cards towards P; P leans forward to look at cards)) (1.0) Uhm (.) I'm baring myself. ((laughs))
>
> P: ((looking down on the cards)) *She's* a:: four six she's an [EIGHT-SIX? ((leaning back in his chair))

C: [eight-six.
P: (1.0) Well (1.0) ((looking into the camera)) Pardon my French (.) ((looking at C)) but I just <u>fucked up</u>. ((both laugh)) I shou — I had the — I had the card to kill *her* and I didn't. ((C smiles and sticks her tongue out towards P)) So you're attacking?
C: ((nodding with her head and pointing with index finger towards P)) You didn't thi — you didn't think I had it in me <u>did</u> you.
P: I didn't know you had tha — I didn't know you had <u>two</u>.
C: (1.0) You knew I had one?
P: No, I didn't know what you had but I — [didn't-
C: [I'm <u>attacking</u> you yes.
P: Yeah I know. *She* doesn't have to tap. That's nice.
C: What does that mean?
P: That means that *she*'s not tapped so if I brought out a *creature* next time_ *she*'s untapped so *she* can still block. Tapped *creatures* can't block_ that's what's so nice about *her*.

C's utterance "off they go" is part of the actual game as with that utterance, despite its non-canonical form, she is in effect attacking P. Her following comment as well as the accompanying chuckles and laugh index the interaction as a continuation of the playful sub-text characterizing the family event between C and her husband, thereby partially mitigating the "attack." Her gaze is directed at him as she utters "I'm baring myself," by which she means that she is letting P know what cards/hand she has.

P's response is his body moving forward so that he can look at her cards. He then provides a meta-comment on the strength of the cards, somewhat perplexed by the unexpected move. He then sits back in his chair and turns his gaze to the camera, giving a disclaimer to possible future audiences of the tape and thus pulling the research event into focus, if only for a few seconds, although the mutual laugh after P utters the explicative occurs in acknowledgment of his having addressed the camera before swearing. However, he then quickly brings the meta-game back to the front stage, and in fact stays in that event for most of the subsequent turns. C on the other hand, proud of her move, teases P by sticking out her tongue and by challenging P to acknowledge that she took him by surprise. However, P does not appear to want to engage in the play but presses on to analyze what had happened, also reinforced by his gaze oriented towards the cards. Subsequently, C turns to the actual game with her utterance "I'm attacking you, yes," which is meant as an indirect command for the actual game to proceed. From this point on, their gaze is directed onto the cards, as they become the focus of attention during the teaching event that is triggered by C's inquiry about a quality of a card ("She doesn't have to tap").

The next excerpt shows how a shift in the event may be brought about by recourse to non-verbal semiotic resources. Excerpt (13) comes after, over several turns, P has dealt a series of damages to C and he seems to be winning the game.

> (13) P: *She*'s a what four-four or a five-five.
> C: Mm-hm, four-four.
> (14.0) ((during which P draws a card and is looking at the cards in his hand, contemplating his next move.))
> P: [Uhm-
> C: [Go ahead.
> (4.0)
> P: I'll do three points of damage to you↑ (1.0)

Considering only the verbal activity in this short segment would lead us to conclude that there is nothing exciting happening other than the meta- and actual games. Looking at what participants are doing non-verbally during the 14 seconds of silence fills this period with meaning, generated solely by drawing on non-verbal semiotic resources. At the start of P's contemplation of his move in quiet, C's gaze wanders between P's face and his hand holding the cards, while P's eyes are fixed on the cards in his hands. After a few seconds, P lifts his right hand and rubs his eyes, then lays his hand around his chin, reinforcing and indexing his contemplation by this gesture, his gaze still on his cards. His hand then slides down as P starts to stroke his chin, a gesture that is even more conventional in indexing inner deliberation. At this point, his gaze moves upwards and meets C's gaze that has been shifting between P's cards and his face since the start of the 14 seconds. As their eyes meet, P's face turns to a slight smirk and then produces a burst of laugh, which C counters with a smile on her part, followed by a yawn, a raised hand and her permissive statement "Go ahead."

So what happened here? The ongoing competition surfaced silently but so did the family event and the intimate relationship. P's stroking his chin did not only indicate a reflection about his move; it also meant (as was made obvious by his smile) that he was contemplating the consequences it would have for C's chances in the game. In other words, knowing that his wife likes to win, P was re-considering whether to engage in a move that may lead to her losing the game. P's turning his gaze towards C and smiling indexed this dilemma, which C readily understood, mainly because the competitive element mitigated by family desire for peace and rapport had been present during most of the game and was brought to the fore just before this incident. C's utterance is immediately understood by P to mean "I don't care, just do it" and is indeed followed by P dealing three points of damage to C.

As we have seen in these two examples, the interactions that took place during the *MTG* session I videotaped were the result of complex semiotic work on the part of participants. While verbal commentary has the advantage that speakers' orientation is more or less warranted by their being within hearing distance, we have seen that oftentimes language has to be supplemented by other semiotic resources for successful interaction. When meaning is carried primarily through non-verbal media, it requires (as we have seen in Excerpt 13) mutual orientation that is non-auditory (e.g. through gaze, touch, smell) before it can take effect. Further, to support my use of a social event as analytic category, certain meanings can only be generated and interpreted ("read") in the context of a particular event. P's excuse for his profanity clearly marks a different event (instantiated by his gaze), as he would usually not do the same in the context of a family event. Finally, although the dyadic nature of the interaction has limited the likelihood of a divergent participation framework, participants at times could find themselves orienting towards and indexing different events. In Excerpt (13), C draws on gesture, intonation and gaze to enact the family event but P seeks to remain in the meta-game event, by looking at the cards instead of C as well as by providing the game analysis typical of the meta-game. As both participants have to display mutual orientation for the interaction to proceed, C eventually abandons her event, at least for the time being. In situations where more than two participants engage in the game, mutual orientation to the same event by all may prove more difficult.

Conclusion

In this chapter, I highlighted the complexity of the interactions that occur during fantasy gameplay and showed how semiotic work done by the participants contributes to the interactional achievement of multiple events and roles. The setting provided certain discourses and afforded semiotic systems that participants could rely on to build action and move their interaction forward. In my analysis of the videotape and transcript, I distinguished between five events that seem to be embedded into one another and foster five types of relationships between participants. While the spousal relationship between P and C existed prior to engaging in the game, other relationships and the events that they constitute and are constituted by emerge through P and C's participation in the game. Each event can be described as involving a certain contextual configuration or sets of semiotic resources, including language, gaze, para-linguistic features and gesture, upon which participants rely. By invoking these resources, participants negotiate events and roles and successfully maneuver the interaction in meaningful ways.

As Fine (1983) pointed out, three factors determine the stability of frames in fantasy gaming: the degree of engrossment; whether a frame is voluntary or mandatory; and how much fun players are having in a particular frame. I propose a fourth dimension: the interactional and narrative structure of the game. In role-playing genres such as *D&D*, players use turns to enhance and deepen the narrative that is being built collaboratively. While the rule book provides a guide for what is possible, players use their creativity to spawn a story and success is measured by the elaborateness of the final narrative (Hendricks, this volume). In CSGs, on the other hand, creativity is evidenced in how players combine and manipulate available cards each turn in order to win; the story, one could argue, assumes secondary status. Further, the narrative is carried solely by what is written on cards; players cannot add or take away anything from the 'story' that develops as they play cards. As a result, unlike role-playing games where the on-line creation of the storyline requires focus and attention (and thus engrossment), *MTG* allows more interactional freedom for its players: First, the fairly restricted eventcast that characterizes verbal action during turns allows for non-game events to emerge. Second, what is happening in the ongoing game is registered on the cards and can be read at any point; thus there is no need for players to keep in mind details of moves, that is, details of the story.

My analysis and discussion in this chapter were based on a one-hour long session of *MTG* played between my husband and me. However, in games with multiple players who are non-intimates, there are still diverse events and roles, some pre-existent and others maybe locally developed, all of which would be called into the foreground by similar semiotic means that were observed in the present analysis. This seems particularly likely given the nature of fantasy card games as complex semiotic genres involving the concurrent deployment of objects, gestures and language to achieve certain types of action within certain types of events. While the various genres within fantasy gaming may differ with respect to accommodating roles and events outside of the game, the centrality of language, embodied action and the material surroundings as semiotic resources to navigate across events will most likely remain.

References

Austin, John L. 1962. *How to Do Things with Words*. Cambridge, MA: Harvard UP.
Coupland, Justine, and Richard Gwyn (Eds.). 2003. *Discourse, the Body, and Identity*. Houndmills: Palgrave Macmillan.
Fairclough, Norman. 1995. *Critical Discourse Analysis: The Critical Study of Language*. London: Longman.

_____. 2003. *Analysing Discourse. Textual Analysis for Social Research.* London/New York: Routledge.

Fine, Gary A. 1983. *Shared Fantasy: Role-Playing Games as Social Worlds.* Chicago: University of Chicago Press.

_____, and Sherryl Kleinmann. 1979. "Rethinking Subculture: An Interactionist Analysis." *American Journal of Sociology* 85 (1):1-20.

Gee, James P. 1996. *Social Linguistics and Literacies: Ideology in Discourses* (2nd ed.). London: Taylor and Francis.

Givón, Talmy. 1979. *On Understanding Grammar.* New York: Academic Press.

Goffman, Erving. 1959. *The Presentation of Self in Everyday Life.* New York: Doubleday.

_____. 1963. *Behavior in Public Places: Notes on the Social Organization of Gatherings.* New York: Free Press.

_____. 1983. "The Interaction Ritual." *American Sociological Review* 48:1–19.

Goodwin, Charles. 1981. *Conversational Organization: Interaction between Speakers and Hearers.* New York: Academic Press.

_____. 2000. "Action and Embodiment Within Situated Human Interaction." *Journal of Pragmatics,* 32: 1489–1522.

_____. 2002. "Time in Action." *Current Anthropology* 43:19–35.

_____. 2003. "The Body in Action." Pp. 19–42 in *Discourse, the Body, and Identity,* edited by J. Coupland and R. Gwyn. Houndmills, UK/New York: Palgrave Macmillan.

Goodwin, Marjorie H. and Charles Goodwin. 1986. "Gesture and Coparticipation in the Activity of Searching for a Word." *Semiotica* 62 (1/2):51–75.

_____. 2001. "Emotion within Situated Activity." p. 239–257 in *Linguistic Anthropology. A Reader,* edited by A. Duranti. Malden, MA/Oxford, UK: Blackwell.

Halliday, Michael A.K. 1985. *An Introduction to Functional Grammar.* London/Baltimore, MD: E. Arnold.

Heath, Shirley. 1985. "The Cross-Cultural Study of Language Acquisition." *Papers and Reports on Child Language Development* 24:1–21.

Hendricks, Sean Q. 2006. "Incorporative Discourse Strategies in Tabletop Fantasy Role-playing Gaming." Pp. 39–56 in *Gaming as Culture: Social Reality, Identity and Experience in Role-Playing, Collectible, and Computer Games,* edited by J. Patrick Williams, Sean Q. Hendricks, and W. Keith Winkler. McFarland.

Kress, Gunther. and Theo Van Leeuwen. 1996. *Reading Images: The Grammar of Visual Design.* London: Routledge.

_____. 2001. *Multimodality.* London: Sage.

Martinec, Radan. 2001. "Interpersonal Resources in Action." *Semiotica* 135 (1/4):117–145.

Myers-Scotton, Carol. 1993. *Dueling Languages.* Oxford: Clarendon.

Sacks, Harvey. 1992. *Lectures on Conversation.* Oxford, UK: Blackwell.

_____, Emanuel A. Schegloff, and Gail Jefferson. 1974. "A Simplest Systematics for the Organization of Turn-taking for Conversation." *Language* 50:696–735.

Scollon, Ron. 2001. "Action and Text: Toward an Integrated Understanding of the Place of Text in Social (Inter)Action." Pp. 139–183 in *Methods in Critical Discourse Analysis,* edited by R. Wodak and M. Meyer. London: Sage.

_____, and Susan W. Scollon. 2003. *Discourses in Place. Language in the Material World.* London/New York: Routledge.

Searle, John R. 1969. *Speech Acts: An Essay in the Philosophy of Language.* London: Cambridge UP.

Wizards of the Coast. 1995. *Magic: The Gathering: The Pocket Player's Guide* (4th ed.). Renton, WA: Wizards of the Coast.

Wolcott, Harry F. 1990. "On Seeking and Rejecting Validity in Qualitative Research." Pp. 121–152 in *Qualitative Inquiry in Education: The Continuing Debate,* edited by E.W. Eisner and A. Peshkin. New York: Teachers College Press.

_____. 1995. *The Art of Fieldwork.* Walnut Creek, CA: AltaMira.

Appendix: Transcription Conventions

Data were transcribed using a modified version of the transcription system described in Sacks, Schegloff and Jefferson (1974).

↑	**upward arrow** marks rising intonation;
?	**question mark** indicates question intonation;
.	**period** marks falling intonation;
::	**colons** indicate that the preceding sound is prolonged; more colons means increased prolongation;
CAPS	**all capitals** indicate increased volume;
_	**underlined** utterances are stressed by a raised pitch;
[	a **left bracket** indicates the start of overlapping speech;
(1.0)	**numbers in parentheses** mark pauses in seconds;
(.)	**period in parentheses** indicates short pause (less than 1 second);
-	**a dash** marks a brief stop or break in the flow of speech;
( )	**single parentheses** indicate non-hearing or uncertain hearing of a word/utterance;
(( ))	**double parentheses** enclose features of the interaction that have not been transcribed, for instance information about gaze or body movement as well as certain audible characteristics of talk;
Italics	**italics** in the transcript and elsewhere indicate card types, specific card names or reference to them.

Notes

1. While my analysis focuses on semiotic patterns characteristic of certain events, I do not mean to imply that events can exhaustively be described in terms of a fixed set of relevant semiotic systems. On the contrary, I illustrate that social events do not occur in identifiable sequences; rather their potential is always present during the game and can be brought to the foreground by way of focus and selection.

2. For a more thorough description of the game, see *Wizards of the Coast* (1995).

3. Some may object to the fact that I was one of the participants in the study, on the grounds that it may preclude an "objective" understanding of the research topic. However, recent perspectives within the qualitative research tradition have advocated the inclusion of participants into the research process, including making sense of the data, precisely because of the incompleteness and relativism of interpretation (cf. Wolcott 1990; 1995). Keeping these positions in mind and given the focus of my study, I argue that my status as participant-researcher as well as my close relation with the co-participant provides me with a richer knowledge of the context (including roles, material surrounding, personae) in which the interaction takes place.

4. Consumption and Authenticity in the Collectible Strategy Games Subculture

J. Patrick Williams

There is a strand of contemporary cultural theory that draws links between people's consumption practices and their personal and collective identities (e.g., Bourdieu 1986; Giddens 1991). One important part of this theoretical strand posits that culture industries organize the production, distribution and consumption of cultural goods in hegemonic ways so as to maximize the rational accumulation of profits. At the same time, culture industries provide people with so-called "choices" about what and how to consume and the resulting authenticity of identities that get constructed (van Leeuwen 2005). If there is a direct correlation between consumption and identity, then we could expect to find this correlation to be highly salient within the organization and expression of collectible strategy game (CSG) subculture, a collection of leisure worlds grounded in the rational consumption and use of *collectible* game items. Through participant observation in and interviews with members of four CSG player networks in the southeast United States, I critically investigate the relationship between consumption practices and the construction of "authentic" subcultural identities.[1] In doing this, I analytically distinguish between *organizational* and *expressive* dimensions of the subculture. The organizational dimension refers to how the gaming industry structures gameplay as well as how an objectified status hierarchy is established. The expressive dimension refers to the intersubjective accomplishment of subcultural identity. In terms of subculture theory, this chapter problematizes the relationship between subcultural consumption and subcultural authenticity. At a broader sociological level, it highlights how individuals simultaneously rely on consumptive cultural practices, yet resist dominant meanings of consumption as they construct a positive image of the (sub)cultural self.

The data presented below come from two ethnographic studies on collectible card games and collectible miniatures games. Although I sought to learn both games for fun, I also approached both with explicit research goals in mind. The first project was between January and May of 1997; the second was from January to November 2004. The research took me to retail gaming stores, gaming club meetings in a university center, and people's homes, where I engaged in recreational and tournament play.

I collected data through participant observation and in-depth interviewing strategies. I spent hundreds of hours actively playing *Magic* and *Mage Knight*, as well as observing others play. Regular members of all four player networks knew that I was a sociologist and that I was researching collectible gaming in addition to learning to play. During many of my participant observation sessions, I kept a notebook handy and occasionally jotted down notes to record verbal and non-verbal behaviors that I found relevant to my research agenda. I regularly wrote fieldnotes after returning home from gameplay. I conducted in-depth interviews with seven *Magic* players and one focus group with five additional players. I made audio recordings of the sessions and transcribed all audio tapes to enable close analysis of participants' talk. In addition, I informally questioned several other *Magic* and *Mage Knight* players about various aspects of the game and made detailed notes about our conversations. In all cases, I assigned pseudonyms to participants to protect their identities and subsequently reduced their pseudonyms to a single letter for this chapter.[2]

Brief Histories of Magic and Mage Knight

Since 1993, when Wizards of the Coast released *Magic: The Gathering*, collectible card games and collectible miniature games have dramatically increased in visibility and usage across fantasy gaming populations. Collectible card games have been produced for many popular sci-fi and fantasy worlds, including *Star Wars*, *Star Trek*, *The Lord of the Rings*, *The X-Files*, *Pokémon* and *Yu-Gi-Oh*. The most popular collectible miniatures games are also based on sci-fi and fantasy, including *Mage Knight*, *MechWarrior*, *Warhammer*, *Dungeons and Dragons*, and comic book-based *HeroClix*. Collectors wishing to stay up-to-date with the items these companies produce and players wishing to be competitive buy or trade for hundreds or even thousands of US dollars worth of cards or miniatures every year, as well as remain cognizant of the latest rules, storylines, and play formats. Being a collectible game player therefore requires both monetary and subcultural commitments.

Collecting is a fundamental aspect of CSG subculture. Owens and Helmer (1996: 12, 16) describe how collectible card games actually comprise two games in one:

> The new card games added another twist: players couldn't buy all [the] cards at once. They could buy a box of 60; they could buy a pack of 8 cards ... or even just a single card. But companies printing the playing cards wouldn't sell all the cards together. Collecting a whole set was like a game itself.... Collectible card games are two games in one: playing the cards and collecting the cards. Both games depend on the luck of the draw, as well as your skill in playing the hand you've been dealt.

CSGs all operate under the same basic format: game producers create items that vary in terms of in-game usability and rarity. With few exceptions, the rarer or more powerful the item, the more collectible it becomes. Gamers seek out these rare and/or powerful items either as a form of curatorial consumption (Tankel and Murphy 1998) or to use during gameplay. In both instances, owning such items enhances their prestige within local, regional, national and international player networks.

The length to which gamers will go to procure these items should not be underestimated. At the annual GenCon fantasy convention in southern California in 2003, a factory-sealed case — 4,800 randomly packaged cards — of *Magic*'s first expansion, *Arabian Nights*, sold at auction for $95,000 (Buehler 2003). *Magic*'s "Power Nine," nine cards considered by many in CSG subculture to comprise the Holy Grail of collectible cards, can be found on EBay selling at $3,000 or more for the set, while first edition copies of the greatest of these cards (the alpha *Black Lotus*) have sold there for more than $2,200. While such cards may be at the extreme end of collectibility, their value reflects how many player-collectors feel about CSGs.

Magic was released in 1993 by Wizards of the Coast, who licensed the game from its inventor, Richard Garfield. According to Garfield, it was the first collectible card game (Garfield 1995). The game was developed on the premise that decks of cards represent the mental repertoire of sorcerers who duel with each other for supremacy on a fantasy world called Dominia. Because every sorcerer's repertoire is the result of her/his unique life experiences, no two deck of cards is likely to be the same. Each *Magic* card has a specific function in the game — generally speaking, there are cards that represent a sorcerer's energy and the spells s/he knows: spells for attack, defense, creature summoning, and so on. Some cards are rarer than others, which is the basis of the collectible aspect of the game — a player might buy dozens of card packs without getting a copy of a particular rare card.[3]

Players typically do not buy ready-to-play decks of cards, though Wizards of the Coast began marketing this option several years ago as preconstructed "theme" decks or championship replica decks. Rather, players buy packs of cards without knowing their exact contents. There are starter packs of sixty cards and booster packs of fifteen cards. Starters cost less than $10 and boosters cost about $3. Gamers choose any number of cards (the exact number might vary, though tournament rules require exactly sixty) and build a deck. The player then finds one or more players with a deck and they duel each other, each using her/his own deck.

In order to keep the game constantly fresh, Wizards of the Coast issues new sets of cards three or four times each year, called expansions. Expansions have an overarching theme based on some part of Dominia. Expansions also introduce new mechanics that alter how the game is played. There are literally billions of potential decks that players can create, but certain combinations of cards will almost always outperform others. While *Magic* may have started out relatively small, the game is now sold in dozens of countries and the cards are printed in several languages, including Chinese, German, Italian and Korean. Wizards of the Coast has also developed World Championship and Grand Prix circuits, where top players compete for tens of thousands of dollars annually.

In some ways, *Mage Knight* follows in the footprints made by *Magic*. However, *Mage Knight* is unique in its own right. Instead of cards, *Mage Knight* is a game of collectible miniature figures invented by Jordan Weisman of WizKids Games in 1999. These small, pre-painted plastic figures resemble humans, elves, orcs, dragons, and other mythical creatures. According to the *Mage Knight* rulebook, each player represents "a powerful warlord: a king, baron, or high wizard who sends his or her troops out to do battle with opposing armies" (WizKids 2003). Miniature figures have been used by strategy war gamers since at least the early 19th century (Fine 1983; Paxson 1971), but what makes *Mage Knight* figures unique is the base on which the figures stands, which includes a "combat dial." This invention created a new way to use miniatures for gameplay by simplifying their use. "No cumbersome record sheets are required to track a unit's combat values and accumulated damage. Instead, all of a unit's combat statistics and abilities are located on the combat dial" (WizKids 2004). Like *Magic* cards, *Mage Knight* figures vary in rarity and power.

Players buy packs of randomly assorted figures and then assemble armies, which they use to battle with or against other players. *Mage Knight* is somewhat more expensive than *Magic*. A starter pack (which comes with a rulebook and some accessories) costs about $20 for eight figures, while a booster pack of four figures costs about $8. A *Mage Knight* army can vary in size from two to as many as perhaps twenty figures. Individual figures have a point value upon which players rely when building armies. Players agree on the total point size of an army (for example 300 points) before playing and then assemble a group of figures that comes as close as possible to that number without going over. Like *Magic*, *Mage Knight* is released in expansions. Each game relies on a different randomizing mechanic. In *Magic*, players shuffle their decks between games while in *Mage Knight*, players use two six-sided dice when they engage in combat. These randomizers are key aspects of the game that help ensure some modicum of equality between players.

Two Dimensions of Subculture

As I sketched out a map of the relationships between consumption and subcultural identity, I found it useful to analytically separate the subculture into two dimensions: organizational and expressive. The former refers to the commodity-oriented organization of CSG subculture, while the latter refers to the intersubjective means through which players develop meaningful identities. I begin by exploring the organizational dimension, emphasizing how gameplay is organized by game producers and how this organization structures an objectified form of status-identity. I then turn to the expressive dimension to show how gamers resist the notion of conspicuous consumption in favor of expressions of cultural identity

The Organizational Dimension

Cultural theories of consumption and taste operate under the notion that "the meaning of our lives is to be found in what we consume" (Storey 1996:114). The now oftentimes taken-for-granted relationship between cultural objects and people's selves emerged out of changes in Western societies that created a culture of consumption. Consumer culture saturates our everyday lives and our social selves, embedding us within consumer-based networks. "Popular culture's emphasis on entertainment and commodification of the self" promotes the idea of "identity as a resource to satisfy individually oriented needs and interests to be whomever you want" (Altheide 2000:12). Overall, there seems to be a growing consensus among many scholars that people rely increasingly on commercially available products, including leisure commodities, to construct status- and cultural identities (Beck 1992; Dayan 1986; Giddens 1991; Hodkinson 2002; Warde 1994).

The organizational dimension of a subculture is characterized by the flow of material and nonmaterial "cultural objects" (Griswold 1994) among producers, distributors and consumers. Understanding that the role-playing game subculture requires material resources to support itself, Fine (1989) outlined a theoretical approach to explain how the gaming industry uses resources to attract and retain participants. Fine's primary focus was on the relationship between material conditions and participation in game subcultures. In order to facilitate the survival and/or growth of a game subculture, companies help develop social infrastructures and distribute material and nonmaterial resources to participants. For example, game producers provide a regular flow of new or "revised" game items (e.g., cards, miniatures, rulebooks, errata, gaming accessories) that must be purchased by participants. In addition producers provide, in conjunction with retailers, opportunities for players to socialize and to construct status- and cultural identities through organized play. Thus, game producers are largely responsible for organizing the material and social dimensions of game subculture. The organization structure is characterized by rules, events, game mechanics, media and markets, all of which shape gamers' consumption practices and their status-identities.

Rules

Rules, at their simplest, prescribe directions for behavior. Almost every facet of gameplay is limited by game and tournament rules issued either by the game companies (at the subcultural level) or informally decreed by local gamers as "house rules" (at the idiocultural level). Rules impact the organization of CSG subculture in two ways. First, the rules require regular monetary investment on the part of players. Second, the rules can be selectively enforced to benefit players with "insider" status.

The game companies' control is perhaps most evident in the publication of official rulebooks. Rulebooks are regularly revised in order to keep gameplay "fair" for all involved. One consequence of new rulebooks, however, is that players must reinvest money in order to meet the newest rules. With each new expansion of *Magic* and *Mage Knight*, the game companies print rulebooks and include them with starter and/or booster packs to provide structure for gameplay. Both companies also regularly publish comprehensive rules and errata on their websites that clarify or change specific rules. Rule changes sometimes make certain cards or figures illegal for tournament play, oftentimes causing players to invest more money in replacement items. Rulebooks do more than simply codify gameplay, however. Both *Magic* and *Mage Knight* rulebooks introduce players to the mythical worlds represented in the games. Rulebooks thus simultaneously structure both the shared fantasy in which gameplay is embedded as well as the mechanics of gameplay.

Companies also require that referees oversee "sanctioned" play (see below). In most cases, local shop owners serve as referees. Referees are responsible for keeping up to date on the latest errata, ensuring that no cheating occurs, and promoting a positive environment in which to play. Referees are able to enforce a "definition of the situation" (Thomas 1923) on gameplay and thus serve an important function in policing the boundary between more central and more marginal players, a hierarchy that is often defined by the most powerful players within a player network (Fine 1983). During one of the first *Mage Knight* tournaments in which I participated, I beat another player, whom I will call "Q." Q was a long-time amateur player and a loyal customer at the local game shop. I had only been playing about six weeks at the time. I placed second overall and Q placed third. When it came time to award the three tournament prizes provided by WizKids for the event, the referee announced that, because Q had let another contestant borrow a figure for the tournament, he earned "fellowship" standing and could take the second-place tournament prize, leaving the third-place prize to me. Not understanding, I questioned the referee. He explained that WizKids had a tournament rule that allowed the referee to reward players who showed a commitment to building "community." The rule is thus selectively enforced by referees to reward players who put the community above themselves.

While rules are well-intentioned, they may be abused. For example, when I once visited a *Mage Knight* tournament simply to observe gameplay, a player told me about another local shop owner who regularly allowed his friends to enter tournaments and to bend or break rules to win rare prizes. When other players complained, the shop owner invoked his status as a referee to make final decisions about gameplay and told players that if they did not agree with the rulings they could remove themselves from the game. One result of such rulings is that central players are likely to win more valuable prizes than more marginal players. The value of the prize is subcultural rather than merely economic; that is, its rarity is coveted more than its cash value (see Csikszentmihalyi and Rochberg-Halton 1981). In short, the value of subcultural items may result in the selective application of rules that create or maintain status hierarchies.

Sanctioned Events

Companies gameplay in ways that require that participants pay to play. Wizards of the Coast supports "Arena" and "Friday Night Magic" tournament leagues, for example. These leagues serve to separate recreational players from more competitive players, giving each an environment in which to play the game. Similarly, WizKids has a sanctioned tournament league in retail stores for games in its product line. For *Mage Knight* and *Magic* players, many tournaments are "constructed events," meaning that players construct an army/deck from among their figures/cards at home and arrive ready to play. Wizards of the Coast charges a fee for participation, while WizKids does not, and each company offers rare items as weekly prizes to the top three finishers. For recreational and competitive players alike, the chance to win limited edition prizes is worth the price to register. One gamer I interviewed felt that players, the companies and retail stores all benefited from the leagues:

> The Friday Night Magic series and ... Arena ... is a way to get people who are semi-casual players or casual players that they want to turn into tournament type players by combining a competitive aspect every Friday at your local game store with prizes and with promotional material [S, interview].

Players benefit because the company and retailer set aside time and space specifically for them to gather and play (see also Fine 1989). The companies benefit because the leagues attract players with the lure of prizes into coming regularly to compete, which increases the likelihood that the players will remain interested in the game and continue to buy game-related products. Retail stores benefit from the foot traffic generated by the company's official support of the league.

Regardless of the fee charged or whether they won a prize, several participants reported that they would regularly buy a few booster packs when they spent time at a retail store. One gamer talked about his small but regular purchases as "natural": "[a]nd another thing that's just great about *Magic* is just like ... I guess it's human nature, but just ... opening a pack of cards and then seeing what you got" [J, interview]. This excerpt can be interpreted in different ways. From a critical perspective, the organization of game play helps ensure that both the company and the retailer benefit monetarily from players' involvement, while the players' "needs" for things are also satisfied (Marcuse 1966[2002]). Yet from a more contemporary "ordinary consumption" perspective (e.g., Granow and Warde 2001), the player's purchases are simply a routinized aspect of his identity. "Consumption is not inherently good or bad, but it is deeply human" (Hine 2002:*x*).

Routinized consumption is common among gamers and game companies understand how lucrative weekly tournament leagues can be in facilitating consumptive practices. Some of these events are "limited format events," which characterize a more formal method of controlling gamers' consumption practices. Unlike a constructed event, a limited format event is one in which players are required to buy the cards/figures at the event in order to participate — no cards/figures can be brought from outside the venue. For example, in *Magic* "sealed draft" tournaments, players purchase one starter pack and two booster packs of cards (totaling about $15), from which they must build a deck with which to compete.[4] In a limited format *Mage Knight* event, players buy three booster packs (totaling about $24) and build a 300-point army.

Even basic tournament formats limit the types of cards/figures that players can legally use. In *Magic*, the company has divided tournaments into several formats, the most popular of which is loosely referred to as "Type 2." According to the company, the idea behind Type 2 was that new and advanced players should have "equal" access to rare and powerful cards, so the company limited the number of expansions that are legal in tournament play to those printed roughly within the previous twelve months— typically three expansions. This way, if a gamer started playing Type 2 *Magic* tournaments today, s/he would have "equal" access to all legal cards because all of them are a year old or less and still available at retail stores. In *Mage Knight*, figures from older expansions are "retired" and become illegal in restricted tournament play as new expansions— usually twice each year — are released.

From many players' perspectives, however, the companies organize their games in such a way so that players are "forced" to buy the newest cards/figures in order to remain competitive. This tests the loyalty and willingness of players to continue investing money in items they believe will be worthless once they cycle out of the Type 2 environment: "from time to time everybody gets burned out and they'll quit ... it happens time and time again. [...] A lot of the game became about money" [C, interview]. Not only is player loyalty tested, but the burn out effect results in an active secondary market where players buy, sell and trade used cards. This secondary market, discussed below, functions as a type of informal organization that channels the (re)distribution of collectible items and thus provides an additional site for consumption.

Game Mechanics

In CSGs, new mechanics are developed and introduced in new expansions. Each of these mechanical changes attempts to revitalize fan interest by changing how the game is played. Yet, such changes in the structure of gameplay are polysemic. Industry spokespeople and many players see the evolution of game mechanics as invigorating because it forces players to think about the game in new ways. Other players, however, argue that the companies engage in a form of "one-upsmanship" with themselves by constantly pushing the limit of game design. One player argued that "because Wizards of the Coast has to make money off *Magic*, they always have to top themselves and, you know make better decks" [J, interview].

Gamers see the constant evolution of game mechanics as part-and-parcel of the Type 2 environment.

By introducing "stronger" mechanics with each expansion, Wizards of the Coast and WizKids assure themselves that players will not remain satisfied with the game as it "used to be." Rather players feel the need to buy the newest items, either to experience new mechanics or to remain competitive. One player told me that, because a couple of his close friends regularly bought new cards that utilized new mechanics, he also felt it was necessary to buy them in order to keep up — it was not fun "doing your best and building what you think is an awesome deck and then going ... and having someone just completely squash you" [K, interview]. As they talked, players also expressed awareness of the marketing strategies in which gaming companies engage. Yet, while the awareness exists, the game subculture is organized in such a way that players still feel the need to consume increasing quantities of cards/figures. Buying and playing new cards/figures not only may improve company profits, but may also act as a source of objectified subcultural status-identities for players who successfully integrate the newest items into gameplay.

Subcultural Media and Markets

Two additional organizational aspects of CSGs are worth mentioning. First, various print and digital media are dedicated to collectible fantasy gaming and provide detailed knowledge sources for new and experienced players alike. Both Wizards of the Coast and WizKids maintain a complex presence on the internet. Each company has a vast inventory of game-related information for players to access. Not only are there pictures and descriptions of almost every card or figure ever produced, the internet also provides a plethora of forums and knowledge vaults that players can tap for deck/army design and strategy tips from pros, as well as amateur player communities. In addition to official company websites, print magazines such *The Duelist*, *Scrye*, and *Inquest* focus explicitly on CSGs. Via these print and digital media, players can find up-to-the-minute rule errata, lists of winning decks or armies, and articles from industry insiders on play developments, strategies, and sneak-peeks at upcoming collectible game products. Both print and electronic media also offer promotional game items to subscribers, thus coaxing more spending by players. For example, magazines will occasionally contain promotional cards or offers to receive promotional items — gamers are more likely to buy a $7 magazine if they receive special offers for "limited edition" items. Similarly, internet sites also advertise limited edition items from time to time. The owners of *Realmworx*, an online *Mage Knight* community, worked with WizKids to produce a series of limited editions relics for use in *Mage Knight* tournament play.

Secondly, retail and secondary markets facilitate the consummation of competitive players' desires for the cards/figures that, according to industry insiders, are certain to help them win games. Retailers and players alike regularly open booster packs and sell rare cards/figures separately. Some players avoid buying booster packs at $3 each (for *Magic*) or $8 each (for *Mage Knight*) and risking not getting the items they want. Instead, they can shop in retail shops and online for cards/figures at prices ranging from less than $1 to more than $50 for a rare card set or a unique figure. This is perhaps most obvious on Ebay, where tens of thousands of auctions exist at any given time.[5] By buying individual cards or figures, players bypass one of the perceived problems of these games—being overwhelmed with multiple copies of useless common items. Once purchased, these unique or rare items equip the player with a powerful arsenal to overcome rival players.

The Objectification of Status-Identity

Together, the rules, tournament formats, game mechanics, media and markets highlight the organization and maintenance of status-identity within the subculture. This organization supports an objectified form of subcultural status-identity. Thornton (1995) uses the term "objectified subcultural capital" to refer to tangible objects—like record albums—that reflect and represent the status of club-going youth, while Csikszentmihalyi (Csikszentmihalyi and Rochberg-Halton 1981) refers more generally to the meaning of objects as status symbols. In the CSG subculture, status is quantified and objectified in two forms: rankings and limited edition cards/figures.

First, status hierarchies are objectified through players' win-loss records and rank, which are recorded by referees at sanctioned events and managed by the game companies. Within both *Magic*'s and *Mage Knight*'s tournament systems, players are ranked according to their win-loss records. Every time I entered a *Mage Knight* tournament, the referee would record my wins and losses for that day. He would then log onto the WizKids website and enter this information into their database, which is immediately available to anyone with a web browser. The win-loss record affects a player's overall rank in the gaming community at the local, state, national and international level. And because most *Mage Knight* players pre-register online for tournaments, they can compare their ranks against other registered players before or after tournaments. Rank has consequences. When doing research, for example, I initially sought out highly ranked players to talk to, uncritically assuming that their knowledge was more valuable to me. Other players similarly gave status to players simply because of their win-loss records, which some players touted at tournaments and social games alike, thereby making status claims.

Second, limited edition and promotional items are coveted by gamers as status markers. In *Magic*, tournament prizes are based on the alternate art concept. As one player explained it, Wizards of the Coast takes the most often-used cards ("staple" cards) and prints different art on them.

> ... So if you win a tournament in Arena or Friday Night Magic, you usu-ally get some kind of staple card, like it used to be *Disenchant*, then *Fire-ball* and *Counterspell*— all had alternate art. [...] I think that's awesome cuz it shows that you're into the game and it gives you that pride like, "Yea, I'm good enough to have an alternate-art *Disenchant*" [S, interview].

In *Mage Knight*, tournament players can win limited edition figures. Whereas standard figures (commons and rares alike) have black/white combat dials, the limited edition figures are printed in black/gold. In both games, players expressed the belief that, by playing these limited edition items, they were displaying their status relative to players who did not have them. The card/figure represented either the time spent in the sub-culture (being "old school") or their skill in tournament play.

This objectified form of identity is build around status, in which gamers are ranked hierarchically. But what does all this *mean* to the play-ers? Are there differences among players that affect the meanings they attributed to games or the game subculture? What about players who pre-ferred the social aspects of gaming over its competitive aspects (Avedon and Sutton-Smith 1971)? In order to shed light on these questions, we can consider the expressive dimension of the subculture.

The Expressive Dimension

Magic and *Mage Knight* each have an organizational dimension that emphasizes and supports monetary commitment from players and how players' identities are linked to these commodities, albeit in objectified form. Many other leisure subcultures are rooted in the consumption of cultural objects as well. The subcultural consumption of commodities does not always follow a dominant (i.e., subculture industry) logic, however. Donnelly and Young (1988) explored the importance of subcultural con-sumption and display among neophyte rock climbers, including "wearing climbing clothes and boots in nonclimbing settings [and] carrying equip-ment, books and magazines about climbing as conspicuously as possible" (p. 229-30). Following suit, Wheaton (2000) noted that some windsurfers focused on consuming and displaying subcultural items such as boards, wetsuits and clothing rather than focusing on improving their windsurfing skills. In these and other cases (e.g., Thornton 1995; Williams 2004), the researchers found that some subculture members deemphasized such con-spicuous consumption in favor of alternative discourses of authenticity.

Wheaton (2000) explored how windsurfers constructed and negotiated subcultural identity vis-à-vis windsurfing commodities. She found that participants "could not "buy" their way into the core of the subculture" (p. 263). Rather, windsurfers expressed "authentic" subcultural identities through alternative means: avoiding popular commodities (which she labels "style denial"), the time they spend at the beach, their surfing skill, and mental and emotional commitment to the sport. Similarly, Williams and Copes (2005) examined how a sense of authenticity among participants in the straightedge subculture extends beyond the physical markers of subcultural identity to include both immaterial concerns (e.g, values and beliefs) and everyday practices. The expressive dimension thus emphasizes cultural identity over and above status-identity and is reminiscent of previous studies on the symbolic work that occurs in everyday life around cultural media and products (e.g., Willis 1990).

These alternative discourses highlight the complex processes through which gamers construct subcultural identity. Player's identities are visible through multiple symbolic markers including the items with which they play, knowledge of the game environment and history, and gaming style or the skills one has in building winning decks/armies. Further, players emphasize the importance of commitment to the gaming community over win-loss records or the accumulation of rare items. In fact, multiple, overlapping processes are involved in the construction of "authentic" identities. In addition to owning and playing collectible game items, gamers also have to demonstrate a broader love for fantasy and fantasy games, a willingness to build community, and skills as a strategist.

Authentic Players Love Games

Being good at any particular game is not a sufficient criterion for other gamers to attribute status to that player. All the players I talked to saw themselves as more than just *Magic* or *Mage Knight* players— they saw themselves as gamers in a broader sense. Nobody I interviewed or asked informally reported being interesting *only* in these CSGs. Rather, they played a variety of other fantasy- and strategy-based games. Players reported playing *Legends of the Five Rings, Star Wars, D&D, Lord of the Rings, Vampire: The Eternal Struggle, Risk*, chess, backgammon, and various PC and console games in addition to RPGs and CSGs.

Much like role-playing games, evenings filled playing CSGs were memorable. Three of the player networks I studied involved regular weekend game sessions that lasted into the middle of night or the next morning. Sleep was lost, but not always missed.

> I remember when I first started playing *Magic*, that was 1997 or so, and
> I went to this guy's house who'd invited me over to play. We'd go in at

like 8 o'clock at night and stop at like 8 o'clock the next morning. We'd
come out from this basement and it would be daylight. It was just brutal, but it was a lot of fun [P, interview].

Such sentiments were shared by many players, who considered the
most enjoyable aspects of playing to be spending time with friends actively
engaged in a shared fantasy they constructed together. Gamers who hosted
late night or all-night sessions in their homes, store owners and game club
officers did not perform organizational roles only for the status that such
work brought (although they were given status by other gamers because
of their official roles, which "proved" their love of games and their commitment to CSG subculture). Rather, they claimed to perform these roles
because of their love for game and game culture.

Authentic Players Are Friendly and Fun

Whereas role-playing games provide opportunities for the development of "collective sociability" (Fine 1983:233), not everyone played *Magic*
for such reasons. Gamers I interviewed drew an emic distinction between
two different player types: recreational and competitive.

I would say that I'm more recreational. You know, I don't like to lose,
but it's a game and I play just to have fun and hang out with my friends
and everything. And there's competitive people who get mad if you
beat them, or they don't like to lose. There's [also] people that really
get on my nerves ... they just make decks so they can beat people at
Magic, and it's sort of like, you take all the fun of it by doing that [J,
interview].

According to J, recreational players play for fun. They enjoy each others' company and look forward to the camaraderie associated with weekly
gaming sessions. While sitting in a university center playing *Magic*, members of one player network were regularly approached by students who
were attracted by gameplay. Almost every week, somebody would exclaim
excitement at seeing us playing a game that they had given up when moving to college. Several of these gamers subsequently retrieved their *Magic*
cards from home and joined our weekly games.

Some of these individuals turned out to be competitive players, a fact
that many core recreational players in the network did not appreciate. "I
enjoy playing with recreational players more than with competitive players just because they're usually nicer and they're not as strung out as the
competitive players, who are worried about whether or not they're gonna
lose" [J, interview]. Recreational players claimed that competitive players
were too concerned with winning and lost sight of the fun of playing.
"When highly competitive players come around to places where you play,
you just get sort of a bad sense about them. [It's] like, this person is not

going to be any fun" [P, interview]. In other words, competitive players concentrated on establishing a status-identity in the group based on winning rather than on a subcultural identity based on having fun.

Several competitive players, who played for the "wrong reasons," were made to feel unwelcome by recreational players, who saw them as unwilling to allow others the chance to have fun. In interviews players told me that competitive players were unfriendly in their play.

> When you play somebody it's nice if somebody does something very effective, you may not be happy about it but you should at least compliment them. Like "good job, you just kicked my butt on that," versus the whole, "Ha I just ground your face into that and you suck." Just verbally abusive basically, a poor sport. Just being mean for the sake of being mean and demoralizing the other guy [K, interview].

Overall, there was a tension expressed between "playing" and "dueling," which affected players' statuses within local player networks. Most players (including me) really wanted to win games. Yet, players managed that desire and their presentation of self so that others labeled them neither as gloaters when they did win, nor as sore losers when they did not.

> Sometimes when a player wins, he gets excited and pokes fun at the losers—this seems to happen in multiplayer games. But in duels, both players are usually very civil. In duels, winners regularly say "I got lucky" while losers regularly look into their deck and say "Oh, just [one] more card[s] and I would have had you." There is thus a constant negotiation between not appearing smug and not appearing as a bad player. These players want to meet in the middle ... keep some consensus and friendliness ... not piss other players off [fieldnotes].

Fine (1983:200) conceptualizes a similar problem of "frame interpretation." A gamer is simultaneously a person and a player.[6] For collectible game players, the self is not divided between person versus player (see also Waskul, this volume), but rather the competitive self versus the recreational self. While the competitive self seeks to win the game and thus higher status, the recreational self must negotiate the "real world" expression of that winning attitude with his desire to "just have fun."

Authentic Players Share Their Wealth

> [A]nyone who tells you that price and collectibility are not important considerations when talking about Type 1 cards is just wrong. *Magic* cards are a collectible (in addition to being a great game) [sic] and we aren't going to mess that up by reprinting the "Power 9" no matter how many times or how many different ways we're asked to do it [Buehler 2003].

As Buehler makes clear, the rarity aspect of CSGs is their keystone and players regularly displayed their rare cards/figures to other players as a way of expressing both their authenticity as subcultural insiders and their status vis-à-vis other players. When trading cards at retail game shops or club meetings, *Magic* players regularly display their most expensive cards on the first pages of their binders— notebooks filled with clear plastic sleeves that hold nine cards each (some players bring multiple binders with hundreds of cards each week). Similarly, when I first went to another *Mage Knight* player's home, he began his tour by showing me where he kept his rarest and most expensive figures. Displaying these rare items gives gamers credibility and status. In Bourdieian terms, the economic capital invested in these items is translated during interaction into cultural capital (Bourdieu 1986).

Such collections of rare and expensive items require monetary commitment to the game. Monetary commitment is expressed most often in mundane forms of consumption, as I regularly noted during my field research.

> Two guys from the local player network were at the *Mage Knight* tournament tonight, and each had brought his son to play. Normally these guys play, but I think it's nice that they're giving up their spots to let their sons play instead. After 2 hours of solid play, I finished the final round and went over to talk to them. I saw *Mage Knight* figures spread all over the table and the garbage can nearby was full of the little colored plastic containers in which the figures are packaged. I learned that they had bought about $50 total of booster packs while they waited on the tournament to end, hoping for an ultra rare figure. One guy had already bought more than $500 worth of the latest expansion; the other, $200 [fieldnotes].

The figures they were searching for in the booster packs would enable them to win more tournaments, thus increasing their objectified status in the collectible game subculture. But the figures also serve a much more irrational means of developing cultural identity as well. Both of these men regularly brought rare and expensive figures with them and openly invited newer players to borrow them for tournament play. When I started playing *Mage Knight*, these two advanced players offered, on separate occasions, to let me borrow unique figures that I did not own but needed to build competitive armies. The respect I gave them was not the result of any rational plan on their part to gain status by offering their figures, nor was it directly related to any objectified measure of status. Rather, they expressed an authentic subcultural identity through sharing the fruits of their conspicuous consumption, which leveled the playing field in an economic sense and allowed players to focus on their army-building and strategy skills. *Magic* players did something similar, offering to let people borrow decks of cards that they constructed themselves so that these players could participate in weekly multiplayer games. One particular player, V, brought thirty or forty constructed decks for play each week. When I first began observing and playing in this network, he offered me decks with which to play when he saw that I did not own many Type 2 cards. In this way, I and other players who either could not or were not willing to make a high monetary commitment to the game could play.

Offering newer or less monetarily committed players figures/decks was also a form of recruitment, in which all of the gamers reported engaging. When new players entered local networks, advanced players often extended more than a temporary loan on items. In fact, advanced players gave me free cards and figures to help me get started when I was introduced to *Magic* and *Mage Knight*. Since both games require an initial investment to build up a basic set of cards/figures from which to construct decks/armies (about $15 for *Magic*; about $30 for *Mage Knight*), giving a new player a deck or army that is ready to play can make a significant difference in whether the new player becomes a regular player. The cards and figures that advanced players gave me were almost never rare or valuable, though a very few players did occasionally give away rare or unique items. Still, having a collection of common items with which to start is better than no deck/army at all.

Authentic Players Are Skilled Players

Collectible game designers work hard to ensure that games remain as balanced as possible given that rare/unique items are oftentimes very powerful relative to common items. Yet, regardless of game designers' desire for balance, some gamers have greater discretionary incomes than others and thus have greater access to the most powerful items. However, players' overemphasis on the monetary aspect of the game was seen by many as a subcultural *faux pas*. For those gamers with less ability or willingness to conspicuously consume cards/figures, their gaming skill was a powerful, alternative form of authenticity.

> It took me a while to realize it, but part of the big thrill of going out to these tournaments ... was the competition. Taking out people who were richer than me, that had more cards than me, that had been in it longer than me, and then whoopin' their ass. And it was just like winning a football game. It was that type of feeling except I didn't have to count on anybody else. It was just me [F, interview].

F, a working-class male who could not afford to buy heavily into new *Magic* expansions, found that he was able to beat many players who had expensive cards because they often lacked the skills necessary to craft a winning deck. He and other tournament players talked about the status they earned because they could enter tournaments with decks of relatively inexpensive common cards and still place in the top three at the end of the night. Implicitly they emphasized skill as a fundamental characteristic of "real" gamers.

Building winning decks takes time and effort. As players engage each other regularly to play, they develop a deeper understanding of game mechanics and begin to envision strategies for constructing and playing decks/armies. Unfortunately for players who love the strategic aspect of the game, many (especially younger) players rely heavily on news columnists and internet forums for tips on building powerful decks/armies. Wizards of the Coast's website and magazine, for example, regularly publish the content of championship-winning decks. Many players copied those decks and took them to local tournaments and social meetings to play.

> I sort of see the game as more strategy-based and you should, maybe not be good at strategy, but at least understand it to win. [...] It doesn't take any skill to go look up online which four cards, when put together, will give you an instant win. [...] That's all there is to it. I think it should it should be something that you have to work at more [K, interview].

Championship-winning decks are often based on an "infinite combo," a combination of a few cards that, when played together, result in an instant victory. Such combos do not sit well with players who cannot win against them, especially when the opponent did not think up the combo her/himself.

> One thing I do have a grudge against are particular players that go online and find deck ideas and [...] just copy the deck. It's like, why do you even play, because you're just copying other people's stuff, so there's no point in playing. [...] I couldn't do that because it would take all the enjoyment out of the game. Because it's not about beating people, it's about having your ideas come to life in a deck and to be able to, through proper strategy, beat an opponent, and not just "oh I have better cards than you" [J, interview].

Gamers who relied on powerful items to assure them of victory were seen as lacking the skills that made them "real" players. The advanced players regularly complained that *Magic* and *Mage Knight* tournaments were overrun with inexperienced players using "over-powered" decks. Though they might place well in tournaments, these players were not respected by older players. As my earliest *Mage Knight* fieldnotes reveal:

> While playing [*Mage Knight*], I told R that I'd watched E take four unique figures and wipe out an older guy, Q, who had about 15 figures, but no uniques (or maybe one). I also told R that I'd looked on Ebay and seen that some items go for a lot of money. R said, "well, that kid is M's son and gets whatever he wants or needs for the game. He builds 'cheese' armies. He puts the most powerful figures out on the field that nobody can touch. I mean, why even show up? If you know you can beat anything that shows up, why even play?" [fieldnotes].

Many (especially more experienced) players considered these players inauthentic because they relied on powerful cards/figures to play the game for them — they did not focus on developing their own skills. Donnelly and Young (1988) observed that the conspicuous display of equipment disappeared among climbers as they became more experienced. Similarly, as Wheaton (2000) discovered, "an antimaterialism ethos was evident from the windsurfers' attitudes to those individuals who purchased equipment they considered to be beyond their proficiency or who tried to demonstrate their subcultural membership or status just by displaying their equipment" (p. 263). The same processes seemed to occur in CSG subculture.

In sum, an "authentic" identity can be achieved through one's skills at strategizing a winning combination of cards/figures without relying on professionals for advice or money for the rarest items. Skilled gamers may also own the same powerful, rare items as the "copy cats" who continually relied on the same deck or army, but they did not play with those items every week. They constantly changed their decks and armies around, searching for new combinations that worked well together. They took risks with new ideas that did not always work, rather than sticking with the same army/deck design every week. Because of their love of gaming, their friendly attitudes toward and willingness to help out new players, and their focus on skill development, longtime gamers developed the sense that they were more "authentic" than some other gamers. Crucially, new players who expressed the same subcultural values and beliefs tended to be treated as authentic gamers from the beginning, while those that focused on the conspicuous consumption of game items did not.

Conclusion

More than a century ago, Thorstein Veblen (1899 [1992]) theorized that a new American bourgeois leisure class engaged in "conspicuous consumption" to define their social identity and status. Subsequent work by subcultural theorists also emphasized how people use consumption for purposes of social distinction (Bourdieu 1984; Hall and Jefferson 1976). In this chapter I have explored consumptive and expressive practices in CSG subculture, specifically in terms of its organizational and expressive dimensions. The dimensions noted are neither exhaustive nor complete. Studying how CSG subculture is codified into specific forms of social practice that mediate the relationship between individual actors and leisure industries serves two purposes. First, it avoids the limitations of relying solely on macro or micro perspectives. Instead, I have tried to emphasize the dialectic relationship between the various cultural structures that constrain their behaviors, on the one hand, and the social psychology of gamers and their behaviors, on the other. Second, studying the cultural dimension of gaming shifts our attention from cause-and-effect models of culture to the process of consuming leisure itself (Butsch 1990).

While contemporary theories of consumption often depict the self as being rooted in conspicuous consumption, the data presented here illuminate more complex processes at work. Gamers *do* pay to play the games they love, and their identities are partially constructed through the commodities they consume. This consumption, however, is not deterministic. Instead, we can understand the complexity of CSG subculture by studying its organization and expressive dimensions. The ways in which game companies design and structure games and their rules, the organization of gameplay in terms of recreation and competition, the organization of game-related knowledge, and the conditions under which gamers may acquire items are all organizational aspects of the subculture that affect how players interact with games and with others in gaming environments.

The organizational dimension of the subculture is important to study because it highlights how CSGs are oriented toward consumption. This organizational structure is both similar to and yet different from many other leisure cultures. On the one hand, subcultural practices are often routinized at "sanctioned" gaming events (e.g., tournaments), just as many other game cultures—poker, bridge, or chess—cohere around organized events. Unlike poker, bridge, or even role-playing and video games, however, collectible game events are more likely to be organized at local retail stores that receive game support from game companies, thus enabling pre-arranged sets of interpersonal relationships and status hierarchies to be offered as commodities (Dayan 1986). The material role retail stores play in facilitating game play is crucial inasmuch as "leisure worlds depend for their existence and for their tensile strength on the presence of a social infrastructure and on the ability to distribute resources that members desire" (Fine 1989:322). In addition, the constant revision of rules and game mechanics, as well as the existence of subcultural media and markets, all come together to nurture the constant consumption of game items.

The expressive dimension of gaming subculture is equally important. The feelings players express about gaming, how they relate to and treat other players, the ways in which players use and share game products, and their emphasis on skills all offer counter arguments to claims that subcultural selves are reducible to consumer products. Giddens (cited in Warde 1994) argues that choice is a crucial feature of self-identity. For gamers, having a choice in how they identify with and play CSGs is key to their continued participation in the subculture. Gamers' identities can be understood in terms of authenticity, a concept that looks beyond conspicuous consumption. Authenticity, however, is not an objectively "real" phenomenon. It a social construction through which some gamers increase in status relative to others. For players of CSGs, that authenticity is embedded within a complex web of subcultural ideas, objects and practices.

Acknowledgments

The author would like to thank the participants of the Georgia Workshop on Culture and Institutions— particularly Liz Cherry, Jim Dowd, David Smilde, and Erin Winter —for their useful feedback on a early draft of the chapter.

References

Alongi, Anthony. 2003. "Before You Bust Those Packs ..." Retrieved Nov. 9th, 2004 (*http://www.wizards.com/default.asp?x=Magiccom/daily/aa83*).

Altheide, David L. 2000. "Identity and the Definition of the Situation in a Mass-Mediated Context." *Symbolic Interaction* 23(1):1–27.

Avedon, Elliott M., and Brian Sutton-Smith. 1971. "Games Used for Recreative Purposes." pp. 239–246 in*The Study of Games*, edited by Elliott M. Avedon and Brian Sutton-Smith. New York: Wiley.

Beck, Ulrich. 1992. *Risk Society*. London: Sage.

Bourdieu, Pierre. 1984. *Distinction: A Social Critique of the Judgment of Taste*, translated by Richard Nice. Cambridge, MA: Harvard University Press.

_____. 1986. "The Forms of Capital." pp. 241–258 in *Handbook of Theory and Research for the Sociology of Education*, edited by John G. Richardson. New York: Greeenwood Press.

Buehler, Randy. 2003. "Classic Developments: Type 1 Restrictions and Supercollectibles." Retrieved Jul. 7th, 2004 (*http://www.wizards.com/default.asp?x=mtgcom/daily/rb102*).

Butsch, Richard. 1990. "Leisure and Hegemony in America." pp. 3–27 in *For Fun and Profit: The Transformation of Leisure into Consumption*, edited by Richard Butsch. Philadelphia, Temple University Press.

Csikszentmihalyi, Mihalyi, and Eugene Rochberg-Halton. 1981. *The Meaning of Things*. Cambridge: University of Cambridge Press.

Dayan, Daniel. 1986. "Copyrighted Subcultures." *American Journal of Sociology* 91(5): 1219–1228.

Donnelly, Peter, and Kevin Young. 1988. "The Construction and Confirmation of Identity in Sport Subcultures." *Sociology of Sport Journal* 5(3): 223–240.

Fine, Gary Alan. 1983. *Shared Fantasy: Role-Playing Games as Social Worlds*. Chicago: University of Chicago Press.

_____. 1989. "Mobilizing Fun: Provisioning Resources in Leisure Worlds." *Sociology of Sport Journal* 6(4): 319–334.

Garfield, Richard. 1995. "Notes from the Designer." pp. A1–A13 in *Magic the Gathering: The Pocket Players' Guide*, edited by Rich Redman and Eric Doohan. Renton, WA: Wizards of the Coast.

Giddens, Anthony. 1991. *Modernity and Self-Identity*. Cambridge: Polity.

Griswold, Wendy. 1994. *Cultures and Societies in a Changing World*. Thousand Oaks: Pine Forge Press.

Granow, Jukka, and Alan Warde (eds.). 2001. *Ordinary Consumption*. London: Routledge.

Hall, Stuart, and Tony Jefferson (eds.). 1976. *Resistance Through Rituals: Youth Subcultures in Post-War Britain*. London: Hutchinson.

Hine, Thomas. 2002. *I Want That! How We All Became Shoppers*. New York: Harper Collins.

Hodkinson, Paul. 2002. *Goth: Identity, Style and Subculture*. Oxford: Berg.

Marcuse, Herbert. 1966 [2002]. *One Dimensional Man*. London: Routledge.

Owens, Thomas, and Diana Helmer. 1996. *Inside Collectible Card Games*. Brookfield, CT: Millbrook Press.

Paxson, E. W. 1971. "War Gaming." pp. 278–301 in *The Study of Games*, edited by Elliott M Avedon and Brian Sutton-Smith. New York: Wiley.

Storey, John. 1996. *Cultural Studies and the Study of Popular Culture: Theories and Methods*. Athens: University of Georgia Press.

Tankel, Jonathan, and Keith Murphy. 1998. "Collecting Comic Books: A Study of the Fan and Curatorial Consumption." pp. 55–68 in *Theorizing Fandom: Fans, Subculture and Identity*, edited by Cheryl Harris and Alison Alexander. Cresskill, NJ: Hampton Press.

Thomas, W. I. 1923. *The Unadjusted Girl*. Boston: Little, Brown, and Co.

Thornton, Sarah. 1995. *Club Cultures: Music, Media and Subcultural Capital*. Cambridge: Polity Press.

van Leeuwen, Theo. 2005. "Discourses of Choice." Presented at the Georgetown Linguistics Society 2005 Student Conference, Washington, DC.

Veblen, Thorstein. 1899[1992]. *The Theory of the Leisure Class*. New Brunswick, NJ: Transaction.

Warde, Alan. 1994. "Consumption, Identity-Formation and Uncertainty." *Sociology* 28(4): 877–898.

Waskul, Dennis D. 2006. "The Role-Playing Game and the Game of Role-Playing: The Ludic Self and Everyday Life." *Gaming as Culture: Social Reality, Identity and Experience in Fantasy Games*, edited by J. Patrick Williams, Sean Q. Hendricks, and W. Keith Winkler. Jefferson, NC: McFarland.

Wheaton, Belinda. 2000. "'Just Do It': Consumption, Commitment, and Identity in the Windsurfing Subculture." *Sociology of Sport Journal* 17: 254–274.

Williams, J. Patrick. 2004. "Authentic Identities: Straightedge, Music and the Internet." Presented at the Southern Sociological Society annual meeting in Atlanta, GA.

_____, and Heith Copes. 2005. "How Edge Are You? Constructing Authentic Identities and Subcultural Boundaries in a Straightedge Internet Forum." *Symbolic Interaction* 28(1)67–89.

Willis, Paul. 1990. *Common Culture: Symbolic Work at Play in the Everyday Cultures of the Young*. Boulder: Westview Press.

Wizards of the Coast, 2004. "Magic Arena League: Nothing Beats It." Retrieved Nov. 9th, 2004 (*http://www.wizards.com/default.asp?x=events/magic/arena*).

WizKids. 2003. *Mage Knight: Complete Rules of Play*. Bellevue, WA: WizKids.

_____. 2004. "What Is a Combat Dial?" Retrieved Nov. 20th, 2004 (*http://www.wizkidsgames.com/mageknight/article.asp?frame=howtoplay&cid=36912*).

Notes

1. I use the term "authentic" here in quotations to mark it as suspect. The reason for this is that many subculture researchers assume the objectivity of authenticity, assigning the labels "insiders" and "outsiders" as if they were real. I do not consider authenticity as real or objective, but as a social construction. Competing definitions of authenticity (or authentic identity) exist in every subculture. A dominant definition will arise through inter-

action among members who share a vision of the ideal subcultural member. Therefore, any definition of authenticity will have certain criteria that must be met. Those who do not meet the criteria tend to get marginalized or excluded from subcultural networks— they are called poseurs, pretenders, or wannabes.

2. I use the third-person pronoun "he" throughout the chapter when referring to participants because everyone I observed and interviewed was male. This should not suggest the absence of females from the subculture, but it should suggest how rare female players are. The reasons for this rarity are beyond the scope of this chapter.

3. In *Magic*, cards are divided in three rarity categories: common, uncommon and rare. In *Mage Knight*, there are six rarity categories: common, uncommon, rare, very rare, super rare, and ultra rare.

4. As the Wizards of the Coast website (Alongi 2003) explains: "How it works: Sealed [draft event] gives you a special pack of a large set and one booster each of the subsequent two expansions. Booster draft has each player (recommend 6 or 8) open one pack at a time, pick one card, and pass to the left (first and third packs ... pass right on the second pack). In both cases, you have to build the best 40-card minimum deck you can from whatever you get."

5. Doing random searches on Ebay, I regularly found more than 30,000 auctions related to *Magic* cards and more than 8,000 related to WizKids' collectible figures (including *Mage Knight*, *MechWarrior*, and *Heroclix*).

6. According to early rulebooks: "*Magic* is a game of battle in which you and your opponents represent powerful sorcerers attempting to drive each other from the lands of Dominia. Your deck holds your tools: creatures, land, spells, and artifacts...." Thus, similar to role-playing gamers, *Magic* and *Mage Knight* players are expected to assume at some level an in-game persona. This persona, however, is not nearly as complex as those developed among role-playing gamers and is typically not salient during play.

5. DESKTOP CONQUISTADORS

Negotiating American Manhood in the Digital Fantasy Role-Playing Game

Kevin Schut

The Fantasy worlds of Norrath, Britannia, Faerun and others are vast, magical landscapes populated by vicious orcs, tough dwarves, and powerful fighters. They are also full to the brim with shapely sorceresses, lithe elvish women and busty female warriors who barely fit into their revealing suits of armor. Fantasy role-playing games (FRPGs) like *EverQuest* (Verant Interactive 1999), *Dungeon Siege* (Gas Powered Games 2002) and *Dungeons and Dragons*[1] as a whole are not subtle about their characterization of women. Neither are they subtle about bloody combat: battle scenes and weapon-fetish pictures are common in Fantasy[2] artwork, and combat is the major feature of most games.

Sex and violence: this is stereotypical guy stuff used to hook males on a host of media products, from comic books to movies to television — and, of course, games. This is just part of the picture, however. Sex and violence *do* have a very masculine appeal, but so do other things. Not all men want the same thing or play games the same way. A close examination of digital FRPGs reveals a number of different masculine ideals running around in the same text. I believe that Fantasy role-playing games are especially powerful texts for mediating what it means to be a man in today's culture. In this chapter, I examine how digital FRPGs offer the possibility of fulfilling multiple standards of manhood. This is not an investigation based on audience reception research; rather, I want to talk about how the text addresses its players. Specifically, I argue that FRPGs, due to their unique combination of computer technology, gaming culture and

100

the Fantasy genre, are particularly effective texts for men to use in negotiating the often-contradictory ideals of respectable manliness, rugged masculinity and eternal boyhood.

What Are Digital FRPGs?

The FRPG is a kind of game that invites the player to take on the role of an adventurer in a pseudo-medieval, magical world. *Dungeons and Dragons* (often referred to as *D&D*), released in 1974 as the first and still most widely played game of its type, is a table-top RPG meant to be played in a face-to-face setting. The Dungeon Master plays the role of collective storyteller and referee, interpreting game rules that define what is and is not possible in the imaginary game-world. The players, meanwhile, role-play warriors, thieves and wizards by describing and sometimes acting out their characters' actions and speech. This setup was incorporated relatively early into text-based computer games wherein the program took the role of Dungeon Master, describing worlds and providing the outcomes of player decisions. In the 1980s, digital FRPGs developed into fully graphic, imaginary worlds in which the player could either see and pilot a character or navigate space via a first-person perspective. Today, FRPGs and Fantasy-themed games are an important part of the digital game market, with titles like *Neverwinter Nights* selling millions of copies.

Not all role-playing games are Fantasy-themed sword-and-sorcery epics, and not all are computerized. In my analysis below, however, I will look at digital Fantasy role-playing games, not only because of their immense popularity, but also because they bring together three apparently different phenomena that in fact link together quite closely in one important regard: they are all sites for the negotiation of American manhood.

Negotiating the Contradictions of Masculinity

Most authors of today's masculinity studies reject the mid–20th century psychologistic notion of gender as in-born and immutable. Rather, they assume that the creation, maintenance and modification of manhood and womanhood is a constant and ongoing process of social construction. Malin (2000), drawing on Durkheim, helpfully describes the ideals of manhood as ritualistic totems: "idealized, ritualized conceptions, conventionalized through repetition and reiteration" (Malin 2000:15). In other words, the idea of what it means to be a man is the result of the ritual work of society. This is not to say that gender norm construction is a unified or internally consistent process. Many scholars argue the opposite — that the models for masculinity are contested ideological ground, where men must either choose between sometimes sharply contrasted alternatives or try to simultaneously live out very contradictory ideals (e.g., Bederman 1995; Pfeil 1995; Pleck 1981; Segal 1997).

While the field of masculinity studies describes a wide array of ideals for men, three in particular seem useful for an analysis of digital FRPGs. A growing body of historical research identifies both respectable manliness and rough masculinity as deeply-rooted models for manhood in American society (Bederman 1995; Horowitz 2001; Norwood 2002; Pendergast 2000; Putney 2001). Historian Woody Register (2001) suggests a third neglected, yet powerful ideal: the eternal boy. All three of these standards remain powerful standards of behavior for today's men. This does *not* mean that the ideologies are as neatly sorted out in everyday experience as I present them here. These ideals coexist and overlap, sometimes in harmony, but sometimes at odds with each other, a point which I will elaborate below.

In *Manliness and Civilization*, Bederman (1995) uses the term "manliness" to denote the Victorian ideals for a middle-class white man: utterly self-controlled, restrained, master of his own destiny, a respectable man possessing enormous strength of character. A proper (white, middle-class) man of the time, therefore, was a true man because of his financial, social and sexual self-restraint, not because of some primal physical power: self-control was the key ingredient of civilized behavior. This ideal of manliness, "respectable manliness," still has power in today's culture, although it has morphed somewhat. With a few notable exceptions, such as within certain Evangelical circles, self-denial and self-control are not standards that fit well with consumer society. However, parts of the image still have traction. A whole series of stock dramatic characters presents a similar ideal in magazines, television, movies, the news and other media: the hardworking and successful businessman, the intelligent and studious researcher, the principled man with integrity, the realistic but essentially upright cop or soldier, and so on. The Victorian standards of extreme self-denial (as described by Bederman) have become less attractive, but respectable or responsible manliness remains a strong gender ideal with deep historical roots.

Bederman (1995) describes "rough masculinity," on the other hand, as a late 19th century reaction to respectable manliness. The new values appropriated gender ideals never discarded by the working classes, ideals which stressed power, physical strength, individualism and the ability to dominate. Bederman notes that various champions of masculinity scorned respectable manliness as being over-effeminate, over-civilized, and out of place in a corporation-dominated world. Vehicles as diverse as the religious Muscular Christianity movement and calculatingly pugnacious President Theodore Roosevelt praised powerful, individualistic men who could control those around them. Today's champions of rough masculinity, although receiving constant skin-deep makeovers, have many of the same elements at the core as early 20th century muscled paragons like Tarzan and Eugene Sandow. The hardly shaven, sledgehammer wielding, working-man of the truck commercial, the sexually irresistible bad-boy, the testosterone laced race car driver, and the extreme athlete or football player all have an overwhelming presence in today's culture. One significant difference is that today's rough masculinity does not draw just on white working-class culture, but also on that of ethnic minorities, such as African-Americans and Hispanic-Americans. Even so, the core values of personal power, physical prowess and heterosexual dominance are still the main features of the rough man (Ehrenreich 2002; Strate 1992).

Register (2001) has also noted a third ideal: the grown-up boy. In his article "Everyday Peter Pans," he describes the "eternal boy," who values a good sense of humor, a carefree attitude, an excitement and zest for life, and, above all, a spirit of playfulness. Register argues that men like amusement park maker Fred Thompson and playful actor Fred Stone exemplified a kind of unapologetic exuberant behavior throughout their adult lives. These men did not idealize the rough-and-tumble world of the bully and the locker-room intimidation we might associate with boyhood, but a kind of carefree escape from responsibility that romantics associate with childhood — thus the reference to Peter Pan. The standard of the eternal boy continues to prosper in our ever more consumer-oriented culture. Popular entertainment frequently shows men experiencing the joy of playing like kids. In movies and commercials, we see the Jim Carrey type comedian, the party-hard frat boy, and the guys who love toys— Circuit City's or Best Buy's adult male customers who, in commercial after commercial, act like grade-school students in a toyshop. It seems that boys also just want to have fun.

These are not the only three ideals that American men encounter in today's culture. New ideals have also appeared, such as the "liberated man." This new kind of ideal man is sensitive to and supportive of the need to dismantle patriarchy in all its forms (Barthel 1992; Pleck 1987; Segal 1997).[3] While this development and others like it are important, I have chosen to focus on respectable manliness, rough masculinity, and eternal boyhood. This is partly because they explain more of the textual features of digital Fantasy role-playing games, and also because they have a historical, deeply set cultural power.

This cultural power does not necessarily translate into stability. While these three models of manhood have had some continuity through the last century, they are not immune to turmoil. Practically all gender theorists believe that the traditional white middle-class ideals of masculinity have been under fire since the late 1960s. Many writers have used the word "crisis" to describe the state of affairs for 1990s American middle-class masculinity. Whether this is an appropriate term, however, it is clear that in the 1980s and 90s, many (if not most) American men were experiencing a kind of debate or confusion over what it meant to be a man (Douglas 1999).

Different scholars cite a variety of causes for these tensions. Many note the role of feminism (Pleck 1981; Robinson 2000; Segal 1997), while others point to economic changes (Faludi 1999; Robinson 2000; Savran 1996), and some note the emotional chasms between baby-boomer men and their fathers (Bly 1990; Faludi 1999; Pfeil 1995). Most point to a combination of factors, as did Ehrenreich (1983), whose *The Hearts of Men* details how a variety of cultural dissidents and scientists contributed to the steady, gradual destruction of the male imperative to support one's family.

But the assault on traditional American manhood did not and does not come solely from without: the three models of masculinity have a host of internal problems. To start with, the standards are impossibly high for most men. "There is only one complete unblushing male in America: a young, married, white, urban, northern, heterosexual Protestant father of a college education, fully employed, of good complexion, weight, and height, and recent record in sports" (Goffman 1963:128). Even if men could more easily meet all these expectations, however, internal inconsistencies would raise insurmountable difficulties.

Manhood is not a unified cultural concept, but a patchwork of different standards, some of which work together, some of which do not. In fact, manhood is often at war with itself. The ideal standards described above are, in many ways, logically inconsistent with each other: a man can choose between very different models, but he cannot live out all of them at once. If a he decides to play the goofball, how will he also manage to be responsible? Can a man be both fun-loving and power-oriented at the same time? Even making a clear choice may not resolve the tension. Whether a man chooses one kind of behavior or another, he will continue to experience calls from the other ideals. The conflicting pulls of these ideologies can cause real stress for men, stress that requires them to constantly negotiate their gender identity.

This is precisely the observation Douglas (1999) makes when she talks about early radio amateurs (who were almost exclusively boys and men) in her radio history, *Listening In*. She argues that amateur radio technology provided an outlet for middle-class men of the 1920s to mediate the pressures of respectable and rough masculinity. Likewise, she points out that men of the 1980s and 1990s had the opportunity to use talk radio to mediate the ideals of the liberated (feminine) man and the rough (traditional) man. The connection between masculinity and technology is nothing new. American popular culture has long associated men with machines: guys stereotypically have special relationships with cars, chainsaws and computers. Avant-garde art and literature also uses technology to symbolize masculinity (or vice versa), as seen in Thomas Pynchon's (1973) obsession with the phallic missile in *Gravity's Rainbow*. What is unique about Douglas' analysis is that she sees technology as a mediation point — a place for men to work out the ideology of masculinity.

Douglas argues that many amateurs used radio as a way out of this dilemma because it allowed middle-class men to live more than one gender ideal simultaneously. On the one hand, the technical learning required for radio operation and its potential life-saving uses encouraged amateurs to think of themselves (and present themselves to the public) as productive contributors to society. At the same time, the wide-reaching ears of the radio and novel exploration it allowed gave its users a sense of unique power.[4] Amateurs had other reasons for being enthusiastic about the newborn medium of radio, but Douglas cogently argues that the discourse of amateur culture reveals that for many men, this new technology was uniquely suited to mediating pressures from the ideologies of gender.

The Digital FRPGs and Their Parts

In the spirit of Douglas' argument, I explore how the text of the FRPG provides opportunities for men to find ways to resolve the conflicts of the different models of manhood. In other words, digital FRPGs act as sites where men can be respectable, rough and playful at the same time. Part of the reason for this is that these games are a meeting point of three related phenomena: FRPGs involve personal computers, they are games and part of the gaming culture, and they are part of the Fantasy genre. Each one of these components is a cultural location where men can mediate masculinities and each provides a range of opportunities for living out different masculine ideals. I am not claiming that personal computers, digital games and Fantasy literature are solely male objects— only that they provide fertile symbolic resources for men to construct gendered identities. After looking at each phenomenon individually, I will draw the separate strands together by examining actual digital FRPG texts for elements that would facilitate the mediation of masculinity.

Personal Computer Culture

The first widely available personal computers did not arrive pre-assembled. They were shipped as kits, because they were hobby items of electronics enthusiasts. In numerous ways, the personal computer hobbyist culture resembles that of radio amateurs. Digital machinery displays many of the same qualities as older electronic technology in that it is a prime site for negotiating masculinity.

First, the personal computer lends itself to the ideals of responsible manliness by being a machine of productivity, a useful tool. It functions as a word processor, a financial spreadsheet machine and a communication tool, and it is customizable to practically any kind of data processing job. The literature surrounding personal computers, such as the glossy monthlies *PC Magazine* or *PC World*, projects the image of a serious, productivity-oriented culture.

At the same time, the personal computer is a power tool that, in an odd way, lends itself to a kind of rough masculinity. Although it is not a physical powerhouse in the same way as a three-quarter-ton pick-up truck, it is a data-processing machine. Whereas we can measure the strength of a diesel engine in horsepower, we can gauge the processor by GHz. Personal computer literature frequently mixes the masculine language of combustion-engines and computer technology. "Maximum Overdrive," screams a recent *Wired* article on enthusiasts who overclock their machines (meaning they run them faster than their rated speeds): "Welcome to the world of overclocking, where silicon lives fast, dies young, and leaves a good-looking corpse" (Doctorow 2003: 112).

Finally, early personal computer enthusiasts loved playing with machines, and this is no different today — the computer works as a toy as well. Like Lego or Erector sets, the computer is a puzzle of components with which hobbyists can fiddle. Well before they had useful software applications, thousands of hobbyists bought and assembled early personal computer kits ("Pop Quiz"; Veit). Today's hardware enthusiasts continue the tradition by experimenting with numerous hardware configurations. They even playfully decorate their machines with functionally useless sculptures and neon lights. In short, the personal computer provides an avenue for men to negotiate the three ideologies of manhood and provides ways to negotiate them. Computer hardware and software are cultural artifacts that are well suited to mediating the contradictions that a present-day man often faces, because the machinery simultaneously allows for a sense of productiveness, a feeling of power and a license to play. These are exactly the same kinds of features exhibited by games played on these computers.

Digital Games and Masculinity

Like the personal computer, the computer game is a prime site for negotiating the ideology of manhood. The actual demographics of the gaming public are debatable. Published industry statistics— released with no discussion of the methodology used to obtain them —claim that over half of the people who purchase computer games and around forty percent of players are women (Entertainment Software Association 2005). But beyond these unverifiable numbers, publicly available statistics on the digital gaming market are sparse. My point, however, is not that most gamers are male, but that the games themselves contain elements that facilitate the negotiation of masculinity. In addition, the discourse of the hardcore gaming culture is stereotypically masculine.

The notion of responsible or productive manliness is not a strong one in digital games and game culture, but it is not wholly absent. A small segment of the digital games market is explicitly educational, and a larger part of it features games with relatively serious, productive themes, such as *Railroad Tycoon* (Microprose Software 1990), *Civilization* (Microprose Software 1991), or *Age of Empires* (Ensemble Studios 1997). Games also have defenders that see supposed entertainment as socially productive. Gee (2003), for instance, has argued that video games are excellent tools for teaching today's computer-savvy youth — better, in fact, than books. Other recent research has shown that games appear to have beneficial effects upon the human brain (Green and Bavelier 2003). Much of this discussion about socially redeeming gaming, however, occurs in non-gamer discourse (such as news magazines and papers), and it is not terribly important in hardcore fan discussions, such the fan magazine *PC Gamer*. Generally speaking, games do not lend themselves to a discourse of responsible manliness as easily as they do to other ideals of manhood.

The ideology of powerful, aggressive manhood — what Kline, Dyer-Witheford and De Peuter (2003) call "militarized masculinity"— plays a major role in the literature surrounding games and in the games themselves. Games allow the player to experience the extraordinary and to break social taboos. Blowing things up and killing enemies quickly became major themes in early video games. Today, popular genres still reveal a fascination with power and domination: racing games, space battle games, fighting games, and war simulations all indulge rough masculine fantasies. Gamers often talk about their pastime in a sort of coarse, locker-room style banter. *PC Gamer* frequently adopts this voice: "When these guys promise ground slippery with blood, they mean it!" ("Preview— Warhammer 40,000" 2004); or "Weep for joy, for there are five new realms to conquer" (Morris 2004).

Game titles such as *Mortal Kombat, Command & Conquer* (Westwood Studios 1995), and *Manhunt* (Rockstar North 2003) also play off this fascination with power and violence. The computer game is an ideal place to vicariously experience the thrill of the racetrack or the glory of imperial conquest.

The story of the eternal boy or masculine playfulness is also a major theme of the game culture — *playing* is the primary purpose, after all. Plenty of games focus on goofy fun, such as the Lucasart adventure games *Sam 'n Max* (LucasArts 1993) or the *Monkey Island* (LucasFilm Games 1990) series. Even more games, however, feature a kind of carefree adventure — make-believe with no serious consequences. This emphasis on playful entertainment is clear in gamer discourse as well. Even at its most hyper-masculine, fan literature is usually jocular or tongue-in-cheek. Although *PC Gamer* abounds with glorification of bloody violence and explosions, the writers are more often than not amusing themselves and their readers by thumbing their noses at conventional opinion and proper morality.

Much of the gaming culture is not purposefully chauvinistic. When gamers try to address issues of sexual inequality in their culture, however, they often reinforce its masculinity via the language they use.[5] Whether or not gamers are mostly men, it is clear that the discourse of game fans is stereotypically male, and that most games offer a site for men to be manly and productive, masculine and powerful, and boyish and fun-loving.

Fantasy Genre

Although the books that appear on the Fantasy rack in today's bookstores have considerable thematic range, generally speaking, they tend to feature magic and imaginary worlds. Epic Fantasy (Tolkien's sort) is a subgenre that plays out all the stereotypes: wizards, kingdoms in peril, demonic threats, powerful warriors, clever thieves, treacherous wilds filled with dangerous monsters, and so forth. This kind of literature is a major inspiration for *D&D* and similar subsequent games. In terms of gender ideals, the Fantasy genre as a whole is hardly uniform: many writers have carved out spaces for non-stereotypical gender ideals, such as the powerful warrior-woman or the peaceful and pastoral man who is a reluctant adventurer. Nevertheless, much Fantasy-themed literature and art provides opportunities for men to negotiate the ideals of respectability, power and play.

The ideology of responsible manliness is surprisingly widespread in Fantasy literature, albeit as something of a throwback to an earlier era. The key here is the emphasis on the manly hero. Instead of hardheaded, business-oriented productivity, novels and games set in magical worlds feature the literary romanticism of pseudo-medieval chivalry, invoking a different kind of responsibility. Epic Fantasy heroes spend their adventuring time trying to defeat evil in order to save a peaceful or helpless society that cannot protect itself. Tolkien's tale of the quest to destroy the evil Ring is a plot that countless novels employ: the reluctant hero leaves on the quest in spite of daunting odds, because he or she knows the value of duty, of responsibility, for others.

Elements in tune with a brutish, forceful masculinity are even more prevalent in both the books and the artwork associated with the Fantasy genre. Militaristic exploits are very prominent: a large portion of Fantasy art shows warriors in battle, and rare is the novel that does not feature superhuman feats of swordplay and derring-do. A party of Fantasy heroes almost always features a warrior (such as *The Lord of the Rings'* Boromir or Gimli) who is the epitome of rough masculinity. Magic also functions as a kind of power technology in Fantasy works. Essentially, magic works as an invisible tool that can re-arrange the world. Fantasy art also generally features sex-roles that epitomize the ideals of rough masculinity. Men appear as powerfully built warriors, trim and agile thieves, or respectable and wise-looking wizards. Women, on the other hand, are almost always, regardless of their character-role, beautiful and voluptuous, with tight fitting, revealing clothes. In other words, men are powerful and women are eye candy.

The exploration of strange and exciting new worlds is the hallmark of the Fantasy novel, and it has the same kind of appeal now that *Peter Pan* had for early 20th century Americans. The Fantasy genre allows the outwardly cynical and mature grown-up to relive the wide-eyed wonder of the boy. First of all, many of the landscapes and urban settings featured in novels are extravagant works of imagination: the preserved forest realm of Lothlorien, the Druid keep of Paranor, the subterranean dark elf city of Menzoberranzan and so on. Second, the wilderness features prominently in many Fantasy works, recalling survival stories such as those made popular for boys in the mid-20th century by authors such as Jim Kjelgard (*Big Red*) and Walter Farley (*The Black Stallion*). Finally, while the cast of characters in any given Fantasy novel often evokes the grim seriousness of a Nordic saga, it just as often can shade into the whimsical, more akin to a Victorian fairy story or *Alice in Wonderland* than *Beowulf*. In short, wonderful worlds, tales of adventure and weird characters all evoke a kind of juvenile atmosphere, even if they are accompanied by grand themes.

Once again, Fantasy literature provides many themes and elements amenable to helping men wrestle with conflicting ideals of manhood. As with both personal computers and digital games, Fantasy literature is more than *just* a tool for men to negotiate their gender identity, but many of its most prominent themes and elements are particularly well suited to helping men be responsible, rough and playful.

Mediation of Masculinity in FRPGs

The computer FRPG represents a meeting point of these three phenomena. Is it reasonable to think that the mix of personal computer culture, digital game culture and fantasy genre themes make these texts particularly useful for negotiating the ideological currents of manhood? To answer that question, I explore worlds in which I have played extensively — a series of licensed *D&D* computer games set in the "Forgotten Realms." This is an imaginary setting for which *D&D* has released dozens of novels and game aids providing descriptions for role-playing sessions.

Game developer and publisher Strategic Simulations Inc. (SSI) released a relatively successful series of Forgotten Realms games in the late 1980s and early 90s, including titles like *Curse of the Azure Bonds* (SSI 1989), and *Pools of Darkness* (SSI 1991). Developer Bioware released another string of licensed games that are among the most successful games ever made for personal computers. *Baldur's Gate* (Bioware Corporation 1998), *Icewind Dale* (Black Isle Studios 2000) (produced by another developer using Bioware's technology), and *Neverwinter Nights* (*NWN*) (Bioware Corporation 2002), along with their various sequels provide players with enormous Fantasy worlds to explore. Although I spent several dozen hours playing through some of the SSI games, most of my research focused on the newer Bioware set. Over the course of a year and a half, I played completely through the single-player campaigns of each of these games, each one taking many dozens of hours of playing time to complete. In addition to the games themselves, I studied publications surrounding the games, such as the game manuals and the *D&D* campaign setting for the Forgotten Realms.

Throughout this process of textual analysis, I encountered a number of frequently repeated thematic elements related to questions of masculine gender ideals. I narrowed these themes to a list of five features of the game that lend themselves to the negotiation of manhood: playing the hero, ideal body types, the themes of exploration and conquest, the importance of increasing a character's power, and elements of playfulness and weirdness. While these are not the only aspects of the games related to issues of masculinity, they provide some of the best evidence that the digital FRPGs facilitate the mediation of manhood.

Playing the Hero

From their very earliest days, FRPGs have had a strong moral element. *D&D* players must choose "alignments" for their characters, a compound description that has two components: one indicating whether they are good, neutral or evil, another measuring how they feel about rules and order — lawful, neutral or chaotic. Thus, a character could be lawful-good (morally good and upright and very strict about following the laws of his or her religion and rulers), neutral-evil (bad, but neither a rebel nor a rule follower) or so on. Playing anti-heroes in FRPGs or other Fantasy-themed games is not unusual. The Forgotten Realms games also allow players to choose characters with an evil alignment, but the overall arc of the single-player story is one of a hero preventing the triumph of an evil enemy. Players can do immoral things such as break promises and kill good creatures, but if they want to progress through the overall story, they need to work to save Neverwinter. Although the limited moral flexibility somewhat tempers its save-the-world character, this hero-story generally slants the game towards a kind of chivalric behavior that demonstrates the presence of the ideal of responsible manliness. At the very least, the game provides an opportunity to be a hero if the player so chooses.

In *NWN*, the single-player campaign automatically plunges the player into a quest to find the magical creatures necessary to stop the plague troubling the city. In *Icewind Dale*, the player must try to stop a powerful demon from taking over the world. In *Pools of Darkness*, the player has to stop the evil god Bane from destroying the entire Moonsea area. The list goes on. In each case, regardless of the player-characters' actual alignments, they must destroy the always-evil enemy so as to solve the major problem of the game. This is a very typical Fantasy genre theme, and plays to a sense of nobility that works well with responsible manliness. None of the games call for much self-sacrifice, as the tragic death of the characters simply means the end of a game (and a return to a saved version where the party is still alive). However, the game-story *does* present the experience almost invariably as a tale of a small band of heroes triumphing in the face of apparently overwhelming odds.

These digital FRPGs, like many others, promote a re-vamped version of medieval chivalry. Like the code of the fabled warriors of the Round Table or the Jedi Knights of the Star Wars universe, the Forgotten Realms games call for their players to smite evil and protect the defenseless. Thus, through perseverance and proper behavior, the upright triumph over the wicked. This emphasis on the player's role as defender of the people nicely echoes the demands of responsible manliness.

Ideal Bodies

Since all the Forgotten Realms digital games are graphic adventures, they have plenty of opportunities to work all the standard themes of Fantasy art: warriors, castles, dungeons, dragons, monsters, and, of course, sexually ideal bodies. The portrayal of humanoids (whether fully human, elven, dwarven or halfling) turns these magical worlds into places of rough, masculine, sexual fantasies. The men are "real" men: old and wise wizards with flowing robes, lean and athletic thieves or bards, or (best of all) ridiculously powerful, muscled warriors. The women are similarly idealized: regardless of profession, almost all of them are curvaceous yet athletic, clothed in lycra-tight apparel and/or armor. In each case, the bodies conform to the ideal standards of the roughly masculine male.

Even the low-resolution graphics of the earlier games do their best to meet these standards. For example, the icon for dark-elf wizards in the combat screen of *Pools of Darkness* (from 1992) consists of a badly pixilated, yet unmistakably curvy woman wearing a bikini and wielding a knife. The portrait artwork for *NWN* is far more impressive in terms of its detail, and no less fantastic in its body themes. The paladin Aribeth, one of the main non-player characters and a very respectable warrior who gives the player's character orders, has a tight-fitting suit of armor that fails to protect anything above her breasts—a strange omission for a seasoned warrior, but not for a Fantasy girl. To say that women are portrayed in a strictly uniform manner is an overstatement. Some female bodies are not so much curvy as athletic, or even tomboyish. But in the material I surveyed, these are the exception, rather than the rule. The portrayal of male bodies is slightly more varied — although very few bodies are out of shape. Their apparel, however, is usually more functional: FRPG men do not gratuitously bare their flesh as a matter of course.

This tendency to treat women as poster-girls is particularly interesting in light of the supposedly interchangeable nature of gender in the *D&D* rules: whether male or female, the character is statistically the same. Yet, the functional empowerment of women is undercut by the swimsuit-model artwork that appeals to masculine sexual fantasy. As in so many other digital games and gaming culture in general, women can join the show as long as they do not interrupt rough masculine fantasies of sex and power (see also Nephew, this volume). To put it more glibly, but no less accurately, a woman is allowed to kick some ass as long as she herself has a nice one. While the texts are a little more ambiguous about ideals for the male body, they tend to be pretty heavy on displaying men with some kind of physical power, either the lean athletic kind or brute muscular type. These body types could certainly fulfill sexual fantasies of players that do not feel the pull of the rough masculine ideal (say, for example, heterosexual female players). I am not arguing that these games are necessarily made with one kind of player in mind nor that unintended players cannot subvert the overt themes of the text. Rather, I am arguing that the presentation of body types in digital FRPGs—as in the Fantasy genre—provide fertile resources for men to play out the rough masculine ideal. Boys and men playing these games can indulge their sexual fantasies by playing as powerful men interacting with pin-up girls.

The Conquistador Complex

The rough masculine ideals of the conquistador, prevalent in personal computer and gaming culture, are also prominent in FRPG games. A big part of all these games is charting out un-discovered territories. In the Bioware games, as the player searches out new places, the game adds them to a map. In the SSI Gold Box games, on the other hand, selecting the "Area" option shows the player a very crude diagram of the whole area — although nothing is marked on it. Either way, exploration is one of the key game activities, meaning that it is a kind of power play. Space is the currency of the game — if you have not visited a place, you cannot use it. In addition, the discovery of new spaces, such as wild forests or strings of caves, especially when they are so artistically attractive (as they are in the newer games), can be exhilarating in and of itself. *NWN*, for example, features the magnificent temples and palaces of Neverwinter, beautiful giant forests, and moldy old dungeons. *Baldur's Gate* and *Icewind Dale* both also feature some gorgeous artwork.

The Forgotten Realms games enhance this excitement: potential danger lurks behind every corner. Exploration is usually a violent ordeal, as it is often impossible to pass through a territory without cleansing it of its native inhabitants, such as hostile orcs, dangerous trolls, poisonous giant spiders, undead skeletons, and the like. Although some creatures and people within these imaginary worlds are perfectly peaceful, the players' characters cannot avoid fights for the whole game — this is one of the key features, something that sells the game.[6] Some encounters in some of the Forgotten Realms games offer the opportunity for adventurers to talk their way out of trouble (and talk their way into it as well), but in most situations, hostile opponents attack at first sight.

Thus, the game combines the rough masculine ideal of the rough-hewn, self-sufficient explorer with the power of the violent warrior. As with the conquistadors of old, new land is a tool to exploit, and inhabitants are either pragmatically useful or deserving of destruction. This display of rough masculinity is a legacy of both digital gaming culture and Fantasy literature. In a nutshell, the purpose of these games is (to paraphrase an old joke about the Army) to go to interesting places, meet interesting creatures, and kill them.

Powering Up

A large part of the addictive appeal of RPGs— as many dedicated gamers can attest — is the steady acquisition of new skills and abilities by the player's character throughout the course of the games. In fact, the FRPG is a vehicle for giving players the opportunity to gain and exercise power not accessible in real life. The common character skills in *D&D* games are surely ones that most members of society do not have: sword-fighting, playing magical music, casting acid arrow spells, lock-picking, and so forth. As the game continues, deeds earn experience points, which allow the player to steadily upgrade their character's military or magical prowess. They also steadily acquire more and more powerful magic items and gobs of treasure that enable them to purchase powerful magic items. By the end of the game, successful characters can fight enormous dragons and powerful magic-users.

On the one hand, this is very much a masculine power trip. These games offer a sense of extraordinary and ever-increasing ability. Much like the old comic book commercials that promised products to turn the ninety-nine pound weakling into a hulking tower of strength, playing the game gives the player the opportunity to pump up a character. The Forgotten Realms games can solidify this sense of power in three ways: presenting opponents with ever-increasing danger, presenting displays of power, and altering numerical representations.

Some of the games steadily turn up the difficulty level of the enemies the player faces. What would have been murderously difficult at the beginning of the game, however, becomes simply challenging later on. This is because the steady accumulation of new levels of power and better weapons means the player can return and make mincemeat of the former obstacles. The newer games also make use of their advanced graphics by showing spectacular displays of power. This is especially true of *NWN*: a low-level magic missile looks cool enough, but the graphic fireworks of a powerful fireball (not available until the player has worked at it for a while) are much more impressive. In both the old and new games, players can watch their characters steadily increase in statistical power: strength stats, attack stats, health stats, number of spells, and more all go up and up.

This is not a theme that appeals only to the standard of rough masculinity, however. This is very much a tale of capitalist acquisition. Essentially, the characters of the RPGs become commodities: as the player invests his or her labor, the value of the avatar increases. While a somewhat bizarre connection to the ideal of responsible manliness, this *is* in fact how the game functions. By faithfully dedicating time and effort to adventuring, the player gains numerous rewards: the story of responsible work in a nutshell.

These power-ups fit the character of the personal computer culture (investments of time and money equal increased ability) and of gaming in general (most games offer steadily increasing challenges and reward successful play with power). All of this plays in very nicely with both the rough masculine fantasy of power and responsible manly goal of rewarded labor — it may very well offer a feeling of capability that is not present in real life and also introduces the capitalist narrative so tied to the American conception of respectable manliness.

Fantastic Playgrounds

The Forgotten Realms games are not all about rough masculine fantasies and desires for responsible manliness—they tap into the boyishness of games as well. An element of wide-eyed wonder, combined with occasional humor, makes this imaginary world something of a virtual playground. The Forgotten Realms games are not comedy games in the sense that the amusing LucasArts adventure games of the 1980s and 90s were. Yet occasional appearances of non-sequiturs, comic characters, and mildly amusing conversations lend a playful air to these games. Minsc, a giant barbarian with a rather silly accent featured in the *Baldur's Gate* series, is a good example of this. Yelling awe-inspiring phrases like "butt-kicking for goodness!" as he heads into battle, he carries a pet "miniature giant space hamster" named Boo. Weird quirks like this certainly lighten the atmosphere of an otherwise non-stop, hack-and-slash affair.

Most of these games' playfulness, however, comes from the Fantasy world itself. The magic and amazing creatures of the Fantasy genre enhance the game's atmosphere of child-like wonder. Dwarves, gnomes, elves, pixies, enchanters, magic swords, strange landscapes, dragon lairs and other fairy tale elements all populate the games' landscapes. The playful elements of the computer game are also prominent in this FRPG: the contest of combat, the make-believe of entering another world, the vicarious glee of casting spells—all taking place with no consequences more serious than a little frustration at having to load up a saved game if things go wrong. All of this spells adventure, very much of the sort featured in Peter Pan: the game invites us to be children who never grow up. In short, these games are very much play-worlds that invite the enactment of eternal boyhood.

Conclusion

A variety of features in the digital FRPG offer men the opportunity to negotiate the often conflicting demands of respectable, rough, and playful ideals of manhood. It should be quite clear that this is an argument of address. Each man (and woman, for that matter) brings a unique perspective to the game that affects the way he or she deals with the themes I have identified. For example, someone who does not feel particularly burdened by the ideal of respectable manliness will probably not feel a strong pull to play an upstanding and decent hero in an FRPG. Many women gamers wreak havoc within the gender stereotypes of digital games. In other words, all readings (or *playings*) are negotiated, and the player is not brainwashed by the game.

To deny the draw of these FRPGs' themes, however, is misguided. The historical trajectory of the development of American models of manhood, traced by a growing body of research, demonstrates the deep-seated cultural force of the rough masculine ideal, the ideal of respectable manliness, and, to a lesser extent, the ideal of the eternal boy. The field of contemporary masculinity studies has documented the constant turmoil that many men experience while trying to work out their gender identities. In other words, a large body of research argues that many men *do* struggle over exactly what it means to be masculine, and they constantly engage with their surrounding culture — including popular movies (Pfeil 1995), talk radio (Douglas 1999), *Playboy* magazine (Ehrenreich 1983), and PromiseKeeper rallies (Faludi 1999), among other components — in an attempt to negotiate these tensions.

Elements of digital FRPGs also correspond to these conflicts. In my survey of the Forgotten Realms series computer games, I discovered a range of common features that play around with the competition of the ideals of manhood. The theme of playing the hero exemplifies the demands of respectable manliness. The themes of ideal bodies, conquistador adventure, and powering up give the opportunity for players to be paragons of rough masculinity. Finally, the theme of fantastic playgrounds provides virtual adventures for the eternal boy.

To recognize that there are more to these games than the elements facilitating the negotiation of masculinity is not to deny the important potential of those elements. Players can do many different things with the same game, and many Fantasy gamers may no longer fit the stereotypical mold of the white middle-class male, but the game themes appealing to this audience still remain. Whether or not the digital FRPG public is predominantly male, for now, these games are ideally geared toward providing players the opportunity to be a Fantasy man: an impossible man who has put it all together.

References

Barthel, Diane. 1992. "When Men Put on Appearances: Advertising and the Social Construction of Masculinity." pp. 137–53 in *Men, Masculinity and the Media, Research on Men and Masculinities*, edited by S. Craig. London: Sage.

Bederman, Gail. 1995. *Manliness and Civilization: A Cultural History of Gender and Race in the United States, 1880–1917*. Chicago: University of Chicago Press.

Bioware Corporation. 1998. "Baldur's Gate." Interplay (Black Isle Studios).

_____. 2002. "Neverwinter Nights." Infogrames.

Black Isle Studios. 2000. "Icewind Dale." Interplay.

Bly, Robert. 1990. *Iron John: A Book About Men*. New York: Vintage Books.

Cook, David. 1989. *Player's Handbook*. Lake Geneva, WI: TSR.

Doctorow, Cory. 2003. "Maximum Overdrive." *Wired*, March, pp. 112–3.

Douglas, Susan. 1999. *Listening In: Radio and the Imagination, from Amos 'n Andy and Edward R. Murrow to Wolfman Jack and Howard Stern*. New York: Times Books.

Ehrenreich, Barbara. 1983. *The Hearts of Men: American Dreams and the Flight from Commitment*. New York: Anchor Books.

Ehrenreich, Nancy. 2002. "Masculinity & American Militarism." *Tikkun* 17.

Ensemble Studios. 1997. "Age of Empires." Microsoft.

Entertainment Software Association. 2005. "Demographic Information." Retrieved February 18, 2005 (*http://www.theesa.com/pressroom.html*).

Faludi, Susan. 1999. *Stiffed: The Betrayal of the American Man*. New York: William Morrow and Company.

Gas Powered Games. 2002. "Dungeon Siege." Microsoft.

Gee, James Paul 2003. "High Score Education: Games, Not School, Are Teaching Kids to Think." *Wired*, May, pp. 91–2.

Goffman, Erving. 1963. *Stigma: Notes on the Management of Spoiled Identity*. Englewood Cliffs, N.J.: Prentice-Hall.

Green, C. Shawn and Daphne Bavelier. 2003. "Action Video Game Modifies Visual Selective Attention." *Nature* 423: 534–7.

Gygax, Gary. 1979. *Dungeon Master's Guide*. Lake Geneva, WI: TSR.

_____, and Dave Arneson. 1974. *Dungeons and Dragons*. Lake Geneva, WI: TSR.

Horowitz, Roger. 2001. "Introduction." pp. 1–10 in Roger Horowitz (ed.), *Boys and Their Toys? Masculinity, Technology, and Class in America*. New York: Routledge.

id Software. 1996. "Quake." id Software.

Kline, Stephen, Nick Dyer-Witheford, and Greig De Peuter. 2003. *Digital Play: The Interaction of Technology, Culture, and Marketing*. Montreal & Kingston, Canada: McGill-Queen's University Press.

"Letters." 2004. *PC Gamer*, February, pp. 4–5.

Looking Glass Studios. 1998. "Thief: the Dark Project." Eidos Interactive.

LucasArts. 1993. "Sam 'n Max Hit the Road." LucasArts.

Lucasfilm Games. 1990. "The Secret of Monkey Island." Lucasfilm Games.

Malin, Brenton J. 2000. "American Masculinity Under Clinton: Popular Media and the

'Crisis of Masculinity.'" Ph.D. dissertation, Department of Communication Studies, University of Iowa, Iowa City, IA.

Maxis Software. 2000. "The Sims." Electronic Arts.

McKinley, Robin. 2000. *Spindle's End*. New York: Putnam's Sons.

Microprose Software. 1990. "Railroad Tycoon." Microprose Software.

_____. 1991. "Sid Meier's Civilization." Microprose Software.

Morris, Dan 2004. "Review — Dungeon Siege: Legends of Aranna." *PC Gamer*, February, pp. 72.

Nephew, Michelle. 2006. "Playing with Identity: Unconscious Desire and Role-playing Games." pp. 120–139 in *Gaming as Culture: Social Reality, Identity and Experience in Fantasy Games*, edited by J. Patrick Willliams, Sean Q. Hendricks, and W. Keith Winkler. Jefferson, NC:McFarland.

Norwood, Stephen H. 2002. *Strike-breaking and Intimidation: Mercenaries and Masculinity in Twentieth-Century America* Chapel Hill, NC: University of North Carolina Press.

Pendergast, Tom. 2000. *Creating the Modern Man: American Magazines and Consumer Culture 1900–1950*. Columbia, MO: University of Missouri Press.

Pfeil, Fred. 1995. *White Guys: Studies in Postmodern Domination and Difference*, Edited by M. Davis and M. Sprinker. London: Verso.

Pleck, Joseph H. 1981. *The Myth of Masculinity*. Cambridge, MA: MIT Press.

_____. 1987. "American Fathering in Historical Perspective." pp. 83–97 in *Changing Men: New Directions in Research on Men and Masculinity*, edited by M. Kimmel. Newbury Park, CA: Sage.

"Pop Quiz: What Was the First Personal Computer?" Blinkenlights Archaeological Institute, Retrieved November 1, 2004 (*http://www.blinkenlights.com/pc.shtml*).

"Preview — Warhammer 40,000: Dawn of War." 2004. *PC Gamer*, February, pp. 50.

Putney, Clifford. 2001. *Muscular Christianity: Manhood and Sports in Protestant America, 1880–1920*. Cambridge, MA: Harvard University Press.

Pynchon, Thomas. 1973. *Gravity's Rainbow*. New York: Viking Press.

Register, Woody. 2001. "Everyday Peter Pans: Work, Manhood, and Consumption in Urban America, 1900–1930." pp. 199–228 in *Boys and Their Toys? Masculinity, Technology, and Class in America*, edited by R. Horowitz. New York: Routledge.

Robinson, Sally. 2000. *Marked Men: White Masculinity in Crisis*. New York: Columbia University Press.

Rockstar North. 2003. "Manhunt." Rockstar Games.

Savran, David. 1996. "The Sadomasochist in the Closet: White Masculinity and the Culture of Victimization." *Differences: A Journal of Feminist Cultural Studies* 8: 127–52.

Segal, Lynne. 1997. *Slow Motion: Changing Masculinities, Changing Men*. London: Virago Press.

SSI. 1989. "Curse of the Azure Bonds." SSI.

_____. 1991. "Pools of Darkness." SSI.

Strate, Lance. 1992. "Beer Commercials: a Manual on Masculinity." pp. 78–92 in *Men, Masculinity and the Media, Research on Men and Masculinities*, edited by S. Craig. London: Sage.

Tweet, Jonathan, Monte Cook, and Skip Williams. 2003a. *Dungeon Master's Guide*. Renton, WA: Wizards of the Coast.

_____. 2003b. *Monster Manual*. Renton, WA: Wizards of the Coast.

_____. 2003c. *Player's Handbook* Renton, WA: Wizards of the Coast.

Veit, Stanley. "Pre-IBM PC Computers." Retrieved November 1, 2004 (http://www.pc-history.org/).

Verant Interactive. 1999. "EverQuest." 989 Studios.

Westwood Studios. 1995. "Command & Conquer." Virgin Interactive.

Notes

1. Citing *Dungeons and Dragons* is more difficult than it might seem because the game transcends any one particular publication. This is partly because the game has a relatively long history, and partly because different rules appear in different books. We could cite the original version (Gygax and Arneson 1974), but it was only available in very limited quantities and is today a very valuable collector's item (thus, hardly representative of the game as a cultural phenomenon). *Advanced Dungeons and Dragons*, both the first (Gygax 1979) and second (Cook 1989) editions, featured many different rules, but were the main version of the game throughout the 1980s and most of the 1990s. Today, the rules of the third edition of *Dungeons and Dragons* are in several core books (as was *Advanced Dungeons and Dragons*): *The Player's Handbook* (Tweet, Cook, and Williams 2003c), *The Dungeon Master's Guide* (Tweet, Cook, and Williams 2003a), and *The Monster Manual* (Tweet, Cook, and Williams 2003b). I would argue that the game in the general sense is all of these and more.

2. Throughout the chapter I use the capitalized "Fantasy" to distinguish the literary/game genre from the broader and more typical uses of the word "fantasy."

3. Actually, the liberated man made his appearance far earlier — at least as early as the Bohemian communities of Greenwich village in the fin de siècle period (Kimmel 1987). However, the model did not have nearly the same widespread currency it does today.

4. And, although Douglas does not consider the ideal of the eternal boy, her evidence and other radio amateur discourse that I have studied suggests that men thought of their radios as toys as well, allowing enthusiasts to play out the role of the eternal boy.

5. For example, in a response to a female fan's letter commenting on the lack of coverage of girl gamers, *PC Gamer* writes: "We've always given the ladies their props, Kata. Who can forget the classic deathmatch duel (May 2001) between our former *Quake* [id Software 1996] champion, Jeremy Williams, and female gamer Kornelia? She annihilated him, making him weep openly. It's one of our fondest memories" ("Letters" 2004). Perhaps not blatant sexism, but still a reinforcement of male dominance through its use of language: you can be part of the club as long as you behave like one of the guys.

6. Conflict games do not actually have to force fighting. The acclaimed *Thief* (Looking Glass Studios, 1998) series, for example, rewards players for stealth. The *Forgotten Realms* games are not like that.

6. PLAYING WITH IDENTITY

Unconscious Desire and Role-Playing Games

Michelle Nephew

Plato's "Ring of Gyges" proposition in *Republic* describes a ring of invisibility that allows a person to commit any crime with impunity. Two questions then arise: what would you do if you found the ring, and how would your chosen course of action challenge moral systems? In both the case of the wearer of this ring and the player of a role-playing game (RPG), magic powers free him to act in a way that defines what he considers correct behavior, making him a free moral agent (Holsworth 1995:55). The conflict between the unrestrained desires of the player characters (PCs) and their own moral judgment is an aspect of role-playing that defines it as a forum for the exploration of issues of identity. This chapter examines the intertwined relationship between the character and the player in RPGs, focusing on the knowledge of self that role-playing engenders.

Because the player is empowered to do more than just interpret the "text" of a role-playing game — because the player has a hand in shaping his character and the game's narrative based on his own experience and desires— he becomes an active manipulator of the text. The role-playing experience takes place primarily in the imagination, where the character becomes a self-reflective representation of the player's fundamental drives. As such, the character can be approached using Freudian psychoanalytic criticism and Laura Mulvey's (1994) work on performance and spectatorship. These perspectives become especially meaningful in the treatment of topics such as the common semantic slippage between the roles of player and character; the complex structure of fantasy presented by role-playing, which addresses Freudian concepts of dreams and transmits a knowledge of self through the wish-fulfillment inherent in character creation; role-playing's ability to affirm the player's fundamental drives, encouraging a sense of self-worth and power while indulging male erotic desire in a way that devalues women; and RPG culture's resistance to disempowerment. By allowing play in regard to identity, role-playing games encourage players to reflexively exhibit a knowledge of self.

Literature Review

The term "role-play"—a translation of the German word *rollenspiel*—was coined by J.L. Moreno in the early 1940s as part of his system of psychotherapy, which differentiated "role-playing" from "role-creating" in that the former gives the individual a greater degree of freedom (Moreno 1943:438). It has since acquired currency in the fields of sociology, social anthropology, social psychology, psychodrama and simulation games, and, of course, the entertainment field through games such as *Dungeons & Dragons* (Tactical Studies Rules, 1974). Role-playing has been used as an educational exercise, tool of analysis, method of resource management, psychological therapy, and recreational activity.

The field of psychology has given role-playing significant scholarly treatment as it relates to medical therapy, in which professionals use the acting of roles to probe the underlying issues a patient might otherwise cover up. Keith Hurley describes this relationship between psychology and role-play, concluding that role-playing skill is an important part of social cognition, communication, and interaction, and reflects an underlying empathy — the ability to imagine oneself in the shoes of another person — in the role-player. Developmental psychologists also maintain that the changes that occur in the play and social interactions of children as they age reflect their "role-taking ability" (Hurley 1994:40).[1] Hurley further notes that correlations have been found between a person's ability to role-play and moral behaviors like helping, sharing, and altruism, and also with general intelligence; "Lack of role-taking skills has been found to be typical of juvenile delinquents ... training in these skills can subsequently result in significantly lower levels of delinquency" (Hurley 1994:41).

Indeed, in the field of psychology, therapeutic methods such as psychodrama, fixed-role therapy, and behavior therapy are based on role-playing techniques. Psychodrama involves the patient acting out concerns so as to confront problems and achieve a catharsis. "Through a process of role-reversals and assumption of various personae the client is encouraged to view their concerns from otherwise unconsidered perspectives" (Hurley 1994:41).

In fixed-role therapy, the patient is given a pattern of behavior that differs from the patient's normal behavior, which he then enacts during therapy sessions and in everyday life. Enacted roles help protect patients as they explore these environments. The behavior therapy technique involves adopting effective social behaviors to replace ineffective ones and is used in assertiveness training. The subject role-plays through several increasingly difficult scenes, while the therapist takes the role of the person with whom the subject wants to become assertive. "It is rather like a role-playing version of systematic desensitization," comments Hurley (1994:42). In psychodrama, fixed-role therapy, and behavior therapy, role-playing is used as a therapeutic method to help the patient achieve a greater self-awareness and understanding of other people and himself.

In this context, cultural studies is able to approach role-playing using psychoanalytic criticisms derived from Sigmund Freud's therapeutic technique as presented in *A General Introduction to Psycho-Analysis*, and by invoking the issues of performance and spectatorship later explored by Laura Mulvey in "Visual Pleasure and Narrative Cinema." In this chapter I develop the argument that role-playing's use as a medical therapy underscores the supposition that during an RPG session a player's character acts as a latent aspect of himself, played out publicly; the role-playing game is a text shaped by unconscious desire.

Player Versus Character

In a role-playing game, the player's unconscious desires are allowed to become manifest in the role taken, since the persona of the character allows the player a disguise behind which to hide. A self-reflexive identity is in this way formed though the display of the player's inner desires, as is first apparent in the difficulties players sometimes have distinguishing between the subject positions of "player" and "character," and in the creation of wish-fulfillment-driven characters.

As in a performance, the player/actor in a role-playing game is "behaving 'as if I am someone else' or as if I am 'beside myself,' or 'not myself,' as when in a trance. But this 'someone else' may also be 'me in another state of feeling/being,' as if there were multiple 'me's in each person" (Schechner quoted in Lancaster 1995:23). This state has been interpreted as identity confusion or self-delusion by opponents of role-playing games, but as a normal function of game play by others who perceive games as "absorbing;" that is, "they pull the minds of the players into them and function preemptively and exclusively" (Wilson 1990:5). This dynamic —

which I think of as "the problem of the player character"—foregrounds the importance of identity in RPGs. Most role-playing games in publication feature a special section — generally near the requisite "Role-playing is Fantasy" disclaimer — that discusses the difference between the "player" and the "character" in the game. *D&D* 3rd Edition, for example, points out the distinction explicitly.

> The action of a Dungeons & Dragons game takes place in the imaginations of the players. Like actors in a movie, players sometimes speak as if they were their characters or as if their fellow players were their characters. These rules even adopt that casual approach, using "you" to refer to and mean "your character." In reality, however, you are no more your character than you are the king when you play chess [Cook 2000:6].

The *Call of Cthulhu* RPG reduces this sentiment to one sentence, saying, "The game is an evolving interaction between players (in the guise of characters unraveling a mystery) and the keeper, who presents the world in which the mystery occurs" (Petersen 1999:23). The distinction between player and character generally becomes moot when participating in a role-playing game, however; saying that "I" as my character "draw my crossbow" as part of the role-playing experience is to engage in the performative rather than merely the descriptive, which is a central goal of the game. As Lancaster observes, when actively role-playing the players don't just describe what their characters do; "what they say is the action itself" (Lancaster 1998:51). You don't just report an act in a game session, but rather indulge in it, identifying with the character you're playing and with the fantasy world of which he is a part. The common usage of the combined term "player character" in gaming literature merely underscores the melding of the two identities that often happens as part of the normal dynamics of a game session.

The process of developing an RPG character is an intensive, lengthy endeavor. As RPG industry insider James Wallis observes, in-depth characterization evolves during play, sometimes taking years as the player develops the character's personality, in the process creating "a library of experiences and references which define their past and present;" character development is an existential process, he concludes (Wallis 1995:86). But if the development of a character is experiential, the problem arises that upon first creating a character, this experience is lacking. For this reason, a new RPG character is often more like his player than different, as the player "fills in the blanks" with his own experience. The character cannot leave behind his player's background, knowledge, and skills, though the two might be completely dissimilar individuals as far as the game's narrative is concerned. The designer of the *Call of Cthulhu* role-playing game recognizes this situation and includes a warning to the game moderators (GMs) who narrate and adjudicate the game and to players: "[a] player has a duty to role-play an investigator within the limits of the investigator's personality and abilities. That is the point of role-playing. Try to know as little or as much as the investigator would in life" (Petersen 1999:23). Wallis describes a similar idea, saying that because the character's personality is little more than sketched out, the character often becomes "a facet of the player's personality, projected onto the archetype, and with the abilities and attitudes of the role" (Wallis 1995:85).

Though there are instances of "self-play," in which players are told by the GM to translate themselves into stats, creating characters who "are" the players as part of the conceit of the game scenario,[2] for the most part players take on a role less obviously self-reflexive. The designer of *Call of Cthulhu* suggests, rather pointedly, that "[i]t is often more fun to create investigators entirely different from the real-life player: a tough private eye, perhaps, or a rude taxi driver, or a tuxedo-clad millionaire dilettante" (Petersen 1999:23). In playing a character who is very different from the player, however, more is sometimes betrayed about the player's unconscious desires than would be had he reproduced himself accurately in fictional form. Nathan Gribble, a teacher who uses fantasy role-playing as a classroom teaching tool, reports:

> Children are happy to play characters who have the same good points that they do, but shy away from creating ones who share their bad points, or with compensatory good ones. A child who thinks they are tough might create a tough player character, but they would be equally happy to create a weak one. A child who feels weak and vulnerable, on the other hand, will certainly not choose a weak character, and would be fairly unlikely to choose a tough one since that would also draw attention to their vulnerability. When children start to come to terms with their own failings, it is sometimes reflected in their choice of player character [Gribble 1994: 103-104].

In this way, a player's perception of self is reflected in his character. This is a situation that recalls the human condition of being made a victim, a scapegoat, or a sacrifice by someone superior (Wilson 1990). In role-playing this situation, however, the players are also often given the means to reverse this power relationship; first by being able to subvert the GM's control of the narrative[3], and second by taking on the roles of mighty warriors, arcane magic-users, or even superheroes, and in this way playing out their own fantasies of power within the game world.[4] Being able to take on the role of someone with superior abilities to your own is an escapist draw for many players (Wallis 1994). In the world of the role-playing game, players are in this way able to reverse the hierarchy of power into which they were born, asserting their own power over the culture that has manipulated them their whole lives. As Martin explains:

> The youth of Generation X were exposed to crass consumerism in the marketing of expensive action figures; preestablished hierarchies; machine culture; and an emphasis on masculine characteristics, aggression, the importance of power and wealth, and human powerlessness. The boys were not merely passive recipients of these messages, however, but learned to manipulate and reject them.... As adolescents, they reacquired some of their power and creativity as human beings through their role games, played among themselves with rules manipulated by them and a Dungeonmaster chosen by them [Martin 1997:118].

Role-playing allows the players to escape a sometimes harsh reality into a dreamworld in which they can re-assert their personal power and individual sense of worth. Make-believe, as promoted by RPGs, replaces the real world with a better one, at least in an act of psychological displacement (Wilson 1990).

Freudian Dreams and Power

Regarding the purpose of dreams, Freud says that "[o]ur relationship with the world which we entered so unwillingly seems to be endurable only with intermission" (Freud 1960:92). This sentiment could as easily apply to the "escapism" of role-playing games. In a Freudian sense, the created realm of the RPG might be considered parallel to that of the dream fantasy. For example, Freud refers to dreams in the context of being a "region" of exploration, similarly to the way that the game world allows players and GMs the perception of space. Indeed, Freud states that dreams transform thoughts into hallucinatory experience (Freud 1960:224), much as the RPG facilitates a group narrative experience based on individual imagining. Freud's concept of the dream also presents dreams as being "a life bearing certain resemblances to our waking life and, at the same time, differing from it widely" (Freud 1960:92). Similarly, though a wide variety of settings are possible in RPGs— ranging from historical to science fiction to high fantasy — each instance follows certain laws of physics (instituted in the form of game mechanics), presents interpersonal relationships between the characters, and takes for granted rules of cause and effect.

Role-playing worlds make sense because of their resemblance to the real world, yet the RPG scenario also places the players in positions of power that may differ drastically from the reality of their everyday lives. Freud posits the idea that dreams are produced as a response to a disturbing stimulation of the body during sleep. As an example, he cites a colleague who claimed that "[w]hilst dreaming, he was made to smell some eau de Cologne, whereon he dreamt he was in Cairo, in the shop of Johann Maria Farina, and this was followed by some crazy adventures" (Freud 1960:96). Similarly, RPG players take the kernel of the adventure provided by the game moderator and transform it into their own narrative. This transformation of the original "stimulation" by the players for their own narrative use often culminates in a story line very different from the one begun by the game moderator, just as the dream often has no resemblance to the physical occurrence that may have prompted it.

Aligning the role-playing experience with Freud's understanding of dreams suggests that the underlying goal of RPGs should also be parallel to that of dreams. Indeed, both instances are often cases of wish-fulfillment. However, the game's storyline perhaps more closely mimics day-dreams in its aim, which Freud states gratify either "the egoistic cravings of ambition or thirst for power, or the erotic desire of the subject" (Freud 1960:103). Daydreams, especially, are subject to the manipulation of the dreamer, and the hero of a daydream is always the dreamer himself, even if transparently identified with another person. As previously noted, players many times create characters almost indistinguishable from themselves, but for the thin shell of a different name and appearance, yet who are able to attempt daring deeds and access phenomenal physical and magical abilities not possible in real life, in this way assuaging the thirst for power that Freud says is a primary motivation for day-dreams.

As a process of wish-fulfillment, role-playing games also actively identify the taboos and desires working within the subculture that engages in it. RPGs not only justify acting these taboos out, but actually sanction this behavior by positioning the players as inherently "good" in the cosmology of the setting. The most basic formulation of this is in *Dungeons & Dragons*, where players take up the roles of characters with a choice of nine moral alignments: Lawful Good, Neutral Good, Chaotic Good, Lawful Neutral, "True" Neutral, Chaotic Neutral, Lawful Evil, Neutral Evil, and Chaotic Evil. Because a character is normally designated by the game as Good — PCs actually take this as a formal game statistic — actions that would be abhorrent in everyday life are more easily rationalized. PCs regularly seek out otherwise harmless creatures in their underground homes and slay them for their treasure,[5] for example, then justify homicide and theft by saying, "Well, it was an Evil creature!"[6] *Dungeons & Dragons* formalized this construction of good versus evil in the internal "Code of Ethics" of Tactical Studies Rules (TSR) — the game's previous publisher — which stated:

Evil shall *never* be portrayed in an attractive light and shall be used only as a foe to illustrate a moral issue. All product shall focus on the struggle of "good vs. injustice and evil," casting the protagonist as an "agent of right" [TSR 1988].

In another example, the game *Vampire: The Masquerade* justifies murder and mayhem as part of an internal struggle between good and evil, as well. Players take the role of vampires who struggle between the conflicting desires of the remnants of their humanity and the impulses of their bestial selves. To live, they must take the lives of others. The rush of feeding on blood is also identified with that of sex or drug use. Even in H.P. Lovecraft's work and the *Call of Cthulhu* RPG based on it, killing masses of Mythos worshipers in the swamps of New Orleans is justified because they are the miscegenate offspring of humans and unnamable alien creatures. In each of these games and many others, by playing out cultural taboos players are imbued with a sense of power and control over their lives that they may feel is lacking in reality.

From a psychological perspective, RPGs navigate the terrain between the dominant culture's conflicted suspicion and fear, and the RPG culture's own resistance to disempowerment. They are sites of conflict taking the form of complex structures of fantasy, which are easily appropriated and reinscribed by the players, and which at their core address the Freudian concepts of dreams and wish-fulfillment. In RPGs, players find a dreamworld of their own creating that affirms their sense of self-worth and power.

Freudian Dreams and Desire

Power is not the only motivator behind day-dreams, or role-playing games for that matter. As noted before, the gratification of erotic desire is as strong a drive in day-dreams as the thirst for power (Freud 1960:103). One way that role-playing provides an outlet for the erotic desires of players is by facilitating the gender inequality that many RPG settings and gaming groups indulge in, while the elements of scopophilia present in role-playing's performative nature demonstrate a second outlet.

In my experience, the participants in the role-playing community are predominantly white, well-educated, middle-class males in their late teens to late twenties,[7] though the role-playing hobby welcomes into its ranks many who would not fit this description. This makes role-players problematic to the dominant culture because, as Jenkins points out, fans can't be dismissed as intellectually inferior; "they often are highly educated, articulate people who come from the middle classes, people who 'should know better'" (Jenkins 1992:18). In reaction to this unresolveable circumstance, fan cultures (Jenkins uses *Star Trek* fans as his example) are instead interpreted by the dominant culture as being brainless consumers, cultivators of worthless knowledge, who place inappropriate importance on devalued cultural material. They are seen as social misfits, emotionally and intellectually immature, unable to separate fantasy from reality, and are feminized or desexualized as a result.

The dominant culture's attempts to feminize and desexualize participants in the RPG fan culture can be seen in the yearly media coverage of GenCon, the United States' largest role-playing convention. Full-page color spreads of convention-goers dressed in medieval armor or as Klingons regularly decorated the *Milwaukee Journal Sentinel's* City pages before the convention moved to Indianapolis in 2003. Other photos showed awkward, aging boys with *Dungeons & Dragons* t-shirts stretched taut across their bellies, holding up their prized custom-painted fantasy miniatures for the camera. Year after year, the media coverage of the event took a "look at the freaks" approach that did, indeed, portray male RPG fans as de-gendered, asexual, and impotent.[8]

The male-oriented settings that many RPGs adopt are a direct contrast to the impotency that society forces on male gamers, however. Consider my own introduction to M.A.R. Barker's world of Tékumel through a monthly gaming group I played in. Because I knew the RPG was associated with the *Empire of the Petal Throne* series of novels, I read Barker's *Man of Gold* (DAW Books, 1984) before our first session to prepare myself. I was immediately struck by the blatant misogyny shown in the construction of this fictional world. For example, the hero leapt from one sexual encounter to another throughout the narrative, literal sexual slavery was rampant, and when the hero couldn't decide between his two lovers he promptly married both in an offhand remark by Barker at the very end of the book. In addition, both of the primary female characters were stigmatized by their society for aspects of their physicality; one had the blue eyes that marked her as a "witch," and the other — when her presence became inconvenient to the plot — was poisoned with an addictive drug that made her a cataleptic. Indeed, the only way women could have the status of men was to declare themselves "aridani"— members of a class of women who take on the social role of men. To my discomfort, this sexist mindset was also reflected in the RPG during game play. My female character was required to declare herself "aridani" before she could go adventuring with the boys, for example, and her sex became an ongoing obstacle for her. But this misogynist attitude was also present, more subtly, in the approach toward women displayed in sourcebooks for the game. For instance, on the cover of the

Tsolyáni Language Part II sourcebook (Imperium Publishing, 1978) is a cartoon that depicts two men having problems understanding the intricate language Barker devised for his world. Some confusion comes up between the words for "shlen beast"—a fantasy beast of burden—and "slave woman." The interaction in the comic implies that there may not be a real difference between the two.

The game world of the *Call of Cthulhu* RPG provides another example of the misogyny that sometimes seems endemic to the hobby, but which provides an outlet for male players' erotic desires. H.P. Lovecraft is known for letting men dominate his stories, with only minor, problematic female appearances. These intrusions are of note in this discussion for their similarity to the positioning as "other" that women often experience in roleplaying, which effectively empowers their male counterparts by devaluing those women. For instance, in "The Thing on the Doorstep" (*Weird Tales*, Jan 1937) Asenath Waite is possessed by her sorcerous father Ephraim, who has displaced her mind with his own. She is, literally, a man wearing a mask of the female. And Asenath must also be considered as non-human; extrapolating from the implications in "The Shadow over Innsmouth" (*The Acolyte*, Winter 1942), she is the product of miscegenation between a human and an aquatic creature, and she has the "Innsmouth look" that confirms her unnatural heritage. Also, when Asenath's husband Edward Derby says that Ephraim (as Asenath) is now attempting to take over his own mind, he comments that she "wanted to be a man—to be fully human" (Lovecraft 1963:288). Here, women are seen as monstrous, as weak-minded and less than human, and as a distortion of the male that seeks to consume the male. Asenath is, in fact, a monstrous female who has trapped her mate and will eventually devour him. In Lovecraft's work, women often obscure the truth, impede the hero, and are positioned as possessions of the primary male as wife, landlady, mother, etc. Bear in mind that Lovecraft's women are usually relegated to minor appearances such as the landlady Mrs. Herrero in "Cool Air" (*Tales of Magic and Mystery*, Mar 1928), Captain Johansen's widow in "The Call of Cthulhu" (*Weird Tales*, Feb 1928), and Wilbur Whateley's "mother" Lavinia in "The Dunwich Horror" (*Weird Tales*, Apr 1929). Women in Lovecraft's stories also represent fecundity, as is shown by the cosmic force Yog-Sothoth who sires a set of twins by Lavinia Whately, but insists on characterizing itself as the female principle. Lovecraft uses women like Lavinia Whately and Asenath Waite as vessels to propagate the unnatural: a woman's sexuality is irrevocably tied to her reproductive capability, which is cast as horrific. And many of these misogynistic elements inevitably make their way into the role-playing game based on these works, either as excerpts and background material in the published game books or by way of the players themselves, who rely on Lovecraft's fiction as direct source material for their own attempts at world-building.

The designers of the *Call of Cthulhu* RPG recognize the existence of these issues in the game, but refuse to overlook the more obvious, cultural forms of "racialism" and misogyny in Lovecraft's work — in particular, they cite the bigotry that was a social norm in the different time periods in which the game is set:

> Historical settings are as real as possible. The world and the United States were very different in the 1890s and 1920s from now, and behaviors most find repugnant today then were ordinary and acceptable. Racism, xenophobia, religious bias, and sexual discrimination as we now perceive them were then normal parts of life, and often loudly espoused. Local, state, and federal laws systematically supported segregation and discrimination of every sort, and social forces of great power underwrote that legislation. Scenario authors can choose to ignore social history as not germane, or decide to incorporate specific elements into their plots. Both sorts of approaches have been published. To preclude information about earlier eras (or about this one) dishonors the memory of those who prized freedom, fairness, and opportunity, perhaps long before we were born [Petersen 1999:24].

But this awareness on their part merely highlights the existence of those games that use historical basis as a justification for sex discrimination and other prejudices.

Take the game *Pendragon* (Chaosium, 1985) as an instance of an RPG firmly based in a gender-biased, historically based world. This game assumes that most player characters will be males, since the game revolves around knights in a pseudo-medieval setting. Andrew Rilstone, a professional in the RPG industry, asserts that it is pointless to censure the game for this; "If you are going to go off to war, or on the quest for the Holy Grail, you are likely to leave the women-folk at home" (Rilstone 1995:6). Rilstone goes on to explain:

> Many role-playing games are set in archaic cultures in which politically incorrect values are the norm: not only the romanticized Middle Ages, but also Victorian England or the 1930s. In such societies, the roles of women and men were more sharply differentiated than they are today. Could it be that, for male gamers, this is part of the appeal? Perhaps it appeals to the same ethos as the Wild Man culture: that some men — particularly, perhaps, rather studious, unathletic "nerds" — yearn for a world of heterosexual male friendships; of hunting honor and warfare [Rilstone 1995:5].

From this perspective, including the historical facts of sexual inequality and other discriminatory practices as part of the game setting allows male players to escape into a game world that validates their own sense of worth by making their characters physically and socially superior to others around them, whether those "others" happen to be monsters or women.[9] The constructed pseudo-histories of many RPGs represent a purposeful blurring of reality and fiction to create this kind of androcentric game environment[10]—an environment already noted as having similarities to Freudian day-dreams as a vehicle for wish-fulfillment. Role-playing games that incorporate historical information usually don't include footnotes to indicate historical sources, for example, so the reader has no way of finding out which elements are only products of the writers' imaginations. This mixing of historical reality and fiction allows the players free rein in constructing their own male-dominated fantasies.

Rilstone goes on to say that in historically based games like *Pendragon*, it is possible to bend the norms and introduce female knights or Valkyrie-like warrior women, but doing this makes the massive assumption that the only way to include female characters is by having them join in the murdering and pillaging; "We admit women into our games, but they have to be macho women, preferably with guns" (Rilstone 1995:6).[11] The issue of gender is dealt with directly in only a few RPGs, often by making female fighter characters into rare but accepted oddities; *Rune* (Atlas Games, 2001) allows for the occasional Viking warrior woman, and *Pendragon* admits the existence of exceptional characters like Joan of Arc, for example.

Casting female characters in typically male roles as a method of disallowing women a place in the game may also occur in part as a product of the influence of fantasy tropes in RPGs, since the fantasy genre traditionally leaves no one with whom women can identify and provides no story structures that break women characters out of the confines imposed by male fantasy. According to Ursula K. LeGuin, the hero-tale common to fantasy is concerned with "the establishment or validation of manhood. It has been the story of a quest, or a conquest, or a test, or a contest. It has involved conflict and sacrifice" (Le Guin, quoted in Oliver 1995:62). Few of these stories feature any women, even fewer have a female protagonist, and the women who do appear are likely to be "men in women's clothing," in that they are driven by what can be seen as stereotypically male egos, motivations, and impulses. These women wear armor and wield swords. They are given qualities inappropriate to their conventional gender roles instead of focusing on a more complex portrayal of women. As one of educator Anna Altmann's students commented, the tokenism of women warriors is "just another case of welding brass tits on the armour" (quoted in Oliver 1995:60). More typically, though, women in fantasy—and in role-playing games like *Call of Cthulhu*—are seen only in relation to the heroes as they take on the roles of mother, wife, lover, or maiden

in distress; women are approached as accessories rather than as protagonists. In fantasy novels, as in RPGs, the hero's relationship to women follows an artificial code of chivalry, especially in "the adoration of a
woman-shaped object" (Le Guin, quoted in Oliver 1995:65).[12]

By drawing on fantasy tropes, pseudo-historical background, and the
work of biased writers like H.P. Lovecraft, role-playing games in this way
disempower women either by masculinizing them or by positioning them
in the roles of devalued and extraneous non-player characters (NPCs) who
are manipulated by the GM. The dominance of the male adventurers is
consistently foregrounded though the game's thinly disguised gender
inequality and focus on combat and violence — the hallmarks of male fantasy — and an outlet for the male players' erotic desires is provided by the
misogyny common to role-playing.

Performance and Spectatorship

The elements of scopophilia present in role-playing as a performative activity based on erotic desire may influence the narratives of RPGs
even more so than the games' questionable portrayals of women do, however. In analyzing dreams, Freud locates the mind as "the stage whereon
the drama of the dream ... is played out" (Freud 1960:94). Dreams, then,
"are a performance and an utterance on the part of the dreamer," Freud
asserts (1960:105). By approaching role-playing by way of Mulvey's (1994)
application of psychoanalysis to the cinema, role-playing can be interpreted as a performance that offers insight into the desires of the players.
This perspective is feasible largely because role-playing is an experiential
endeavor; a setting sourcebook has no life of its own lying on a table, until
the players create the role-playing act through their portrayals of their
characters. Frein asserts that, because of this, "role-playing seems to be a
close cousin of drama. A role-playing game, like a play, needs to be embodied and occurring through time" (Frein 1995:74–75). Live action role-
playing, in particular, highlights the performative qualities of role-playing,
and ties it to performance theory.

Live action role-playing (or LARPing) emerged in 1982 with the formation of the Treasure Trap club at Peckforton Castle in the United King-
dom. Its members played a *Dungeons & Dragons*-like game that took the
mechanics of table-top RPGs and made them "live." As Jay Gooby, events
organizer for the international live role-playing society The Adventurers'
Guild, explains, the actions of the players replaced the die rolls normally
used in role-playing games to determine whether a particular feat suc-

ceeded or failed (Gooby 1994:16); in a LARP, role-playing is enacted in an outwardly performative manner:

> Sword fighting, running, leaping and hiding actually took place. Spells were "cast" by quoting a line followed by the effect of the spell: "By the power of the fire elements—Fireblast!" Those having the spell cast at them reacted appropriately, role-playing its effect upon them. Physical combat occurred by way of "safe" weapons. These were swords, axes, maces, etc. all constructed from high-density foam glued over a rigid central core and covered with appropriately colored tape.[...] Certain conventions were also introduced to simulate the impossible: a hand in the air signified invisibility, a call of "Time-freeze" indicated that the players in a game should shut their eyes and halt in their current positions—time effectively was held—until "Time-in" was called, thus permitting instantaneous actions such as teleports or transformations to occur [Gooby 1994:16-17].

Like standard pen-and-paper RPGs, LARPs can be linear, event-based adventures, or character-dependent, interactive scenarios. The step from pen-and-paper RPGs to live action role-playing, however, brings role-playing even closer to modes of performance such as the theatrical improvisation of the *commedia dell'arte* of the fourteenth to the eighteenth century. Both are improvised, created by the players on the spot. There are no scripts, though there are stock characters and situations that appear in different combinations. And though *commedia dell'arte* featured characters who were old favorites—those who audiences saw over and over—particular actors individualized their own roles, distinguishing them from other portrayals of the same characters. "Actors would take a stock character and give them more and more of a personality, making a name for themselves in the process" (Cule 1994:37). Similarly, RPG characters are many times stock figures with no home, family, friends, or real personality of their own. James Wallis states that "characters created within the confines of a game's rules can survive being two-dimensional, or even one-dimensional, because they will function as a template, a blank sheet for the player to project a personality onto" (Wallis 1994:72).

On the stage of the RPG, however, the performance can become problematic in relation to gender. In particular, a certain anxiety often makes itself apparent when a player of one sex role-plays a character of the opposite sex. In one of my own first experiences with gaming, a male gamer created and played a female character that illustrates an extreme case. "Her" name was Ballistic, and she was described as a black Aeon Flux, shaved bald and loaded down with armor and weaponry. She was a cold-blooded killer, and had a completely unfeeling personality. Ballistic is typical of one common method of cross-gender role-playing: that of the frigid, withdrawn, masculinized female character. Another troubling female character sometimes created by male players is the "vamp." When these "mysterious and sultry" sex-driven women appear in role-playing sessions, they lose no time in attempting to seduce every male in sight, PC and NPC alike.

One way of approaching problematic occurrences of males playing stereotyped female characters, either as overly sexualized vixens or as masculinized, frigid combat machines (and of females playing sometimes equally problematic male characters) is from the perspective of Mulvey's (1994) theory of spectatorship. In the performative space where the audience has the freedom to become actor — where players act the parts of their individual characters while viewing the actions of others— the oversexed female persona taken on by the male player seems to fall into the category of an extended scopophilic act that has been given the opportunity to manifest itself in the narrative, influencing the plot rather than being restrained by the inherent distance between actor and audience present in cinema. Scopophilia refers to "taking other people as objects, subjecting them to a controlling and curious gaze" and thus taking "pleasure in using another person as an object of sexual stimulation" (Mulvey 1994:424–425). In the case of cinema, "the determining male gaze projects its fantasy onto the female figure, which is styled accordingly" (Mulvey 1994:425). In the RPG, this styling of the female figure around male fantasy is literally enacted upon the male player's female character, resulting in a hyper-sexual seductress equivalent to the cinematic *femme fatale*. Pushing the analogy a bit further: just as the appearance of the woman in cinema works against the development of a story-line, so too does the presence of the vamp character in a role-playing group. The woman in cinema halts the action of the film in favor of extended erotic displays such as dance numbers, and the vamp character often leads role-playing groups into tangential situations, such as bar scenes, where the female character is inevitably propositioned by any and all male characters in attendance, generally halting the forward movement of the plot.

As a result of situating himself as both subject and object by playing a female character, the male gamer finds himself with two options from which to choose his role-playing strategy, just as the male cinematic character is limited to two reactions to the woman as icon. These are, voyeurism: a "preoccupation with the re-enactment of the original trauma ... counterbalanced by the devaluation, punishment or saving of the guilty object"; or fetishistic scopophilia: the "substitution of a fetish object or turning [of] the represented figure itself into a fetish so that it becomes reassuring rather than dangerous" (Mulvey 1994:427). The male gamer playing a vamp generally chooses the second option, resulting in character sketches that resemble dark versions of a Barbie® doll in sprayed-on spandex, with a (non)personality to match. The male-generated female character "bursts through the world of illusion as an intrusive, static, one-dimensional fetish" (Mulvey 1994:430).

The flip side of this coin is the masculinized female character played by a male gamer; what I have described as the "Ballistic" character. This seems to represent an acting-out of narcissistic scopophilia in an identification with the character, with a hint of wish-fulfillment thrown in, as well. The male gamer is able to picture his character as a militaristic mercenary in this guise, but must strip her of femininity and personality to accomplish this. Again, he is limited to voyeurism or fetishistic scopophilia in his approach to synthesizing these reactions, but this time he chooses voyeurism; he is able to demystify the female character by acting her as an exaggerated male, which thus devalues the feminine as necessarily "weak" by privileging the amplified masculine traits of the character.

Although my perception of the dynamic at work in the case of the woman player acting in the guise of a male character is necessarily biased by my own gender, and limited by the fact that at most games I am the lone female at the table, it seems to me that female gamers role-play male characters in a more restrained way than their male counterparts play female characters. Emma Kolstad, a woman role-player on the Strange Aeons online discussion list, suggested that "since western society has conditioned us to find women's bodies attractive (hence their use in advertising) but does not glorify men's bodies in the same manner, men experience more of a thrill or mystique when they play women than women do when they play men" (Antunes 1995:63–64). This erotic thrill is a possible motivator for the extremism sometimes shown in the cross-gender character choices of male players, which female players don't often seem to reciprocate. In my observations of female-played male characters, however, I have noted that women are more likely to err on the side of creating male characters who exude an excessive (transgressive) sexuality, sometimes even crossing into overt homosexuality, as I admit one of my own male characters once did. The female player in this case acts much as the male player does through his *femme fatale*, rather than playing up her character's physical power through a "macho" approach.

However, Mulvey asserts that "the male figure cannot bear the burden of sexual objectification. Man is reluctant to gaze at his exhibitionist like" (Mulvey 1994:426). In role-playing, this reluctance takes the form of a semantic slippage demonstrating the anxiety a transgressive woman provokes in the dominant culture, most often represented in the patriarchal figure of the GM. In both LARPs and traditional RPGs, gamers usually perceive the characters of other players as looking similar to their players, and so characters often treat other characters as the players themselves would treat each other. When one of the players is a woman playing a male character, or a man playing a female character, pronouns become confused and conceptual difficulties arise. For example, in the several times that I've played male characters, I've needed to call constant attention to the fact that I am a *male* as far as pronouns go in reference to my character, otherwise risking the (usually male) game moderator describing semantically conflicted events: "Thor the Barbarian walks out the door of the pub. She's leading the tavern wench by the hand and giving you guys her 'don't bother me for a few hours' look." Instances like this show the subversiveness available to enterprising gamers in regard to acted gender constructions.

While manifestations of visual pleasure may not be "intrinsic to film," Mulvey claims that "it is only in the film form that they can reach a perfect and beautiful contradiction" (Mulvey 1994:430). I would disagree with this, citing role-playing as an example of an unprecedented instance in which these contradictions are emphasized by the flexibility of the boundaries between subject and object positions— those of audience and character. This dynamic allows role-playing games the advantage of subtly working against the traditional split between spectacle and narrative.

Conclusion

Role-playing is a self-reflective endeavor, and as such RPG narratives present a complex structure of fantasy; characters are more than just their players' senses and limbs, they are their representatives in the game world, and representations of their players' inner selves. Players inevitably begin role-playing by creating characters who emphasize some aspect of their own personality or physicality into heroic proportions in an overt display of wish-fulfillment; this melding of player and character identities allows the player's perception of self to be reflected in his character, and provides the player with a means to gratify erotic desire and the thirst for power, just as do dreams in a Freudian framework. The game worlds of many RPGs are constructed based on male power fantasies to take advantage of this phenomenon, providing, for example, moral judgments of good and evil that never overlap as PCs are defined as inherently good, and confrontations that involve firepower, destruction, and super-human abilities so as to emphasize and reinforce stereotypes of masculine power and yet still empower male players who are feminized and desexualized by the dominant culture. The addition of elements of male erotic fantasy to those game worlds further supports gender inequality and ambiguity in relation to gender construction, but also positions role-playing as a locus for issues of identity, performance, and spectatorship.

References

Antunes, Sandy. 1995. "Leaping into Cross-Gender Role-Play." *Interactive Fantasy* 1.3: 62–67.

Arnholm, Anders. 2002. "What Is 'Macho Women with Guns'?" Retrieved Dec 28, 2002. (*http://www.acc.umu.se/~balp/rpg/Macho_Back.html*).

Cook, Monte, Jonathan Tweet, and Skip Williams. 2000. *Dungeons & Dragons Player's Handbook.* 3rd ed. Renton, WA: Wizards of the Coast Inc.

Cule, Michael. 1994. "Improvisation in the Theatre: As Discipline, Tool, and Political Statement." *Inter*action* 1.1: 36–39.

Dancey, Ryan S. 2000. *Adventure Game Industry Market Research Summary.* Version 1.0. Wizards of the Coast, Inc.

Frein, Mark. 1995. "Role-Playing Defined." *Interactive Fantasy* 1.4: 74–76.

Freud, Sigmund. 1960. *A General Introduction to Psycho-Analysis.* NY: Washington Square P.

Gold, Lee. 1995. "Self-Censorship." *Interactive Fantasy* 1.4: 94–105.

Gooby, Jay. 1994. "Live Role-Playing: The Meta-Play." *Inter*action* 1.1: 16–20.

Gribble, Nathan. 1994. "The Munchkin Examined." *Interactive Fantasy* 1.2: 101–108.

Holsworth, Mark S. 1995. "Walk a Mile in Someone Else's Shoes" *Interactive Fantasy* 1.4: 52–58.

Hurley, Keith. 1994. "Uses of Role-playing Within Psychology and Psychotherapy." *Inter*action* 1.1: 40–47.

Jenkins, Henry. 1992. *Textual Poachers: Television Fans & Participatory Culture.* New York: Routledge.

Lancaster, Kurt. 1995. "Cyber-Performances," ed. Andrew Rilstone. *Interactive Fantasy* 1:4: 21–31.

_____. Autumn 1998. "The Longing for Prelapsarian Fantasies in Role-Playing Games." *Foundation* 74: 48–53.

Lovecraft, H. P. 1963. *The Dunwich Horror and Others.* Sauk City, WI: Arkham House.

Martin, Catherine E. et. al. August 1997. "Perspectives on Generation X: The Role of Play in the Formation of Male Personalities." *Popular Culture Review* 8:2: 109–119.

Masters, Phil. 1995. "Horror: Motifs and Actualities." *Interactive Fantasy* 1.4: 68–73.

Moreno, J. L. 1943. "The Concept of Sociodrama: A New Approach to the Problem of Inter-Cultural Relations." *Sociometry* VI: 434–449.

Mulvey, Laura. 1994. "Visual Pleasure and Narrative Cinema." pp. 422–431 in *Contemporary Literary Criticism.* Ed. Robert Con Davis and Ronald Schleifer. NY: Longman.

Oliver, Martin. 1995. "The Circle Stands Unbroken." *Interactive Fantasy* 1.4: 59–67.

Petersen, Sandy and Lynn Willis. 1999. *Call of Cthulhu.* 5.6 ed. Oakland, CA: Chaosium, Inc.

Rilstone, Andrew. 1995. "Editorial." *Interactive Fantasy* 1.3: 4–6.

Selman, R. L. 1976. "Social Cognitive Understanding: A Guide to Educational and Clinical Practice." pp. 299–316 in *Moral Development and Behaviour: Theory, Research, and Social Issues.* Ed. T. Likona. New York: Holt, Rinehart, and Winston.

TSR. 1988. "Code of Ethics." Lake Geneva, WI: Tactical Studies Rules.

Wallis, James. 1994. "Realism vs Playability?: Rules, Environments and Characterization." *Inter*action* 1.1: 66–83.

_____. 1995. "Through a Mask, Darkly." *Interactive Fantasy* 1.3: 78–95.

Wilson, R. Rawdon. 1990. *In Palamedes' Shadow: Explorations in Play, Game, and Narrative Theory.* Boston: Northeastern U.P.

Notes

1. The acquisition of role-taking skill has been divided into the following five stages by R.L. Selman in *Social Cognitive Understanding*:

Stage 0: The egocentric viewpoint (0–5 years), during which children can't imagine others taking different perspectives on social situations.

Stage 1: Social information role taking (5–8 years), when the child is not aware that others might perceive a situation differently from the child's outlook.

Stage 2: Self-reflection (8–10 years), during which a child understands that people are aware of the thoughts and feelings of others, and that of the child himself. This mutual awareness affects each person's perspective.

Stage 3: Mutual role-taking (10–12 years), allows a child to put himself in another's situation, and understands that others can do the same.

Stage 4: Social and conventional role-taking (12–15 years), at which point the child understands that there are viewpoints shared by social groups that facilitate communication within the group.

2. A few games, like the translation of the French RPG *TRAUMA* (Darcsyde Productions, 1992), even use self-play as their primary conceit. In this game, the players are expected to play themselves as characters, facing terrible modern-day situations like hijackings, drug wars, conspiracies, and so on.

3. Players often go "off-track," deciding to get drunk at a roadside tavern instead of progressing with their mission, for instance; they sometimes "fudge" rolls when the GM isn't looking; they react to the narrative in ways the GM didn't foresee, sometimes doing things like killing an innocuous NPC who was intended to be crucial to the development of the plot; and they "withdraw" from the game when bored with the direction of the narrative or unhappy with the GM's determinations, refusing to participate actively and only rolling dice when necessary. Unruly players have many methods at their disposal to defuse the game moderator's authority.

4. Exceptions to the tendency for role-playing games to cast players in the roles of superhuman characters do occur in the RPG hobby. Take, for instance, the game *Ars Magica* (Lion Rampant, 1988). In this historically based game of medieval fantasy, players can choose to role-play the powerful magi who control forces of magic present in the year 1220, but just as often they take on the roles of the mundane companions who use their skills to aid those magi, or the servant "grogs" who care for the others in the covenant. Similarly, in the *Call of Cthulhu* RPG the players become mundane scholars, detectives, and policemen uncovering the schemes of all-powerful alien entities. Note, though, that in both of these cases the "Joe Average" characters become empowered by aiding or confounding extraordinary beings ... their identity is still defined by their relationships with the superhuman entities and world-shattering events typical of a fantasy realm.

5. The outcome of each battle in an RPG is predetermined for the most part — the player characters almost always win in encounters with foes, and in those cases where they don't, the GM has probably made victory impossible as part of a plot device. Again, this only works to empower the player characters. Because players often play a thinly veiled version of themselves, severe or permanent harm to their characters is hard to deal with, and so generally avoided by GMs or purposefully used to narrative effect. As Phil Masters asserts, "To the extent that players genuinely identify with their characters—a situation which many games declare to be their highest aim — any serious and prolonged threat to a character's life and well-being should be frightening" (1995:69).

6. I've been in at least one game where this assumption has been turned around by the GM, however. Our party encountered a group of Evil lizard-man kobolds squatting in a mine, and after eradicating them had to deal with the lone kobold orphan child crying that her family was dead. This completely derailed the adventure — which had been a typical dungeon crawl scenario until this point — and threw the entire party into a moral dilemma. By confounding "readerly" expectations in this way, the GM exposed and interrogated the subsumed taboos and desires inherent in the game.

7. Market research released by Wizards of the Coast seems to support this observation. Figures from 2000 focus on 12- to 35-year-olds as the company's target market, and show that only 19 percent of monthly tabletop RPG players are female (Dancey 2000).

8. While male gamers are often desexualized by the dominant culture, the opposite can be said of female gamers. Despite the nearly 1:4 ratio of female to male gamers (see footnote 7), chubby yet scantily-clad women in chainmail bikinis and gypsy garb inevitably appear in disproportionate numbers in the pages of the newspaper, "booth babes" litter

the exhibitor hall selling product at their booths, and male gamers feel justified in collecting photos of all the women at the show (which I can attest to from experience). The gaming convention becomes a haven for the same objectification of women that permeates the role-playing experience itself.

9. As an example of how role-playing games allow male players to validate their own sense of worth by making their characters physically superior to women, consider the anecdotes of how women gamers' characters have been "raped" by male PCs during game sessions. As Lee Gold asserts, this kind of alienating tactic is "often used as a way of discouraging girls from joining an all-male player group" (1995:104).

10. The argument can be made that it's not valid to judge a game, based on a fictionalized historical setting, against modern-day concepts of political correctness. For example, if one were playing an RPG set in colonial America, then slavery would necessarily be part of the setting, though slavery is obviously abhorrent. A game set in a medieval time period could similarly be expected to have serious inequalities between men and women. However, consider that such a game would likely portray slavery as an evil; in fact, the "Code of Ethics" applied to material for *Dungeons & Dragons* as early as 1988 states "Slavery is not to be depicted in a favorable light; it should only be represented as a cruel and inhuman institution to be abolished." Sexism, on the other hand, is generally accepted as a norm in role-playing; that same code allows "heroic" proportions and nudity as acceptable "when done in a manner that complies with good taste and social standard." Rape, "graphic lust," and "sexual perversion" are proscribed, but no suggestion is ever made that overt sexism should be avoided, though alcohol abuse, disrespect for law enforcement officers, slang, and attacks on religion are all important enough to be mentioned.

The fact that so many role-playing games accept misogyny as an intrinsic part of their background rather than make changes to a created history that is already imbued with fantasy merely highlights gender as a locus of conflict in role-playing games. Indeed, games like *Ars Magica* (Lion Rampant, 1988) and *Vampire: The Dark Ages* (White Wolf, 1996) level the playing field between the sexes by isolating characters in an historically artificial egalitarian subculture — whether it be a covenant of scholarly mages or the secretive society of vampires among whom sex need not be relevant — proving that this can be done without unduly disrupting the illusion of historicity. Because the game is fantasy, inequality can easily be written out of the setting, yet the fact that so many RPG designers and the players who follow their lead insist on maintaining gender disparities implies a deeper purpose behind the practice.

11. *Macho Women with Guns* is actually the name of a real role-playing game designed by Greg Porter, and first published in 1988 by Blacksburg Tactical Research Center. A fan site for the game explains, "Macho Women with Guns is the game of a world twisted beyond the bounds of chauvinism and reason. Where no one is immune to lethal doses of satire, and nothing is too sacred to be dragged through the mud. Where we are hopefully so biased and contradictory and blatantly offensive that no one in their right minds would think to take us seriously" (Arnholm). In this way, the role-playing game is translated into a satire that interrogates the assumptions about gender that appear in many RPGs.

12. One more common method of objectifying women in role-playing games is perpetrated by the hobby's publishers. Despite including game material that's exclusionary or vilifying of female characters, RPG sourcebooks more often than not feature illustrations of what few women do appear that rather obviously play to male fantasy. Scant, diaphanous, revealing costumes are the norm, making the bodies of those female characters the objects of the players' gazes and desires.

7. THE BUSINESS AND THE CULTURE OF GAMING

W. Keith Winkler

Traditionally, when speaking of American business industries, one thinks of corporations based on an industrial-capitalist model driven largely by the factors of competition and self-interest. In relation to these firms, the typical American consumer is accustomed to being courted by these corporate providers of goods and services through elaborate marketing and advertising strategies. The employees of these corporations constantly hear the mantra of increasing operational efficiency and improving the firm's bottom line. The consumers are reactive and industry firms are proactive. Corporate providers of goods and services chase the consumers, or more accurately, their dollars.

The gaming industry functions in a distinctly different manner.[1] Certain elements are intrinsic to doing business, so there are naturally manufacturers and consumers, competition and advertising, but almost every firm in the gaming industry is small and privately held, which means comprehensive financial data are not publicly available. Most importantly, the members of the gaming industry, from manufacturer to consumer, are almost all members of the "gamer" subculture, which creates a unifying effect that is very rare in other business industries.

This chapter will explore the business of gaming, but also the culture of gaming and how these dimensions influence and overlap with one another. My key argument is two-pronged: a) the gaming industry is a distinct, niche industry which can be analyzed by traditional business methods and evaluated by traditional corporate models within the limits of available data, but one which functions in an unconventional (some would say dysfunctional) manner; b) the individuals that make up the industry (at any level) are themselves gamers, and share a common subculture: the gamer or gamer-geek subculture. This shared sense of identity impacts relationships among participants in the industry in a manner quite distinct from more traditional corporate industries. This interaction of being an enthusiastic gamer on one hand, but also trying to run an efficient and competitive corporation on the other, can lead to rigors and challenges not faced in more mainstream industries, and creates a unique atmosphere in which the line between proactive, corporate provider chasing savvy, reactive consumer tends to blur and fade.

Defining the Industry Structure

Steve Jackson, a well-known manufacturer in the industry, published a "2004 Report to Stakeholders," which served as a voluntary annual report. Therein, he disclosed a mixture of financial and operational data, as well as an overall opinion on the state of the industry:

> Steve Jackson Games Incorporated has a single stockholder ... me. But we have a great many STAKEholders — that is, people who have a stake in the success of the business. These include our employees, our distributors, the retailers who carry our line, and, of course, the people who PLAY our games! Less obvious stakeholders, but very real, are the creative talents who produce our games, the printers who create the finished product, and the convention organizers who depend on us for game programming, prizes, and so on [*www.sjgames.com*].

Jackson's statement provides an industry model that will be used in this chapter to analyze the different divisions within the industry; from the people who make products to the people who buy them. In essence, there are four divisions: manufacturing, distributing, retailing, and consuming.

Manufacturing is the division wherein a product is developed. It is represented by firms that make new products, and as such, is where much of the creative energy of an industry is employed. This division includes creation and development, marketing and advertising, and a sales staff, who communicate with distributors. Given that industry products begin their life-cycle in manufacturing, this division contains a high degree of risk. Products can fail for a number of reasons, including lack of appeal to consumers, or even lack of appeal to distributors; the former would result in poor sales at the retail division, while the latter would ensure the product was barely present in retail stores and thus unavailable for consumers to accept or reject. On the other hand, a successful product generates not only revenue, but makes it easier for subsequent products to move through the distribution and retail channels. With each additional successful product, the manufacturer becomes known as a producer of quality content, a source of reliable revenue, and therefore becomes a more influential participant in the industry.

Distributing is represented by the "middle men," who are often the best friend or worst enemy of a manufacturer. A manufacturer sells a product to a distributor, who in turn sells it to a retailer where the customers purchase it. The distributor needs to have warehouse space and a staff of buyers who are knowledgeable about what products are coming out from a large number of manufacturers. Buyers working for a distributor need to know their retail accounts and have a good sense of how products are selling in a large number of retail locations. A good distributor with a knowledgeable staff can inform retailers and do a bit of marketing from within the product channel. A strong advocate for a particular product within the channel, especially at the distributor division, can translate into increased sales for manufacturers and better product assortment for retailers. Conversely, an incompetent buyer, or one who actively dislikes and discourages a manufacturer's products, can have a negative financial impact on a manufacturer, and cause a retailer to have limited or no access to those products, which could translate into lost business.

The next division is retailing. The retailer needs a store with a good location, space to display the products, promotional materials, and enough staff to meet the needs and demands of customers. An efficient retailer knows each product's percentage of total sales, makes an effort to cross-promote similar products, and generally tries to tailor merchandise to maximize visibility of new, hot products, or offers incentives to move aging back inventory.

The fourth division is consuming, represented by the people who buy gaming products. This division normally interacts with the retailer, not the manufacturer or distributor, much as retailers generally deal with the distributors, not the manufacturers. Thus, the acquisition of merchandise is the result of multiple dyadic economic interactions between various divisions.

The Gaming Industry

While identifying gaming industry divisions may be straightforward, describing the gaming industry itself is more difficult. This difficulty is not due to lack of products or locations that sell gaming wares, but rather because of the diverse nature of products, and the differences among industry participants. In fact, the gaming industry can be seen as part of a larger industry of fantasy and sci-fi products that also includes closely associated industries. Examples include: fantasy and science fiction novels, comic books, Japanese anime and manga, science fiction or fantasy television shows and movies (e.g. *Star Trek, Buffy the Vampire Slayer, Star Wars, Lord of the Rings* trilogy), collectible action figures and other toys. These are all cultural products that many participants in the gaming industry will have knowledge of and own. They are related, and oftentimes influence the industry, but are constrained or determined by it. At Dragon*Con 2004, a major industry convention held every year in Atlanta, Georgia, during Labor Day weekend, one manufacturer suggested that the term "Hobby game industry" served to delineate gaming from the "book trade or mass market" industry. The most notable difference is that gaming industry products are not generally purchased at mainstream retailers, like Wal-Mart, or booksellers, like Borders. The top one or two manufacturers may have accounts with large retailers, but the majority of gaming industry products are sold in specialty stores. These specialty gaming stores often sell comic books or other related merchandise in addition to gaming products.

This dichotomy between mass-market and specialty-market can aid in deciding if a product is part of the gaming industry, or part of the larger entertainment industry. For example, a mass market game, such as *Monopoly*, would not generally be found in a gaming store, but a specialty or novelty version, such as *Lord of the Rings Monopoly*, probably would be available. Additionally, some products that started out as specific to the gaming industry, have crossed over into the larger entertainment industry. One can find *Magic: The Gathering* collectible trading cards in supermarkets, gas stations, and other non-specialized locations, but *.hack//ENEMY* collectible trading cards still require a visit to a specialized gaming store.

When discussing the gaming industry in this chapter, our discussion shall be limited to three categories of games: role-playing games (RPGs), collectible strategy games (CSGs)—which are exemplified by collectible trading card games (CCGs) and collectible miniature games—and on-line, multiplayer video games. The latter category may either be played on personal computers (PC) or on a gaming console such as Sony's PlayStation2, or Microsoft's Xbox. It could also be argued that video games (PC or console) are actually an entirely different industry, since many of the important firms are large, publicly held corporations whose products are sold by large commercial retailers, and because the scale and scope of operations of an average computer game company so far exceeds that of a role-playing or collectible card game company. This is true to a point, but one must consider that much of the development of computer games is done either by small, third-party developers, many of whom are privately held companies of enthusiastic gamers, or by amateurs who distribute their games through freeware distribution networks. In addition, RPGs and CSGs have been successfully licensed and developed for play on PCs or gaming consoles, so the inclusion of video games (specifically, on-line multiplayer games) is within the scope of this chapter. In short, like any social phenomenon, the boundaries of the gaming industry are not rigidly defined, and there are overlapping and related industries.

The gaming industry is not a wealthy one. Wages are relatively low, and skilled writers, artists and programmers are often lured away by larger, more mainstream corporate industries. The enthusiasm for gaming, and the fact that almost all of the industry participants are gamers and derive personal enjoyment and excitement from the industry helps to offset the low wages and relative small size of the industry. The gaming industry simply does not have the economic leverage to command and retain top talent, but it does offer a less restrictive, more creative environment in which to work, and this carries significant weight with many creative individuals, and makes the industry attractive for entrepreneurs that do not subscribe to conventional corporate models.

The division of manufacturers, often called "publishers" since many gaming products are books, have substantial variation in their business models based on what type of product (RPG, CSG, or video game) they are producing. Creating a new game requires the design and development of setting and system, contracting artists to provide artwork, having a staff of layout and graphic design personnel, and ultimately printing or producing the game. However, there also needs to be a marketing and advertising staff to alert customers to this new product, and a sales staff to talk to the distributors. Most RPG and CSG manufacturers are quite small in terms of personnel. It is not uncommon for job functions to overlap, so that the lead game designer may also do layout and editing work as well. Computer game manufacturers may be very large corporations, such as Atari or Electronic Arts, but they traditionally outsource the development of the game to small firms with a similar corporate climate of wearing multiple hats. In this sense, a manufacturer or publisher in the gaming industry can deviate quite a bit from the more functionally divided personnel structure of a non-gaming manufacturer. In the case of many companies in the industry, the creative person that often had the initial idea for a new game is also the corporate officer that runs the company. As we shall discuss later, this is often not the most effective or desirable combination.

A distributor, as mentioned above, needs to have the necessary infrastructure to receive products from numerous manufacturers and then ship them to an even larger number of retailers. Product knowledge and personal relationships are invaluable to a buyer, and many retailers look to their distributor for information or suggestions of what products to stock. As stated above, there is a potentially positive and negative consequence of this reliance on a distributor's knowledge and personal connections; furthermore, as distributors consolidate or successfully expand their business, the industry risks being dominated by a handful of distributors who wield enormous influence on how products and information flow through the industry.

The retailer for the gaming industry makes an effort to cross-promote similar games, will run demonstrations of games (RPG, CSG, or video) in the store, and needs a knowledgeable staff that actually plays the games that are sold, as most consumers want to be informed before they make a purchase. The retail store owner and staff are usually active gamers, and may even game regularly with their customers.

In terms of consumers, there is no set type of gamer. Gamers can range in age from children to gray-haired adults. Collectible trading card games tend to be more popular with children, and in the case of such games as *Pokemon* or *Yu-Gi-Oh!*, there are popular Saturday morning cartoons, lunchboxes, backpacks and other cross-promotional strategies that are clearly aimed at children. However, a game like *Magic: The Gathering* which launched the collectible trading card game category in 1993 (see Williams, this volume), includes players who may well have started as children, but are now young adults and are still playing. Role-playing games, which have only formally existed for about 30 years, tend to attract teenagers and young adults, but the main consumer base is aging. The nature of role-playing games is such that they are open-ended storytelling, and once a set group of players is established, they tend to stay together and age together. RPG customers tend to be loyal, and will stick with a game for months or years before switching to a new game (often by the same manufacturer). Video games encompass a wide age-range and type of gamer, and are more accessible to the casual gamer. The advantage of on-line video game play is that one does not need to gather other players locally and coordinate schedules as with RPGs and CSGs. Instead, one merely needs to find virtual players. In an increasingly interconnected internet world, that is rarely a problem.

All four divisions need one another. First, it would simply not be cost effective for most manufacturers to mail one or two copies of a new product to hundreds of different retail stores. The returns and damages alone would make such a system very hard to maintain and economically ineffective. Secondly, the distributors are often the retailers' source of information for new products, or even new companies. This 'inside the channel' marketing is very advantageous, especially if a struggling or new manufacturer does not have the money for an elaborate marketing campaign, or a direct mail program to retailers. Finally, there is the cash flow consideration. It is more advantageous for the manufacturers if a relatively small number of distributors order a relatively large number of products, and the manufacturers can then better manage their cash flow based on the payment terms they maintain with each distributor. Imagine trying to juggle hundreds of different accounts, each totaling relatively small amounts of dollars with different net payment terms? It is simply not functional for the average gaming manufacturer from a cash flow or staff perspective.

There is a limited pool of consumer dollars, and manufacturers and retailers come and go. Many of the participants in the gaming industry go into business because they enjoy their hobby or pastime to such a degree that they want to do it for a living. This yields very passionate and knowledgeable participants, but does not necessarily correlate with good business acumen. Flash-in-the-pan products (and companies) are not unknown, and cash flow issues, late shipments, late payments, and all manner of other operational problems have historically been part of the industry. Instability among manufacturers and retailers makes distributors nervous, and causes them to order conservatively. This can lead to a general level of wariness in all divisions of the industry, and cause product shortages in the supply channels. Consumers, already participants in the industry, are accustomed to hearing that the release date for an anticipated product was pushed back a month, or that a distributor is currently out-of-stock on an item (because they ordered conservatively) and cannot meet the retailers' orders. While the existing gaming customer will abide, a new customer may well be deterred from engaging with the gaming industry and culture by what he or she perceives as unprofessional behavior by a potentially failing business.

Gamer Subculture and Identity

The individuals that make up the industry in any given division are almost[2] all members of the same subculture: the *gamer* (or *gamer-geek*) subculture. They are fundamentally excited by what their competitors are doing! They not only play their competitors' games, they buy their competitors' games, or they trade their own product for their competitors' products. This sense of "we're all gamers" creates a very non-traditional business atmosphere. Certainly, every company is in the industry to succeed and make a profit, but the stereotypical, cut-throat, corporate business climate is not as prevalent.

The gamer, or gamer-geek, subculture that permeates the industry is marked by modes of dress, specific linguistic jargon, and a sense of solidarity. Gamers often wear clothing that references specific games, comics, television shows or movies that are not widely known outside of a small following. Even relatively well-known references, such as *Star Wars* or *Star Trek*, are pursued by gamers to a much finer level of understanding than an average television or movie viewer. For example, an ardent gamer who is also a fan of *Star Wars*, may be able to tell the difference in rank pins worn on the uniforms of Imperial soldiers, or even know the rank, titles, and planets of origin for major and minor characters. In addition to modes of dress, there are also modes of discourse which serve to unify gamers. Gamers employ a wide array of jargon, so that on-line video gamers may speak of "buffs," "mobs," and "aggro," and collectible trading card gamers may talk of "tapping" and "mana" while role-players are enthusiastically discussing "armor class," and the "plus" rating of magical items. Gamer discourse is also laden with quotes from movies, television and comics, usually drawn from the fantasy and science fiction genres.

Gamers will self-identify as gamers or gamer-geeks, as illustrated in an article from October 16, 2004 on CNN.com addressing the 30th anniversary of *Dungeons & Dragons*. "Some 4 million people play D&D regularly. Many of them laugh at a common suggestion that fantasy gamers are geeks: Of course they are, they say" (CNN.com). It is this shared subculture, more than a collection of demographic traits, which defines a gamer. Certainly, attempts have been made to characterize the "average" gamer: white, male, mid-teens to late 30's, usually middle class, intelligent and articulate, with stunted social skills. Attending a gaming convention, such as Dragon*Con, would certainly not disprove this characterization, but it falls far short of capturing all of those that would identify themselves as gamers, and is therefore closer to a stereotype than an actual demographic representation.

The small size of the industry, coupled with a shared sense of subcultural identity, discourages the harsh competitive strategies that might be found in larger, more mainstream industries. There is also the sense that if one company in the industry is doing well, then that will translate into sales for others (for example, those that sell support products like dice and card protectors); the perception is such that any money being spent in the industry is good for the entire industry. Again, from a manufacturer's standpoint, these are competitors, and they want to succeed, but they are also genuinely interested in the products they are competing with, and feel a connection to the owners and employees of the other industry firms.

The shared sense of identity and feeling of inclusiveness that encompasses all four divisions of the gaming industry and parts of related industries (e.g., comics) is the most important aspect of this industry and differentiates it from many other businesses. Attending a large gaming industry convention, with representatives from all four divisions, is very different from a typical corporate conference. Instead of clean-cut corporate executives in suits and ties, toting briefcases, handing out business cards and networking to meet influential contacts, one is likely to see a diverse crowd of people dressed casually in jeans and tee shirts (or more outlandishly in costumes), toting backpacks, and chatting enthusiastically not only with other players of their favorite game, but with the individuals that created and designed that game. A non-gamer (such as a corporate executive whose conference was held in the same hotel as the gaming convention) who stumbled into a gaming convention would find it difficult to know what many of the designs (i.e., *Hello Kitty*, *Dragon Ball Z*, the Rebel and Imperial insignias from *Star Wars*) and slogans (i.e., "Natural 20!" or "One Frag Left") on the tee shirts referenced, although he or she might recognize designs and costumes that referenced mainstream movies and TV shows such as *Star Trek* or *Buffy the Vampire Slayer*. Not only manner and style of dress would set apart a gamer and a non-gamer at a gaming convention, but naturally the discourse would be very specific to the games being played, bought and sold. Whether the executive walked away mildly amused, or cursing the "geeks and freaks" that he or she encountered, one thing would be evident: these people formed a distinct group, and the non-gaming corporate executive was not part of it.

This is not meant to imply that everyone exists in some kind of gaming utopia, or that everyone wears iconic clothing with obscure game and media references. We are talking about an industry full of diverse people and personalities, engaged in competitive, for-profit, business practices, and there are certainly conflicts and clashes along personal and business lines. Likewise, there are natural divisions among gamers. A role-playing gamer that started as a child on collectible card games may now find all such games, even ones he or she has not played, indicative of childhood and thus juvenile. A young professional who came to gaming through PC video games might have no interest in RPGs or CSGs, beyond a basic aesthetic appreciation (art, design, etc.) The cultural component is very strong but it is subtle and complex, and is characterized by the level of enthusiasm that an industry participant has for all products and aspects of the gaming industry, not just enthusiasm for how his or her product, company, or favorite game is doing relative to the rest of the industry. As a counterpoint, consider that the CEO of Coca-Cola will most likely never have a can of Pepsi's latest beverage sitting on his desk, no matter how great it tastes, while most gaming company employees have multiple products from multiple competitors in their offices, homes, cars, etc.

While there is a unifying gamer culture, the actual businesses that comprise the industry are quite diverse, and herein lie some of the challenges of working in the gaming industry. The camaraderie is tempered with the practical necessity of running a successful business venture. The gaming industry consists of a large number of manufacturers (one or two very large firms and companies as small as one or two people), about 10–15 U.S. distributors (approximately 40–50 worldwide) and numerous specialty retail shops (many of whom are also selling comics or related merchandise). It consists largely of privately held companies, but these companies are run by gamers, who have an incredible amount of personal interest and energy invested in the industry. There are industry organizations, such as GAMA, the Game Manufacturers Association, or GPA, the Game Publishers Association, that attempt to represent the industry, but in fact, there is no single organization that acts as a voice of the gaming industry.

This references the idea that success for one company in the industry is good for the entire industry. Financial success and operational efficiency are definite goals and are pursued to greater or lesser degrees of success by the industry firms, but for every shareholder of a gaming company, there are many times more stakeholders. These stakeholders are not just the consumers that play the games, but as Jackson states, anyone who has a stake in the success of a particular business. In this sense, then, the distinction of stakeholders, not shareholders, seems especially relevant to an industry that undoubtedly shares a common spirit and common identity, but whose member firms differ greatly in terms of efficiency, profitability and professionalism.

Those companies that do dominate the industry are dominant because they have learned, often painfully, to balance the culture of gaming versus the business of gaming. As firms grow more successful in the industry, it becomes necessary to adopt more and more traditional business processes. It becomes necessary to have better control of costs, to understand and maintain reliable cash flow, and to continue delivering quality content to one's loyal consumers. For example, failing to adopt better business controls could lead to: layoffs as payroll balloons due to excessive hiring in the wake of success; cash flow problems (e.g. the manufacturer gets paid from the distributor in 90 days, but owes the printer in 30 days and fails to account for this two month difference); a loss of customers as players perceive the growing firm to have lost its creative edge; having "sold out" to a more mainstream demographic.

Consider this statement made by the president of a leading manufacturer: "This hobby has a steep learning curve. You don't pick up a book and hop right in. You're either taught how to play, or you read for *four hours* and learn how to for yourself. It's not a mainstream hobby; it requires too much active participation from the participants to ever capture a significant part of our society who have been spoon fed passive entertainment all their lives." Or as another industry insider, working with sales and distribution, said: "Gaming is niche in the U.S. It's a place for geeks, nerds, some pervs, and Wookies."

Conclusion

In this chapter, we have explored the interrelationship of the business of gaming and the culture of gaming. The business of gaming can best be described as a niche market, comprised of a small industry of specialized manufacturers, distributors, retailers, and consumers. The gaming industry is relatively stable, with a consumer base that is loyal. The business practices are not as rigorous as in more traditional corporate industries and the competition between firms is more akin to friendly rivalry than cut-throat maneuvering. The industry produces numerous entertainment products, and this chapter has focused on the three main categories of role-playing games (RPG), collectible strategy games (CSG) and on-line, multiplayer video games. In this sense, the industry is a part of the larger multimedia entertainment industry, but occupies a niche market, remaining largely unknown or misunderstood to the majority of American pop culture.

The culture of gaming is characterized by a shared sense of identity among the majority of industry participants. There is a general sense of solidarity among gamers, irrespective of one's place in the industry. Again, this is not meant to imply that there are no differences or conflict among gamers; we are not speaking of an idyllic world where everyone gets along. Businesses clash in competition or debate actions taken by other firms in the industry, and opinions range widely on what is or is not best for the industry on any given day. Gamers are often passionate about the games they play and this can naturally lead to competitive conflicts, and like any consumer base, tastes and preferences vary among gamers so that a game loved by one person is loathed by another.

It is necessary to remember that we are speaking about an industry that makes games; entertainment for a largely specialized fan-base, with some presence in the popular culture. It certainly would seem that making games, especially games that one already likes to play, would be the dream job, but it is like any other job: it is hard work and serious business. I was often asked, "So you work for a game company? Do you just play games all day?" On one hand, I can understand this question, as it is much less common to meet people that 'make games' for a living, but on the other hand, few would assume the employees of Coca-Cola sit around "drinking Coke" all day. I think the main element that makes the business of gaming so difficult to define relative to other industries, and in the minds of many people, is that the gaming industry traffics primarily in ideas. As Michael Tinney, president of White Wolf, Inc., a leading industry manufacturer, stated, "We're competing with creativity and ideas, not cheaper razor blades and corner kiosks. Fans either like the theme of a product or they don't. If they're not excited about a game, they won't pretend to be in that world during their free time." The gaming industry competes for their consumers' daydreams: would you rather do battle with a rival wizard with your deck of *Magic* cards, raid the lair of the evil dragon with your fellow *D&D* players, or fire up your Xbox and lead a virtual team of fellow *Halo 2* players on a search and destroy mission?

Obviously, the gaming industry is engaged in interactive multimedia entertainment, a fast-paced and fickle domain where success depends on understanding and connecting to the customer base. That is why the culture of gamers is so integral to the business of gaming. So why does it work? Why would so many people tolerate what seems to be an inefficient, dysfunctional industry that could benefit from a top down reorganization? The system works because the primary gaming product is an idea, not an item, and ideas require a different business environment than mass produced commodities. There needs to be room for creativity and experimentation, and a structure that was too rigid, too controlling, would hamper that creativity. Certainly there are creative industries that mass-produce ideas, such as Hollywood, but that is passive entertainment. While there are many Americans that prefer independent, foreign or art films, a large segment of society has been conditioned to accept Hollywood's idea of what a movie experience should entail. One key difference between the gaming industry and the movie industry is the facet of active engagement. Gaming requires one to engage with the game and with other players, thereby simultaneously mediating and constructing one's experience. Watching a movie is passive, and the viewer exerts no control or influence over the movie experience, short of turning it off or leaving the theater.

This is not to imply, however, that there is no room for a more business-minded approach. Indeed, the gaming industry could benefit greatly by borrowing several of the business world's *processes*. A process that improved inventory control would be an asset to just about any manufacturer, distributor, or retailer, but a rigid theoretical model that dictated when the business should order and reorder would not be particularly useful. Likewise, improving basic processes such as creating a production schedule for the entire year, or reliably collecting and accounting for foreign translation royalties, or even paying freelance authors, artists, and programmers in a timely and professional manner (assuming they deliver the contracted work in a timely and professional manner) would provide a competitive edge to a gaming industry firm. It is no surprise that the dominant enterprises in the gaming industry (publisher, distributor and retailer) have very good processes in place, and run their businesses seriously, but it is always based on the relationship and feedback of the consumer base, and never on what the "model projects" for the quarter.

Finally, the gaming industry as a business and a culture is, to borrow an overused metaphor, like two sides of a coin (also known as a two-sided die). The business side wants to make games that will meet the consumers' wants and needs. They want to be successful so they can support their families, and have a better lifestyle. But the same people are also gamers, and therefore have a much better understanding of the wants and needs that drive their customers. Any improvement in lifestyle would most likely give them more time and money to game, which is to say that given the limited wealth in the industry, most participants are not engaged in the industry to strike it rich and retire early. This depth of knowledge and customer understanding cannot be replicated by a focus group or marketing survey. Again, to reiterate, there are differences, stark differences, among gamers. All gamers do not like the same game, and often have strong feelings about certain manufacturers or genres of game, but overall the sense of community is present, and the shared culture of gaming is what unites very disparate people in a very unorthodox industry.

Acknowledgments

I would like to acknowledge my fellow editors, Patrick Williams and Sean Hendricks, for their hard work, patience, and enthusiasm. I would also like to thank all my friends and colleagues in the gaming industry, but especially Bill Bridges, Andrew Greenberg, Michael Tinney, Chris Wiese, Fred Yelk and everyone at HDI and White Wolf, and Dragon*Con 2004.

References

Associated Press. 2004. "Gamers Mark 30 Years of *Dungeons & Dragons*." CNN.com, October 16. Retrieved October 16, 2004 (*http://www.cnn.com/ 2004/SHOWBIZ/10/16/dungeons.dragons.ap/index.html*).

Connected Home Media. 2004. "Video Game Sales Break $7 Billion in 2003." Retrieved October 18, 2004 (*http://www.connectedhomemag.com/HomeTheater/Articles/ Index.cfm?ArticleID=41565*).

Griepp, Milton. 2004. "Game Market Mixed in 2003 — Wide Variation in Category." ICv2 Retailers Guide to Games, Q2 2004, pp. 2, 4.

"Report to Stakeholders: 2004." 2004. Steve Jackson Games. Retrieved October 18, 2004 (*http://www.sjgames.com/general/report.html*).

Tinney, Michael. 2004. Personal Communication. November 4, 2004.

Williams, J. Patrick. 2006."Consumption and Authenticity in the Collectible Strategy Games Subculture." Pp. 77-99 in *Gaming as Culture: Social Reality, Identity and Experience in Role-Playing, Collectible, and Computer Games*, edited by J. Patrick Williams, Sean Q. Hendricks, and W. Keith Winkler. Jefferson, NC: McFarland.

Notes

1. The gaming industry is briefly defined, for terms of this chapter, as those firms that create role-playing games (RPGs), collectible strategy games (CSGs), or on-line video games (PC or console), as well as a range of support products for these main categories. Included in the industry are also the retail stores that sell the games, the distributors that move the product from the manufacturer to the retailer, and the end consumer.

2. I say "almost" because recent years have seen the entrance of a few major corporate players. For example, Hasbro, Inc. purchased Wizards of the Coast, the makers of *Magic: The Gathering* in 1999, and The Topps Company, Inc. acquired WizKids in 2003. While the management and staff of Wizards of the Coast and WizKids are certainly still part of the gamer subculture, I would not include the executive officers and board of directors of Hasbro or The Topps Company.

8. ONLINE GAMING AND THE INTERACTIONAL SELF

Identity Interplay in Situated Practice

Florence Chee
Marcelo Vieta
Richard Smith

In recent years the popular media have asserted that massively multi-player online role playing games (MMORPGs) like *EverQuest* are highly addictive (Frankel 2002). Consequently, public opinion has rallied to this latest panic, changing the way in which society views the world online affecting the world offline. According to popular belief, these games have caused players to forsake "real life" obligations and "significant" offline relationships in order to pursue the "fake" and "trivial" online. In this chapter we bring the examination of online games into a broader context by linking the online worlds of gamers with their offline worlds. We explore phenomena that indicate that these worlds are more integrated than they initially appear.

In this paper we interpret ethnographic data from *EverQuest* and its social spaces using the sociological phenomenology of Schutz (Schutz 1962; 1970; Schutz and Luckmann, 1973). We argue that the interplay between the everyday, situated lives of online interactive gamers and their activities in games such as *EverQuest* is much more enmeshed and certainly not the root cause for dysfunction as has been suggested by some. Indeed, using the work of Schutz for phenomenological clarification, we argue here that online games are no more addictive and disconnecting than other sites of play, gaming, or other social activity. Rather, they are ways of re-enchanting life and of sustaining meaningful community experiences.

Popular accounts of the dangers of gaming fall into a discourse about the Internet as a lonely and risky place where online users are likely to be depressed and dislocated from the wider, offline population. The Internet and all the mysteries therein are talked about on the evening news as if danger to personal and psychological safety existed in quantities much greater than those found in the real world. In a well-known study that gave ammunition to pessimistic views of the Internet in the popular press, Kraut et al. (1998) concluded that the Internet is a paradox: it is both a social technology and one that decreases quality time offline, leading to reduced psychological wellbeing. Nie and Erbring (2000), in a separate and also widely-circulated study, found that the more we use the Internet the less time we spend with "real people." In addition, Putnam, in his popular book *Bowling Alone* (2000), makes the claim that we are increasingly turning into "suburban hermits," preferring to stay home with our televisions and computers rather than to engage in civic life. These critical studies highlight the views of contemporary philosophers such as Borgmann (1999) and Dreyfus (2001), who make the claim that the Internet fractures the individual from the more authentic connections of face-to-face life. They argue that real community and human connection cannot be sustained effectively on the network. In addition to these and other increasingly negative accounts of online activity, a growing body of ethnographic and survey-based research has tried to provide a more balanced account of the place of Internet mediation in our everyday lives. These projects are grounded in the human and social philosophies of experience and many show that cyberspace and, as we shall contend in this chapter, online gaming spaces, are more mundanely placed in our daily lives (Bakardjieva 2000; Bargh, McKenna, and Fitzsimmons 2002; Herring, Scheidt, Bonus, and Wright 2004; Howard, Rainie, and Jones 2002; Markham 1998; Markman 2003; McKenna, Green, and Gleeson 2002; Nardi, Schiano, Gumbrecht, and Swartz 2004; Papacharissi 2002; Romero 2003; Slater 1998; Walker 2000; Wellman and Gulia, 1999; Wynn and Katz 1997).

We propose that video game interactions, rather than being addictive sites of social discord, are constructions of a greater need for community grounded in a "will-to-communicate" (Jaspers 1957/1997). This will-to-communicate remains in place even during computational interactions such as those experienced in MMORPGs (Vieta 2004). We re-evaluate technologically pessimistic notions such as the addictive quality of interactive video games by looking at the activity from the perspective of the lived-experience of users (Bakardjieva 2000; Markham 1998; Vieta 2004). As we will discuss, the socio-phenomenological work of Schutz helps us build an interpretive path within gamers' lived-experiences.

Methodology

Our informants contributed their experiences and narratives in the thick, descriptive manner typical of ethnographic studies. In addition to the researcher's participant-observation, informal interviews, and supplementary research, we use the testimonies of *EverQuest* informants from formal, in-depth interviews. Though this data is not intended to be representative and generalized to the greater population of players, the data gathered and ideas presented here do touch upon some insights that we doubt could have been collected by methods other than ethnography. The answers to questions in the findings highlight even more intriguing questions for future research, such as implications for online communities and notions of addiction.

The ethnography discussed took place over a two-year period from 2002 to 2004. In that time, Chee created her own avatar and conducted participant-observation in the land of Norrath on the Terris-Thule server. In the *EverQuest* participant observation portion, approximately one-hundred and fifty hours were spent playing, participating in online forums, and conducting general online research. Chee documented events by taking fieldnotes while playing, keeping a post-session reflections journal, posting a public web log (blog), and taking screenshots. Rather than introduce herself as a researcher to everyone in the game, the researcher made an active decision not to do so, as it was more appropriate to the inquiry of this study to concentrate on the experiences of the game at hand. The situation called for Chee to be a player first, and researcher second. The authors believed that the decision was sound and justified, as no players online were pulled aside for purposes of answering the research protocol, and ethics clearance of confidentiality and informed consent was gained for informants explicitly chosen for interview offline. In game, the researcher slipped into the natural role of player, with the motives any player would have: to "level up," and have fun. This experience was integral to the study because it directly impacted her ability to understand the stories of other players, the phenomenological game experience of a relatively new *EverQuest* player, and possible reasons why players see a game like *EverQuest* as an opportunity to participate in an engaging community.

In many respects, Chee's experiences in the land of Norrath closely matched the experiences of what people have come to know as traditional ethnography. That is, immersing oneself for an extended period of time in a given field site while attempting to build rapport through networking, experiencing what it is like to live as a local through daily life and guidance from acclimatized locals. Unlike offline ethnography, however, Chee could be very much in control of the character she choose to be instead of having her attributes assigned due to accident of birth. It was possible for the researcher to immediately become a resident of Kelethin and instantly assimilate the attributes of being a Wood Elf along with that race's programmed tensions with other races, and to be an *EverQuest* community member like everyone else.

Description of Interview Participants

This fieldwork laid the foundation for general observations of players in the game and outside the game, in formal interviews for which we gained ethics clearance and ensured confidentiality of informant identities to the extent they wished. We present some key insights from four informants who were recruited by a combination of snowball and convenience-sampling methods, as was appropriate for a micro-study of this nature. Throughout this chapter, the testimonies of our informants are discussed, along with some additional unique issues arising from the online game environment that might not arise in strictly non-computational communities. The interviews were conducted on males in their mid-twenties, reflecting the average age of *EverQuest* players according to Yee (2001). However, their professional offline activities were quite different.

Our first contact is a habitual early adopter of games. He is a college student who "joined the bandwagon, bought it, played it, and [thought] it was pretty incredible." He got started on *EverQuest* after reading about the game in magazines and online when it was launched. The longest he has played in one sitting is ten hours. His primary observations about the types of people online are that there are different motives for playing. "Some people are in it for being in a guild, some people are in it for the loot, items, and some people are in it to help others." Originally, none of his offline friends played the game, but he says he "made friends online."

Our second contact is a young professional working in the technology industry. He travels often and is very busy with work. In addition to online games, he has always enjoyed tabletop role-playing games and is also a competitive billiards player. The longest he has played in one sitting is eighteen hours. He started playing *EverQuest* because he knew one of his friends liked the game. When asked the reason he found the game so compelling, he stated: "The gameplay really sucks, but I had to play it. I don't know why. I've given up dates, I've ignored my friends, neglected sleep and food and hygiene. I've done it all." He has become a member of a very elite guild and quite serious about the game, as we will describe.

Our third contact is a part-time student and part-time employee. He also seems to be the most dedicated *EverQuest* player of the four informants, possessing two top-level avatars. Though his average time during one sitting has not exceeded twelve hours, he would play about twelve hours almost every day and outplay the other informants in hours amassed per week. At the time of the interview, he was playing about six hours a day, after finishing work or school. When asked what he liked about *EverQuest*, he stated: "It was such a huge world, and it was the social interaction. You'd have to talk to people all over the world, which I found was pretty amazing."

The fourth contact was a paradox. He was quiet, mysterious, and initially almost too withdrawn to interview. What he did end up telling us out about himself and his interaction with the online game however was very interesting and valuable for our understanding. He works in shipping and packing, often working thirteen-hour days. His work schedule impacted his ability to achieve and sustain deep sleep, agitating a condition which predisposed him to insomnia. While he did have medication for his physiological disorder, he talked about his troubles in obtaining adequate mental rest. While surfing the Web, he came across a discussion about *EverQuest*. He decided to try it as a way to unwind from his day. It soon became more than just unwinding for him; while his professional occupation did not seem mentally fulfilling, he found that he could engage his mental activity to a greater degree online. Quiet in person, yet social and powerful online, he summarized his experience in as positive a way as one can proclaim: "*EverQuest* saved my life."

How could this game have such an important role in someone's life? In order to lend some greater context for our phenomenological analysis, we briefly describe the game of *EverQuest*.

A Brief Description of EverQuest

Upon logging on, the world laid out before a player is impressive. The graphics capabilities of 1999 have definitely since been outdone, but the visual cues are still enough to give the player an indication of being 'in' a geographical location. One can be in a forest, walking around a town with stone buildings, or sailing across a vast ocean. In order to participate in this initially strange land, one must first go through the laborious but often pleasurable task of going through numerous windows to choose the looks and attributes of a character or avatar. A player can choose among many different traits for any given character. The options are too wide-ranging to name all here, but some are race (Human, Wood Elf, Dark Elf, Dwarf, and so on), class (Warrior, Druid, Enchanter, Bard, and so on) and corresponding attributes like wisdom and agility, expressed in numeric values.

From that point on, the player is born, almost naked, into a home zone which corresponds to the chosen race. On a screen surrounded by windows for chatting, character inventory, spells, and other such miscellany, one can see the environment from first person view or toggle between other views. There are other people online running around, chatting in order to accomplish the daily tasks of buying equipment, selling loot, or killing a monster. These players have names displayed above their heads for all to see. There is also very likely a guild name displayed under the player's name, meaning that the player belongs to a particular group, called a guild, and that the player is reasonably committed to that peer group, with its own rules and code of conduct. It is ultimately up to the player to ensure the avatar is fed, clothed, and advancing in levels. As one might already gather, the *EverQuest* game world is much too large to describe in its totality, and one can spend endless amounts of time exploring the world. It is immersive, impressive, and an exercise of the imagination.

EverQuest is one of the most popular MMORPGs in North American history. In 2002, subscriptions exceeded 430,000 gamers (Taylor 2002), and 2004 estimates situate the number as greater than half a million players. At any given time, around 2000 players per server are going about their daily business online, totaling 100,000 active users at peak times. But, perhaps more intriguing to the social scientist, *EverQuest* is a fascinating case study because of its reputation for being an especially addictive game and one that has been the subject of lawsuits and policies addressing that alleged addictiveness (Death of a game addict, 2002). People often spend as much time with *EverQuest* as they would in a second job (10–40+ hours per week). According to Castronova (2001), "avatars in virtual worlds must work to do anything interesting at all" (p. 17). Our informants distinguished between engaging in interactive engagement, like gaming, and passive consumption, like watching television. They felt that their active participation in *EverQuest* highlighted the feeling of being social and productive — and this, we claim, makes their activity not an addiction. Schutz's notion of the "working self" will help us unravel what these social and productive experiences might mean. As Taylor (2002) finds, games like *EverQuest* place the user in many settings containing both online and offline friends, strangers, and people across the world, who may be virtually next to you in avatar form. Even a superficial examination reveals that the game is much more than the computer entertaining a player by facilitating a little interaction — the game is the nexus of a vast online community, complete with its own modes of human expression in art, culture, conflict, and resolution.

Phenomenological Perspectives: MMORPGs as Online Communities

Rethinking gamer social groupings and their online environments as communities is not as radical a move on our part as would first appear if we think of online environments as intimately intertwined with the greater life-world of gamers. Communication theorist James Carey points out the importance of the similar etymological roots of the words "communication" and "community" linking communication closely to the life-world (Carey 1989). Philosophers of community have known the link between communication and community for a long time. "Community through communication is found, to be sure, already among the merely living existences; it is in consciousness as such, and it is in spirit [as an] openness in the will-to-communicate" (Jaspers 1957/1997).

Further, as Feenberg and Bakardjieva (2002) and Anderson (1983) rightly point out, the notion of community is both an empirically observable co-presencing of individuals and, at the same time, an "imaginary" social construct. By considering both realities when defining online community, Feenberg and Bakardjieva (2002) and Mynatt, O'Day, Adler, and Ito (1998) have shown that the "real" versus "virtual" community debate is a dead-end when describing actual practices of computer-mediated communities and for designing appropriate community tools. Indeed, in a now-classic work on the concept of community, Anderson (1983:16–18) argues that all communities, from the "primordial village" to social groupings as large as the nation state are all "imagined" and so, it would seem, all virtual in that sense.

For all these reasons, a significant distinction between face-to-face community and virtual community seems superfluous. As an alternative, we introduce Schutz's theories of intersubjectivity as a substitute to the real/virtual community dichotomy, which will, we hope, add weight to our assertion that the worlds forged in online communities like *EverQuest*, while imagined, are no less real than communities in the world of flesh-and-blood.

Schutz's Working/Partial Self and the Interactional Selves of *EverQuest*ians

Although mostly ignored by gaming researchers and Internet studies in general, Schutz provides theories of interaction and community that are useful for theorizing mediated experience (Bakardjieva 2000; Vieta 2004). Schutz's phenomenological theories of the "working self" (Schutz

1970), of the myriad "provinces of reality" (1962; 1973) we all possess, and the interplay of both concepts within our "intersubjective" life-worlds have been especially fruitful for us in understanding the Internet-mediated life of *EverQuest*. Schutz's theories of worldly praxis and intersubjectivity are useful for grasping how the online phenomenological experiences of gamers are intertwined with their offline lives, and vice versa. It is necessary to realize that the interactions of gamers are not merely play and fantasy but also social interactions that occur within intersubjective and existentially-rooted and real engagements that are also intimately linked to gamers' offline lives.

One of Schutz's (1970) key "phenomenological baselines" (p. 53–7) is his concept of the working self (p. 68–71). It is the part of the interactional self[1] that acts onto the world, manipulates things, and strives to fulfill projects by somehow changing some aspect of that world. Moreover, the working self's acts of worldly transformation happen in an individual's "wide-awake" "plane of consciousness," where we have the fullest attention to our existential surroundings in the "vivid present" (1970:69). That is, as the working self acts onto the world, that part of us is already-always in the present.

Similar to George H. Mead's I/me framework, the interactional self emerges explicitly as a dialectic between this *working self* and the *"partial self"* (Schutz 1962 emphasis added). What Schutz adds is an explicit action theory encapsulated in the notion of a future-oriented "project" (Schutz, 1962:24) that is characterized, as Barber (2002) explains, "by the intention to bring about ... [a] ... projected state of affairs" (sec. 2). At the same time, *the partial self* is that part of us which is socially determined (Schutz 1962:216, emphasis added). The partial self is the reflective role taker, accessed through circumspection and reflection (Schutz 1962:216). The partial self is passive, recollecting "performed past acts" from its socio-biographical stock of knowledge by referring "to a system of correlated acts to which it belongs" (p. 216). In essence, as observers of ourselves, we use our socio-biographical and historical "determinates" to connect to and inform our ongoing projects and completed actions (Barber, 2002). In this chapter we argue that player experiences in *EverQuest* follow similar *working* (action, projection) and *partial* (reflective) experiences.

Schutz's 'self' is one which is rooted simultaneously in agency and action of the working self *and* reflection and recollection of the partial self. To Schutz, the world is one of "well circumscribed objects" (Schutz 1962:208) encountered through "eminently [and imminently] practical interest" (p. 208). We "gear into" the world, manipulate and use things in the world, and both change and are changed by the things we manipulate and use. That is, this world is overseen by a "pragmatic motive that governs our natural attitude toward the world of daily life" (p. 209). However, there is a tension in the way we encounter the world. We give agency to our plans, purposes and actions while transforming objects in the world. The world mitigates our efforts to change it as it resists those attempts at transformation. These resistances often alter the ultimate outcomes to our projects and actions.[2]

Critically for Schutz, this working involvement with the world is not solitary. Unlike Martin Heidegger's concept of *Dasein*, Schutz explicitly adds intersubjectivity to this worldly encounter: "The world is from the outset not a private world but an intersubjective world, common to all of us" (p. 208). We live with others. We are social creatures. We actively pursue worldly transformation "with our fellow men" (p. 209) within the common ground shared by working selves mutually engaging with the world's things and with each other. Thus, this shared world is Schutz's "outer world," (p. 69) made up of the "manipulatory sphere" (p. 203) of life. That is, the outer world of action is a world where things are done by "gearing into" and manipulating things in shared common projects with others as found in one's participation in *EverQuest*. But, while one shares the outer world, the reflective attitude of the partial self is situated in inner experiences, which are not directly shared with others. The outer world, rather, is where we engage in our purposeful pursuits with others and where our life-worlds merge and overlap with common interest, shared situations, and shared meanings and values. This is what we mean by the term "intersubjectivity." Borrowing from Edmund Husserl, Schutz claims that we cannot avoid this intersubjectiveness to life. Further, this intersubjective world of everyday life is "the scene" (p. 209) where work, action, and interaction happen. We believe the world of Norrath is part of this outer world made up of intersubjectively attuned working selves. When working within *EverQuest*, gamers are engaged in purposeful pursuits with others. As such, we will show that these pursuits cannot be dismissed merely as irrelevant play, nor can they be tar-brushed as simply "addictive" practices. It is a medium with which people form legitimate community, with mutual projects and plans. *EverQuest* appears, phenomenologically, to be an arena for meaningful human communication and social life and a medium for our will-to-communicate.

Importantly for our ensuing analysis, Schutz's usage of "work" is *not* to be confused here with economic work values and employment, although this could certainly be a subset of Schutz's concept of work, as we will show with Castronova's economic analysis of *EverQuest*. Rather, for Schutz, "work" is, more broadly, any *engagement* in the world that is rooted in "purposive action" (p. 211).³ Thus, on *EverQuest*, we claim that gamers engage in work, change and are changed by work in the world of Norrath, and share this work with others in online realities that never quite leave players' offline, situated lives.⁴

Towards a Phenomenology of EverQuest

What makes games like *EverQuest* so compelling? The player informants touched upon a number of different points in their interviews, but some very interesting themes emerged that have not been highlighted in previous studies. One such theme is the development of the player-driven economy that can more broadly be interpreted as working selves gearing into Norrath. In addition, "grouping" and/or more the more committal form of joining a guild, forming an avatar cohort, and feelings of obligation to the community were compelling factors in one's decision to play the game for prolonged periods of time.

One of the questions this paper attempts to answer is whether the world of *EverQuest* can be considered an outer world or a closed world of fantasy. Perhaps *EverQuest* isn't a closed world of fantasy but an outer world of intersubjective ways of gearing into its outer worldliness in community. As our informants ultimately show us, *EverQuest* is a world of doing, of acting, of gearing into things, of manipulating things and doing these things collaboratively. In short, *EverQuest* activity is rooted in *real* kinds of community based-actions and interactions.

The question then shifts from the authenticity of actions within *EverQuest*, to instead, what degree real interactions happen in the game. Do players actually gear into the world of *EverQuest* as we are suggesting? Do they share in common projects together? We must answer affirmatively here because players have and continue to view the *EverQuest* world as "work," both as a sphere made of manipulatory things, Schutz's "well circumscribed Objects," and as online locales of economic kinds of work. The informants Chee interviewed reveal *EverQuest* as a productive and engaging space in how there are everyday tasks, errands, and obligations to be done which are intimately linked with player conceptions of "real time" that also require emotional and bodily commitments:

> There's no point in logging on for a short time. It's kinda like going into work for an hour. It just doesn't make sense. You spend more effort in trying to log on for 10 minutes than you would playing the game. You have to log on for at least an hour. Even an hour seems too short. Probably about 3 hours before you find a good group to join yourself with and to get everything sort of in time, and actually start gaining stuff. There's just no way you can do it in half an hour/an hour.

Thus, our evidence shows that the *EverQuest* world is an outer world of work as suggested by Schutz. The world of flesh-and-blood engages the self with the other, just like *EverQuest* players engage with others and gear into the things of the world on *EverQuest* and its communally-created realities. As mentioned earlier, Castronova found working realities (trading weapons, for example) within the game. While Schutz's concept of work, as we have explained, is not necessarily economic work but a broader notion of engagement with the world, Castronova discusses both economic and motor-practical notions of work at play on *EverQuest*:

> The typical user devotes hundreds of hours (and hundreds of dollars, in some cases) to develop the avatar. These ordinary people, who seem to have become bored and frustrated by ordinary web commerce, engage energetically and enthusiastically in avatar-based on-line markets [Castronova 2001:3].

In *EverQuest*, we also encountered working selves that were economically working and motor-practically working, as well as "worked over" worlds. We witnessed gamers' avatars running errands, working collaboratively, building their surrounding life-world structures, and even, as Castronova reports, engaging in "free market" exchanges of *EverQuest* goods and services. Players reported the "rush" and the feelings of accomplishment they felt as they geared into the world of Norrath together, as they helped fellow players accomplish goals and by acting on the virtual spaces and objects of Norrath pragmatically. For example, players were seen going into wooded areas of Norrath to forage for goods that they could either eat, store, or trade or sell. An interesting element of the game is also the ability for an avatar to be under the influence of alcohol. Players can buy and consume *EverQuest* alcohol, changing their in-game experiences. Things look fuzzier on the computer screen and one's avatar even moves differently.

Chee also experienced exchanges with gamers that showed that while gamers view these shared events and engagements as lived and even vividly visceral experiences, gamers also described "projected states of affairs" (Schutz, 1962:212) that were shared with other gamers in the "bodily movements" (p. 212) of gamers' avatars. Through commands one can laugh, cry, or even mourn a body. These are what Schutz would call "wide awake" descriptions of their online activities that constitute "the reality of the world of daily life" (p. 212) of these gamers. Castranova (2001) would agree:

> These communications allow social interactions that are not a simulation of human interactions; they are human interactions, merely extended into a new forum. As with any human society, it is through communication that the VW (Virtual World) society confers status and standing [Castronova, 2001:14].

Gamers were well aware of their own and other's avatars' movements, the spaces of Norrath they shared with other gamers via the traces of embodied selves left by other avatars, and the shared projects with others in guilds and raids:

> So you have to rely on other people to make it happen for you, and when you find other people who have similar interests in the game, and want to achieve the same thing you do—which is essentially just to get to that next level, then it works really well. I really enjoy hanging around with those people, and spend the time ... they ask you to do stuff like wake up at 3:30 in the morning so you can kill the dragon you have been camping for 2 days ... and you do it. You give your phone number.

Further, Castronova's work supports our analysis in that he also claims that the worlds of *EverQuest* worked over by gamers are "inherently social" (2001:18). Castronova, however, adds an economic dimension to the work of a player, further delineating Schutz's notions of work and intersubjectivity in *EverQuest*. He does this by pointing out an economic dimension to avatar interactions on *EverQuest* that is interlaced with the same motivators and drives that inspire one to engage economically in the non-computational realm of the life-world:

> Moreover, since the VWs are inherently social, the achievements are relative: it is not having powerful weapons that really makes a difference in prestige. In a postindustrial society, it is social status, more than anything else, that drives people to work so diligently all their lives. In this respect, VWs are truly a simulacrum of Earth society [Castronova, 2001:18].

Therefore, players can be said to gear into the world of *EverQuest* both economically and motor-practically via the mediation of their avatars as "extensions" of themselves (McLuhan 1964). These players feel as if they are changing the world of *EverQuest* as it changes them. Further, the same things that tend to motivate people in the non-computational world drive gamers just as much. Some motivators include: prestige, acquisitions, social standing, friendship, camaraderie, connection and community. Players talk about their experiences online like they are "doing"—projecting goals and making things happen together with others. When our informants described what they did in *EverQuest*, their language was a language of work in Schutz's sense. That is, their descriptions indicated attempts to change the world of *EverQuest* and, at the same time, be changed by it. The descriptions spoke of interactions:

> [In a group,] I need someone to heal, which would be a Cleric; an Enchanter's 'slow' so they hit me less often, some higher damage output players like a Rogue, or a Ranger, or a Wizard to kill them faster,

but then they don't have any hit points so they need a Cleric as well to keep them alive ... Druids are fun because you can solo. You have to be in an outdoors zone, but you can kill 5–8 mobs [mobile objects] at a time. You can just run them around behind you.

When probed further, the descriptions changed from primarily economic to resemble Schutz's deeper definition of work as "doing," as gearing into something on Norrath collaboratively and intersubjectively. When Chee first asked what motivated players and how things were done, she got this response:

I remember before when there weren't a lot of level 60 enchanters, and they said oh, well this is an opportunity to make lots of money. I would give them 100 [for casting a spell]. But now I just give people 50 and there's no argument. I just give them 50 plat and that's it. Same thing worked with porting around for Druids and Wizards. They made tons of money just by porting people around. Ever since the books came out, they don't make any more money. The only way you can make money is to go to certain areas, remote areas, where there aren't any. That's where most of them port.

When Chee asked her contact about his view of productivity in *EverQuest* versus a game like Medal of Honor, which is not Massively Multiplayer, he admits to another level of "productivity." He talks about projecting intentions, goals, accomplishing tasks and of manipulating things. In seeing things emerge and grow, one can notice the level of intersubjectivity in the projecting and manipulating that players do, as predicted by Schutz:

I dunno, I'd say yes, playing *EverQuest* would probably be more productive. Cause if you're on a raid and you help people get their epic weapon or something that's more productive if someone got an item they really really wanted. Unlike when you're playing *Medal of Honor*, especially single player mode, which is you and the computer pretty much. To me that's less productive.

In the above quote the player talks about *helping others* be more productive. His response articulates the collaboration and interconnections that take place among *EverQuest* players. Moreover, it alludes to Schutz's notion of mutual projects, of gearing into the world of *EverQuest*, and of accomplishing things communally, with others, in future oriented tasks.

Thus, the social groups and interactions carried out on *EverQuest* should not be merely considered as an economic model, nor should *EverQuest* be dismissed as a game that is rife with the possibilities for addictive behaviors. Rather, the *EverQuest* interactions we witnessed were expressed as acts of mutually interested gamers interacting with each other via the mediations of their chosen and earned avatars, sharing in common projects. As Vieta (2004:194–198) shows, Schutz also articulated his theory of intersubjectivity as a theory of community that he termed the "in-group" (1970:80–85). Schutz claimed that members of in-groups are able to sustain the group long-term by framing their communal interactions within four in-group characteristics that guarantee cohesion and group continuity. What we have been describing thus far map to Schutz's requirements for the cohesion of an in-group. *EverQuest* gamers guaranteed group "consistency" and "coherency" in the world of Norrath via shared "values, beliefs, and myths" and the practices of specific "rituals and ways of communicating" between avatars and players (Vieta 2004:194). Most guilds have member policies and codes of conduct. Stealing the kill of another player can be grounds for dismissal as can be vulgar or offensive language. The system by and large relies on the integrity and self-policing of community members, who in most cases solve problems internally.

As other types of communities, those forged via the mediation of player avatars on *EverQuest* are also based on notions of reciprocity, consideration of others, and deep collaboration of working selves in mutual projects of interest. Thus, when the claim is made that *EverQuest* leads ultimately to addictive behaviors, such notions are problematic. If we can call *EverQuest* interactions addictive, then what is to stop us from calling a strong commitment to a soccer team, chess club, or homework addictive? Who is to decide these normative values? It is interesting to note that most people who have labeled games like *EverQuest* as addictive tend to be non-players who have never set eyes on the world of Norrath.

From Addiction to Intersubjectivity to Interaction

Players who call themselves addicted are often using that term to articulate what they later elaborate upon as unavoidable obligations to their peers. They are engaged in acts of community. When we asked one player what indicated that *EverQuest* was an addiction, he said:

> When you can't really get off. 5 o'clock in the morning, you have a headache, but you still don't want to get off. Either I was with a good group, or there was something I needed to do in the game like get a new weapon, or I needed to get a certain amount of experience points or something like that.

As the dialogue proceeds, the respondent touches upon his dependency on the game, but when pressed further, what he describes is actually the language of the work self interacting with others and acting on the world of Norrath. Tellingly, he reveals the interactional dependency of others on

him and his social commitments that strongly resemble the social commitments of non-computational life:

> [When playing a crucial character] there's the aspect that you didn't
> want to be a loser and just drop from a group after you get something.
> You didn't want to do that, especially, when I was playing a cleric I was
> the only healer, and healers are hard to come by. If I dropped from the
> group, it would mean that the group would be practically destroyed.

Another player shows similar sentiments of commitment to fellow
players and this deep connection between his non-computational and computational realities that suggests phenomenological effacements between
his online and offline realities:

> You needed reliable people that stuck around for the hours that you
> need to play. People like that you're committed, and not just here for
> a minute and abandoning your group and ruining the whole night. You
> would have to stay on, find the opportunity, gather a force big enough
> to take it, and it's a dragon, it's a tough mob, before anyone else does
> or else you lose. First in force gets to take the mob down, that's the rule
> that *EverQuest* set. So, the one player that was camping it was on for 2
> days, 24 hours straight in shifts with a friend of theirs, waiting for this
> thing to pop. And then, you need to get first in force so often it would
> pop overnight and no one was on, so she [the guild leader] got a call
> list of phone numbers of everyone in her guild. I was sleeping one night,
> it was a work night. The phone rang at about 3:45am, and they told me
> Rage is up. So I get up and boot my computer, log on, and park in the
> right area, and we killed the creature and went back to bed [Laughs].

Not only do we see the deep commitments players have towards their
EverQuest social groupings, but the suggestion that the experiences of gearing into the world of Norrath are not simply whimsical activities of partial selves engaged in realms of fantasy. Rather, they are deep social
involvements between future directed and co-responsible working selves
committed to meaningful mutual projects in the "Now and Here," as
Schutz puts it. There is also, for example, interplay between the player's
online activities and offline realities of work and sleep. Indeed, if players'
activities were rooted in, mere fantasy worlds that prevented them from
"produc[ing]" in the "external world," why would they feel such social
pressure to not drop from their groups or to be reliable people? Why does
it ultimately matter that "the group would be practically destroyed" if he
left it? It matters because these experiences are not simply inconsequen-
tial acts of fantasy. For these players, *EverQuest* holds deeply meaningful
and shared experiences that are rooted in community values and recipro-
cal projects. The above experiences of both gamers are deeply circumscribed social acts with deep investments of emotion and time. Their

descriptions are sentiments of socially committed people intimately and intersubjectively linked to their fellow *EverQuest* gamers in communal formations of respect and reciprocity. In short, the working selves of our players, as mediated by *EverQuest*, together with the partial selves that are reflecting on their experiences, have deeply cohered with others on Norrath. Both respondents are relating situations where gamers have socially geared into the world of Norrath in, "a commonality of projective means, sharing in the processes and values that are intersubjectively constituted and agreed upon" by fellow community gamers (Vieta 2004:205). These are sentiments of real community members engaging in real community activities in ways that are intricately entangled with offline situations.

EverQuest's Offline/Online Links

Our players experienced *EverQuest* not only cognitively but also viscerally and bodily. They lost sleep while engaging with *EverQuest*. They described physical discomfort and even pain when engaging in *EverQuest* activities. They also articulated the tensions that can emerge when they neglect their loved ones who do not share their *EverQuest* activities. Further, when describing their online interactions, the players interviewed referred to the other characters they knew on Norrath as "people," not avatars. We recall an interesting portion of a conversation with one of our players, when Chee asked him what gradually cut his thirty hours playing per week:

> My girlfriend helped [me spend less time online.] It was also the idea that there was starting to become too much of a gap between the high level characters and the low level players, and then they were finding all the new [items] so there was nothing left for us. When I started advancing levels there was nothing new that I could search out. I couldn't explore the higher level areas without spending a LOT more time on the game, and so I was basically stagnating. I couldn't gain levels as quickly as I used to, so there was no sense of accomplishment.

What caused this player to reduce his online hours was not medication or counseling in the conventional sense. Instead, he made a choice of replacing one activity with another, as is often the case with such behaviors. His motives were a combination of wanting to spend more time with his girlfriend, who was getting progressively more annoyed with him because of his online commitments, and his in-game level stagnation, causing his interest in the game to ultimately to wane. This decision was not arrived at easily, as there were deep tensions between offline lives and online activities that could not be kept separate. Indeed, what seemed to

ultimately drive this player to reduce his *EverQuest* activities was the wan-
ing sense of accomplishment he was feeling each time he logged on. These
tensions resolved differently for the player who woke up in the middle of
the night to play with his guild mates; his commitment to fellow players
was so great that he felt compelled to do these things to assist his *EverQuest*
community members in their tasks while fully aware that he had to be at
work in a few hours. These are *not* the sentiments of people who have disconnected their offline lives from their online ones. They are the sentiments
of individuals who, like many, struggle to make sense of the myriad tensions of their intersubjectively attenuated life-worlds. For the players, these
intersubjective realities, when engaging in *EverQuest*, express themselves
in the tensions between their merged offline/online realities that resonate
within vague and indeterminately overlapping dimensions of their life-
worlds.

Conclusion

After looking at gaming from a socio-phenomenological point of
view, one might question how the behaviors exhibited in these online environments are vastly separated from or any less important than those exhibited through other media or life-world settings. Our application of Schutz's
phenomenology of intersubjective interaction highlights the importance
for social researchers, game designers, and policy makers to ask themselves
if the computational worlds of *EverQuest* are radically different from the
non-computational worlds of flesh and blood before conceptualizing the
gamer, designing the games, and legislating restrictive policies in regards
to gaming activities. Studying game players at their level, as ethnography
helps us to achieve, is of paramount importance when trying to understand the motivations truly at work within mediated environments like
EverQuest. Rather than being a world of fantasy set apart from real life, we
have attempted to show in this paper that, phenomenologically, the realities of gamers are not clearly distinguishable between offline and online
realities. Rather, the online interactions of gamers are deeply embedded
within their offline lives, and vice-versa.

We use Schutz's theories to help us see two major socio-phenomenological actualities in *EverQuest* gaming practices. First, involvement in
EverQuest life intimately links the offline desires, passions, and pursuits
of players on multiple levels of social and phenomenological interest that
have been, to date, sorely neglected. Second, the actions that players *do*
when engaging in their online activities are largely perceived as *real* engage-

ments with *real* fellow gamers involved in *real* forms of community. To these players, life in Norrath is associated with community life. As such, we hope the work in this chapter has hinted at the possibilities for further understanding the ways interactive games and the way online activities interplay with offline lives and the sense of self.

Therefore, it seems that either calling an immersive multiplayer game such as *EverQuest* "just a game" or contrarily, claiming that it has the power to destructively influence the "real" lives of users assists in creating ill-informed and simplistic views of complex social formations that can take place via the mediation of a game. We have shown in this chapter that, phenomenologically, there is no strong case to be made that such a sharp dichotomous separation exists. The life-world of players and the ways community experience is described are just too complex and too integrated into the everyday life of everyone concerned to make strong assumptions regarding the linear influences of MMORPGs on the lives of users.

Acknowledgments

The authors would like to acknowledge the support of the New Media Innovation Center (NewMIC), Centre for Policy Research on Science and Technology (CPROST), and the School of Communication, Faculty of Applied Sciences at Simon Fraser University in Vancouver, British Columbia, Canada. The spirit of collaboration facilitated by all the organizations above was invaluable during this endeavor. Last but not least, this could not have been done without the time and contributions of the many informants and community members, online and offline.

References

Anderson, Benedict R. 1983. *Imagined Communities: Reflections on the Origin and Spread of Nationalism.* London: Verso.

Bakardjieva, Maria. 2000. "The Internet in Everyday Life: Computer Networking from the Standpoint of the Domestic User." Ph.D. dissertation, School of Communication, Simon Fraser University, Burnaby, BC.

Barber, Michael. 2002. "Alfred Schutz." *Stanford Encyclopedia of Philosophy.* Retrieved December 4, 2002 (*http://plato.stanford.edu/entries/schutz/*).

Bargh, John A., Katelyn Y.A. McKenna, and Grainne M. Fitzsimmons. 2002. "Can You See the Real Me? Activation and Expression of the 'True Self' on the Internet." *Journal of Social Issues* 58:33–48.

Borgmann, Albert. 1999. *Holding On to Reality: The Nature of Information at the Turn of the Millennium.* Chicago, IL: University of Chicago Press.

Carey, James W. 1989. *Communication as Culture: Essays on Media and Society.* Boston, MA: Unwin Hyman.

Castronova, E. 2001. "Virtual Worlds: A First-Hand Account of Market and Society on the Cyberian Frontier." *Gruter Institute Working Papers on Law, Economics and Evolutionary Biology*. Retrieved April 15, 2003 (*http://www.bepress.com/giwp/default/vol2/iss1/art1/current_article.html*).

Dreyfus, Hubert L. 2001. *On the Internet*. London, UK: Routledge.

Feenberg, Andrew. 1995. "From Information to Communication: The French Experience with Videotex." pp. 144–165 in *Alternative Modernity: The Technical Turn in Philosophy and Social Theory*. Berkeley, CA: University of California Press.

_____. 2004. "Active and Passive Bodies: Comments on Don Ihde's 'Bodies in Technology.'" *Techne: Journal of the Society for Philosophy and Technology* 7:2. Retrieved April 15, 2004 (*http://scholar.lib.vt.edu/ejournals/SPT/v7n2/feenberg.html*).

_____, and Bakardjieva, Maria. 2002. "Community Technology and Democratic Rationalization." *The Information Society* 18: 181–192.

Frankel, Jon 2002. "EverQuest or Evercrack?" *The Early Show*, CBSNews.com. Retrieved November 22, 2004 (*http://www.cbsnews.com/stories/2002/05/28/earlyshow/living/caught/main510302.shtml*).

Herring, Susan C., Lois Ann Scheidt, Sabrina Bonus, and Elijah Wright. 2004. "Bridging the Gap: A Genre Analysis of Weblogs." Paper presented at 37th Hawaii International Conference on Systems Science. Hawaii, USA.

Howard, Philip N., Lee Rainie, and Steve Jones. 2002. "Days and Nights on the Internet." pp. 45–73 in *The Internet in Everyday Life*, edited by B. Wellman and C. Haythornthwaite, Oxford, UK: Blackwell Publishers.

Jaspers, Karl. 1957/1997. *Reason and Existenz: Five Lectures*. Milwaukee, WI: Marquette University Press.

Kraut, Robert, Michael Patterson, Vicki Lundmark, Sara Kiesler, Tridas Mukhopadhyay, and William Scherlis. 1998. "Internet Paradox: A Social Technology that Reduces Social Involvement and Psychological Well-Being?" *American Psychologist* 53: 1017–1031.

Markham, Annette N. 1998. *Life Online: Researching Real Experience in Virtual Space*. Walnut Creek, CA: Altamira Press.

Markman, Kris. 2003. "Taking the Flesh with Me: Embodied Interaction as Framework for Studying Internet Communication." Paper presented at Association of Internet Researchers Fourth Annual Conference (AoIR 4.0: Broadening the Band). Toronto, Canada.

McKenna, Katelyn Y.A., Amie S. Green, and Marci E.J. Gleeson. 2002. "Relationship Building on the Internet: What's the Big Attraction." *Journal of Social Issues* 58: 9–31.

McLuhan, Marshall. 1964. *Understanding Media: The Extensions of Man*. New York, NY: McGraw-Hill.

Miller, Hugh and Jill Arnold. 2002. "Self in Web Home Pages: Gender, Identity, and Power in Cyberpsace." pp. 73–94 in *Towards CyberPsychology: Mind, Cognition, and Society in the Internet Age*, edited by G. Riva & C. Galimberti. Amsterdam, Netherlands: Amsterdam, IOS Press Mynatt, Elizabeth D., Vicki L. O'Day, Annette Adler, and Mizuko Ito. 1998. "Network Communities: Something Old, Something New, Something Borrowed...." *Computer Supported Cooperative Work: The journal of Collaborative Computing* 7:123–156.

Nardi, Bonnie, Diane Schiano, Michelle Gumbrecht, and Luke Swartz. 2004. "'I'm Blogging This': A Closer Look at Why People Blog." Retrieved March 12, 2004 (*http://www.ics.uci.edu/~jpd/classes/ics234cw04/nardi.pdf*).

Nie, N.H. and L. Erbring 2000. "Internet and Society: A Preliminary Report." *Stanford Institute for the Quantitative Study of Society*. Retrieved July 5, 2004 (*http://www.stanford.edu/group/siqss*).

Papacharissi, Zizi. 2002. "The Self Online: The Utility of Personal Home Pages." *Journal of Broadcast and Electronic Media* 46: 246–268.

Poster, Mark. 2001. *What's the Matter with the Internet?* Minneapolis, MN: University of Minnesota Press.

Putnam, Robert D. 2000. *Bowling Alone: The Collapse and Revival of American Community*. New York, NY: Simon & Schuster.

Romero, Aaron Alzola. 2003. "/WHOIS? Identity: Collectivity and the Self in IRC." *PsychNology Journal* 1: 87–130.

Schutz, Alfred. 1962. *Collected Papers Vol. I*. The Hague, Netherlands: M. Nijhoff.

_____. 1970. *On Phenomenology and Social Relations; Selected Writings*. Chicago, IL: University of Chicago Press.

_____, and Thomas Luckmann. 1973. *The Structures of the Life-World*. Evanston IL: Northwestern University Press

Slater, Don. 1998. "Trading Sexpics on IRC: Embodiment and Authenticity on the Internet." *Body & Society* 4: 91–117.

Taylor, T. L. 2002. "Multiple Pleasures: Women and Online Gaming." *Convergence: The Journal of Research into New Media Technologies* 9: 24–26.

Vieta, Marcelo. 2004. "Interactions Through the Screen: The Interactional Self as a Theory for Internet-Mediated Communication." MA Thesis, School of Communication, Simon Fraser University, Burnaby, BC.

Walker, Katherine. 2000. "'It's Difficult to Hide It': The Presentation of Self on Internet Home Pages." *Qualitative Sociology* 23: 99–120.

Wellman, Barry and Milena Gulia. 1999. "Net-Surfers Don't Ride Alone: Virtual Communities as Communities." pp. 331–366 in *Networks in the Global Village: Life in Contemporary Communities*, edited by B. Wellman. Boulder, CO: Westview Press

Wynn, Eleanor and James E. Katz. 1997. "Hyperbole Over Cyberpsace: Self-Presentation and Social Boundaries in Internet Home Pages and Discourse." *The Information Society* 13: 297–327.

Yee, Nicholas 2001. "The Norrathian Scrolls: A Study of *EverQuest* (version 2.5)." Retrieved November 22, 2004 (*http://www.nickyee.com/eqt/home.html*).

Notes

1. Blending the action theories of human-computer interaction researchers such as Dourish (2001) and Suchman (1987) and the critical hermeneutics of technology of Ihde (1983; 1990) and Feenberg (1999), Vieta (2004) has worked through Schutz's theories with several related phenomenological and social interactional theories of embodiment and praxical worldly encounter (i.e., Husserl, Heidegger, Mead, Merleau-Ponty, Ihde). In this analysis, Vieta has suggested that such theories of "lived experience" can help us understand how users phenomenologically integrate Internet-mediated social interactions into their everyday lives. Taking a cue from American phenomenologists of technology Don Ihde (1983: 14) and Schutz (1970: 163-199), Vieta developed a working concept he called the "interactional self" to encapsulate how the related aspects of worldly encounter and lived experience of existential phenomenology and social interaction theory help us understand the intimate phenomenological connections between online realities and offline sociability. Further, the acts of apprehending the things of the world, anticipating a future, and experiencing others within the sedimented reality of everyday life characterize the interactional self, as with the self of symbolic interactionists, projecting onto others as others and things project upon it. The intersubjective theories of interaction of Schutz prove to be central in beginning to decipher how closely linked online sociability is to offline situations. Indeed, approaching the Internet-mediation from an interactional perspective, Castells emphasizes that the Internet is "an extension of life as it is, in all its dimensions, and with all its modalities" (p. 119). Miller & Arnold's ethnographic study of expressions of online identity echoes Castells' sentiments: "the things people do on the Web, and the selves presented there, should not be expected to be distinct and separated from actions and self in other areas of life" (Miller & Arnold). Schutz and the interactional self concept help us see that, despite all the hype surrounding gamer addictions and "time wasted" playing MMPORG games, Castells' and Miller & Arnold's views of the deep interconnections—

rather than the deep separations— between online and offline life might also apply to social interactions on *EverQuest*.

2. As Schutz explains: "Our bodily movements ... gear, so to speak, into the world, modifying or changing its objects and their mutual relationships. On the other hand, these objects offer resistance to our acts which we have either to overcome or to which we have to yield.... World, in this sense, is something that we have to modify by our actions or that modifies our actions" (p. 209).

3. This is akin to the *Canadian Oxford Dictionary*'s (1998) definition of work as a noun — "*n.* 1) the application of mental or physical effort to a *purpose*; the use of energy" — or as a transitive verb — "*v.* ... 9) *tr.* a) bring about; produce as a result" (1676). That is, as a noun, "work" for Schutz means an action or "a doing" that changes something for a greater purpose (e.g., "It took collaborative work to build that house"). As a transitive verb, work produces results (e.g., "They worked the fields in order to prepare for the harvest"). Notice how each of these definitions of "work" is future oriented; work, in these definitions is

directional in that it moves an action, desire, or project forward. It projects. As such, the working self is the part of the self that is "directed towards the objects and objectives to be brought about" (Schutz, 1970, p. 70) from the present into a world of future oriented and open-ended "anticipations" (p. 70). That is, the working self is always in the present, rooted to a past of recollections via the partial self, but already-always directed towards future goals.

4. To Schutz, then, work is action in the outer world, based upon a project and characterized by the intention to bring about the projected state of affairs by bodily movements. Among all the described forms of spontaneity that of working is the most important one for the constitution of the reality of the world of daily life ... the wide awake self integrates in its working an by its working its present, past and future into a specific dimension of time; it realizes itself as a totality in its working acts; it communicates with Others through working acts; it organizes the different spatial perspectives of the world of daily life through working acts (p. 212).

9. INVOKING THE AVATAR

Gaming Skills as Cultural and Out-of-Game Capital

Heather L. Mello

Few leisure activities are as engrossing and enriching as fantasy role-play gaming (FRPG), a unique game form where "fantasy, imagination, and reality intersect" (Waskul and Lust 2004:334). Role-playing games require of players a myriad of abilities, skills, knowledges and awarenesses. If these characteristics are learned during actual game play, gamers may be unaware of any benefits beyond fun. Such learning takes place outside of formal education but is very much an example of situated cognition, "thinking as tied to a body that has experiences in the world" (Gee 2003:8). When experiential learning takes place within a subculture that has its own values and norms, such learning may be translated into various forms of cultural, social and human capital, having application not only in the subculture, but outside as well.

Prior fantasy gaming research has focused on gaming's structural, cultural and procedural aspects–its limitations as well as its vibrancy. The seminal sociological FRPG study, by Gary Alan Fine (1983), focused on the subcultural viability of the gaming world, described how gamers develop meaning within the subculture, and explored play within the gaming context itself. Daniel Mackay (2001) related FRPG to impromptu performance art while exploring the social, cultural and aesthetic structures of the genre.

These researchers explore FRPG as a newly forming but increasingly salient leisure subculture with its own norms, values, styles and habits. These researchers however, do not concentrate on these subcultural characteristics as ends in themselves. Rather, these characteristics represent the singular formalization of the FRPG subculture.

Studying the "shared fantasy" of gaming, Fine's research (1983) spans many months of immersion in-subculture and is based in a combination of participant observation and interviews. Oddly enough, his book is prefaced with a justification. Speaking to academicians, Fine defensively balances his enjoyment of the research with its scientific merit. He then assures the hedonistic reader that, while sociologically significant, these games are indeed fun (1983:xi).

Like Fine, many gamers feel a need to defend their interest in gaming lifestyles. Misperceptions of gaming abound, including a simple belief that gamers spend so much time gaming because they don't have "real" lives. As gamers typically spend large amounts of time in-game, sometimes equaling an entire weekend each week, the questionability of the benefits of this lifestyle is an issue many gamers have become accustomed to, if not comfortable with.

James Gee recognized this question in studying the learning and literacy benefits of playing video games. He called this "the problem of content" (2003:20), wherein only academic or intellectual knowledge is considered important. Activity disconnected from such learning, entered into for simple entertainment, is meaningless. Gee's study incorporates an alternative perspective of learning, acknowledging that learning need not be located in any particular area of knowledge or be based on any particular form of literacy. He posits that learning takes place in any "semiotic domain," communicating different sets of meanings through traditional media as well as other modes of transmission — including even the roles people play in life (2003:17).

For Gee, this learning has especial application in negotiating a changing world that values computer-based technology and digital imagery, a world where randomly scattered signs carry significant meaning. Furthermore, cooperation in the diverse cultural and linguistic landscape requires more than traditional knowledge and modes of learning. This situated cognition, thinking while playing games, encourages students to "keep at it," through the games' intrinsic rewards. According to Gee, schools could take a lesson from video games, which might result not only in higher test scores, but also in deeper learning directly applied to life.

Applying Gee's concepts to FRPG is an easy task as many video games are based on FRPG. In FRPG, gamers play at fantastical avatars: characters or personas created within a structured, cooperatively imagined environment. Because these avatars are individually personified, FRPG offers imaginative freedom through which players take these characters in unforeseen directions, in which players' imaginations contribute to the game's shared fantasy. However, the enveloping structure, or social reality, keeps the avatars from ranging too far from the cooperative, social context in which they are personified and developed. The nature of learned skills reflects the social and imaginative structure of the FRPG format.

My first gaming experience introduced me to the world of *Dungeons and Dragons (D&D)*, which remains the archetypical fantasy role-playing game. During ninth grade study hall, a friend played game-master — the powerful, hidden overseer of fantastical quests — and initiated five classmates, including me, to finding treasure in an old castle's dank recesses. Immediately entranced, I saw two worlds before me. The first world was the bland, beige concrete dungeon of my Earth Science classroom, which receded from primary view. The emerging second world was an exciting, yet frightening series of dark chambers accessed with only the light from one hand-held torch. Equipped with a staff and a bag for my otherworldly stuff, I found myself, as Pickaxe the Halfling thief, quickly rifling through piles of skeletons to fill that bag with gold coins. When one of those skeletons stood up as I was picking its decaying pockets, my hair stood on end and adrenaline coursed through my very real, bi-worldly veins.

Having read Tolkien's *The Hobbit*, I had a general conception of Halflings as a fantasy race to which hobbits belong. From news and popular media, I pretty much assumed that rifling through the deads' pockets was compatible with thiefly acts in dungeons. This early into gaming, Pickaxe did not have much in the way of her own personality or experiences. For most gamers this is where gaming begins. There are sets of rules, fellow gamers and a game-master to guide play and announce outcomes of general play through the probabilities determined by varying sided dice.[1]

What starts out as a single game session may stretch on through years, becoming a grand campaign where players animate their characters through unpredictable yet largely formatted adventures. When I first played that Halfling thief, I had only her image in my mind, pieced together from books and other media and my internalized knowledge of such characters.[2] Once created, the avatar then grew primarily as a result of role-play: the more years lived, the deeper and more individuated the personality and game play; the more treasure found, the richer the character; the more monsters fought, the higher the character's experience (which is measured using an accumulating point system). These gaming experiences in the shared environment also drive growth for the gamer in-subculture and as a person.

FRPG constitutes a unique game format with far ranging opportunities for self-development within the gaming subculture (as gamers) as well as in a gamer's rest-of-life (as student, friend, worker, and so on). In the remainder of this chapter I explore the fantasy role-playing subculture at a gaming and science fiction convention and examine the contributions made to personhood by focusing on ideal player characteristics and the out-of-game use of the in-game-derived skills. The aforementioned contributions to personhood represent three basic forms, cultural, social and human capital.

Borrowing from Farkas (1996), the FRPG subculture may be understood as a Weberian status group having its own system of rewards and privileges, situated within and among other status groups, the widest being mainstream culture. In a particular status group, preferred "skills, habits, and styles," act as "mechanisms of cultural influence" (1996:12), which can be referred to as cultural capital. I propose that ideal player characteristics are those mechanisms of influence which help garner such subculturally valued rewards and privileges as gamer prestige and, since we are talking about a leisure subculture, maximization of fun.

Social capital, according to Coleman (1988), is a functional resource of relations between two or more persons and, in this study, includes social norms and skills, social networks, gaming lore and knowledge. Rather than being individually defined, social capital may facilitate action in achieving desired ends within the FRPG community and even in the wider culture. In-subculture, desired ends may consist of friendships and invitations to join gaming groups. Out-of-subculture, desired ends may include the ability to enter into a variety of rewarding social relations.

The last contribution to personhood is human capital, described by Coleman (1988) as individually acquired skills and knowledge. In Coleman's study of social capital and its contribution to human capital, this form of human capital is most easily understood as skills and knowledge derived from formal education. Remembering Gee's alternative perspective of learning, however, I extend the educational arena to the semiotic domain of gaming, in which the knowledge and skills gained have particular application, but are not necessarily confined.

In sum, this research is concerned with the sociocultural environment surrounding game-play as well as how framing and roles within gaming contexts enable growth for the persons who enter these realities. How do FRPG and the gaming environment, roles, role-play and interaction contribute to personhood outside of this environment? More specifically, how do normative understandings of ideal player characteristics facilitate the development of cultural capital (through game play) and social and human capital (in players' rest-of-lives)?

Methods

This research was conducted in fall 2004 over three days at Dragon*Con, a nationally recognized science fiction, fantasy and FRPG convention in Atlanta, Georgia that attracts over twenty thousand fans each year to all of its activities, of which gaming is but one. I volunteered at the gaming tables during the convention, inviting those who signed up to complete a questionnaire or to participate in an interview. Survey materials remained available while I was not working, but the majority were completed while I was working. In addition, I attended several forums aimed at initiating novice gamers. The primary sources of data are 74 open-ended questionnaires and eight open-ended qualitative interviews.

The questionnaires asked gamers demographically-based questions, gaming format preference, and self-reported social orientation (introvert to extrovert). The major focus of this study is on three specific questions: 1) What do you respect most in other gamers? 2) Have you ever used something learned in gaming outside of the gaming format? 3) Have you ever used a character aspect outside of the gaming format?

The interviews gave me a chance to gain a deeper understanding of gamers' answers to these survey questions. Interviews averaged one hour in duration and were recorded, with notes taken to ensure clarity and to allow for review of certain points or ideas. Afterwards, data were analyzed and compared with questionnaires for themes, trends or special examples in relation to these.

A total of 74 gamers completed the questionnaires. Male and female respondents account for 73% and 27% of total respondents respectively. Seven men and one woman agreed to be interviewed. All interviewees completed the surveys and their data are included in all table data. Gamers' ages ranged from 17 to 55 years, with an average age of 32. Respondents averaged 17 years of gaming experience, ranging from 1 to 30 years. Respondents had begun gaming as early as 7 years old and as late as 40. These are chronological figures, however, that do not consider the quantity and quality of play over these years.

Format preference relates to the two major forms of FRPG, table-top and live action. Table-top role-play gaming (RPG) refers to described and seated pantomimed action, whereas live-action role-play gaming (LARP) is more akin to theater, with costumes and dramatic physical role-play.[3] In both formats, gamers play at fantasy roles within an imagined environment, but the formats differ in their use of space, the amount and nature of bodily movement and use of props. In both, players gain skills within smaller idiocultural gaming circles, honing these skills and learning new modes of play as these circles intersect with the larger gaming society. Preferred gaming format was asked as a closed-ended question with the choices of RPG, LARP and both equally. Research materials were laid out where I worked at the RPG sign-up table, which would account for the 61 respondents claiming RPG as their preferred format. Another 13 preferred both formats equally. No respondent claimed LARP preference exclusively. Five interviewees preferred LARP and RPG games equally, while the three remaining preferred RPG games exclusively. There was no single LARP sign-up table, as participants went to the LARP system of their choice to sign up for proprietary games. I went around the LARP tables, asking attendees to complete surveys and place them in the box at the RPG table. Although the paper incorporates both RPG and LARP gamers in analysis, the lack of primary or exclusive LARP respondents limits the range of understanding of the subcultural ideals and contributions to personhood gained within the LARP format.

Discussion of Gaming Skills and Character Use

FRPG takes place within both idiocultural and larger subcultural contexts. These social contexts, not the rules of game play alone, drive gamer and avatar growth. I asked gamers what they respect most in other gamers as an open-ended question. The responses of sixty-three gamers fall into eight basic attributes (Table 1). In this section, I will connect responses to particular forms of cultural capital and the rewards and privileges that may be gained. Respondents also indicated social capital skill gains: social norms and skills, networks and knowledge facilitating action toward valued ends.

Table 1: What Do You Respect Most in Other Gamers?

Attribute	Number	Percent*
Role-playing	41	65.1%
Creativity	24	38.1%
Team Work	16	25.4%
Analytical Thinking	10	15.9%
Sense of Humor	10	15.9%
Rules Knowledge	7	11.1%
Flexibility/Adaptability	6	9.5%
Keep Outside Life Separate	6	9.5%

*N=63

The ability to role-play was the most respected skill reported. The next attribute, creativity, was connected to role-play as well. Creative role-play is the crux of FRPG. The general idea of FRPG is to play at being fictional, most times fantastical characters in the game setting. Whether LARP or RPG, new characters start out as frameworks of personality traits and skill sets. RPG systems primarily use player preference and dice or matrices to generate these personality traits and skill sets from lists of possible traits, races and occupations. LARP systems generally combine RPG character generation methods with player preference and playing group need. After generation, the player animates the character within the shared fantasy.

Respondents considering role-play as the skill they most respected indicated different foci. Simple role-play or acting ability was indicated with a desire to play with gamers more concerned with fun and character development than 'with stats.' Respondents desired to play with gamers who could "truly role-play a character, not just act," "get in and stay in character," "be the character," and play "in-depth characters." Other respected role-play skills aim against typecasting, including the ability "to play different characters over time," and "to play characters different from their [the gamer's] personality." Noting the ability to go beyond acting and to play against type as respected attributes, one interviewee reflected on RPG:

> ... I don't mean they spoke the part and acted, I mean, I have a friend and he got a grandmother, and he did the little old woman voice and he shook when he did the character ... and the guy who did the grandmother, he's the assistant D.A. in the city close to me [Cary, personal interview].

Getting into character, going beyond acting, infers the ability to convince other players that one "truly" is the character. Another interviewee differentiated immersive role-play between RPG and LARP settings.

> If you're playing a table-top game ... its mostly just speaking at that point. And the ability to make others forget sometimes that they actually aren't speaking to the person who is being played, the part being played. In a live-action game, its taken to the next level, because live-action players dress the part, act the part physically, speak the part as do table-top players but no where near to the degree ... in live-action gaming, immersing yourself into the character, while costume and props aren't necessarily required, it's taken to a whole new level [Warren, personal interview].

At gaming conventions and other pay-to-play RPG and LARP venues, this skill includes the ability to role-play unfamiliar characters on the spot.

... here's your character now play it. You didn't get to create one and
start from scratch, and build it, they handed you a character. It might
be the opposite gender, it might be a child and some of those people,
they can do voices, they can do the mannerisms, they just became the
character after just reading the description ... and I tried so hard to
emulate those people when I gamed. And, I think I was pretty good at
it after a while [Cary, personal interview].

Responses indicated that ideal role-play — as the ability to develop and
play at a character unlike the player's own personality creatively, convincingly and consistently — is a social norm within gaming aimed at developing characters beyond their initial framework. These responses point to
freer and deeper character development than acting is generally understood to be, wherein parts are enacted from scripts. Skilled role-play gains
prestige for the gamer, becomes a preferred style model, and makes gaming more fun because it is a positive sanction encouraging players to
develop their role-playing skills. One respondent described "the ability to
truly role-play. Nothing is more satisfying than to be in a game with someone who truly becomes their character." Here, role-play is a respected skill
contributing to the game's level of engrossment. Another respondent stated
that it was "so much fun to confront problems between characters."

Addressing group role-play tendencies, Mackay (2001) noted that first
person performance in-character by one player engendered first person
performances in response. It is much easier to imagine having audience
with the elf queen in her palace when she speaks to you in her high, lilt-
ing voice and not through the voice of the guy who usually brings the
nachos to the games each week. I asked interviewees how gamers acquired
these skills. While many recognized this as innate ability, most felt that it
certainly could be learned with environment as an important catalyst. I
first became aware of the extensive potential for character development at
conventions where attendees had characters that had "been alive" for many
years. I noticed substantively different game environments, where gamers
used in-character voices, body postures and gestures as opposed to mere
descriptions of avatar activity, which resulted in very high levels of engrossment.

At Dragon*Con, a panel of speakers in a gaming forum addressed
this very topic, noting maturation and exposure within the gaming environment as the crucial difference between role-play and roll-play, where
players roll dice and mechanically animate their characters according to
how the dice dictate action. Two interviewees reflected on mentoring and
environment as a "mechanism of influence" leading to the evolution of
ideal RPG role-play styles:

You might hear it referred to as high school gaming mentality. That's when a lot of young people get involved in gaming ... it's rolling the dice, beating up the bad guys through whatever mechanical means ... you break out of that mentality and evolve into real aspects of role-play, that is putting aspects behind characters, telling stories. Until you're exposed to that style you may not fall into that [Don, personal interview].

I recently started game-mastering a group of people absolutely new to role-playing ... it's interesting to watch how they role-play with each other. But then I bring in one or two of my friends who are really experienced role-players ... the reaction is fantastic. You can almost see their pupils widen. And they realize, "wow, you can really take this beyond where we've taken it," or "oh, that's how you do it" [Warren, personal interview].

Keeping outside life separate interrelates with the attributes of role-play, creativity, flexibility and adaptability. Discussion of this skill can be confusing as boundaries between "real world," game structure and fantasy world are at times porous. There are three general nodes of interaction that affect fair and fun game play: person to persona, player to persona, and player to player. The person-persona boundary insists that gamers pursue playing avatars as separate entities rather than as extensions of their own personalities or occupations. More specifically, character action and knowledge must adhere to character traits and history. A brainless, illiterate fighter should not be able to read an intricate map, no matter how often he opens it, though his animator may design complex computer programs. Being able to successfully separate these aspects keeps the game fair by preventing gain for one player at the expense of others, and keeps the gaming scenario "realistic."

The player-persona boundary becomes especially important for gamers immersed in the gaming subculture and social networks. Experienced gamers may be well versed in all forms of demons or bureaucrats encountered in-game, but should not gauge character action, preparation or response on that knowledge, called in-subculture "player knowledge." A form of social capital, player knowledge shared in gaming networks may be difficult to separate out from current campaigns.

> ... you have modules that run multiple times over the course of either a convention or its life ... and people are going to talk. Be it person to person or posts on internet bulletin boards or mail servers ... so word's going to get out about what is contained in a particular scenario. Even if it's not the ultimate resolution to the scenario, it could be as simple as, "wow, I couldn't believe we had to fight that vampire in this module." And all of a sudden you go, "wait a minute there's a vampire in here" [Warren, personal interview].

Some gamers avoid reading "spoilers" on internet bulletin boards, while others are infamous for seeking them out, especially for rewards in tournament play at cons for the most damage caused or experience points gained.

Among players, norms encourage keeping personal lives, problems and schedules from interfering with game play in order to increase engrossment and enjoyment for gamers. One respondent commented, "people may well work out problems through gaming, but I'd rather those situations not resemble therapy sessions."

Gaming researchers spend much time commenting on this inability to completely keep frames of reference separate. Fine (1983:187) comments on the constant interaction between the frameworks of person, player and character.[4] Waskul and Lust (2004) found that although players understand gaming as identity play, they inevitably add to their characters elements of their own personalities, personal or player knowledge. Rather than taking place solely within separated frames of reference, the participant occupies a "liminal role in the boundaries of the person, player and persona" (p. 333).

In bridging the apparent gap between ideal identity-play and less than perfect boundary maintenance, I infer that recognition of this difficulty drives respect for role-playing ability. Were it easy, other skills would likely garner primary gamer respect. In fact, despite calling the process of animating avatars within FRPG "role-playing," in the sociological sense this is, in actuality, "playing-at roles."[5]

Sociologically, gamers cannot role-play the characters they animate because they do not occupy their structurally-linked statuses, e.g. vampire, elf or spy. They can, however, play at being vampires, elves, and spies. Skillful gaming seems more a matter of *how* and *how well* one plays-at a character-styles and skills-not whether this is perfectly possible, especially since many of these characters have never been "real" statuses to occupy.

> How do you play an elf? How do they talk? I mean, you can see the Tolkien movies and stuff, but that's his version of an elf. What's your version of an elf? Well, what I would do, depending on the characters, I would find a television character that I thought might be kinda like that. Hawkeye Pierce of MASH, who has a carefree, very cavalier attitude except when it means business ... so I took that character for my favorite role-playing character that I started from scratch [Cary, personal interview].

Considering video games, Gee (2003:54) described an identity situated between the "real-world" player and the virtual persona. This "projective identity" is a projection of the player into the game and the player's project-in-the-making, a growing identity. Applied to FRPG and taking into account ideals of playing characters against type, the avatar exists because of the individual choices of the gamer *and* as a result of game mechanics and experience in the shared fantasy. In fact, the term avatar more aptly fits what are commonly called characters. An avatar is more than a scripted being, developing as part of and apart from the animator. The avatar may be understood as "a ready-made or customized form· of representation" of the gamer in-fantasy (Hillis 2003:73). In the interview extract above, Cary describes piecing parts of his elf character together, from a vision of an elf gained from strips of mythology and gaming media as well as from a television show character. The book and television strips set up the avatar, influencing the representation and reflecting the animator's preferences and experiences.

Teamwork includes comments that express gamers' respect for cooperation. FRPG is cooperative venturing where characters work together in pursuit of the mission or task. Players must also cooperate to ensure a satisfying and fun game for all involved. There are instances where this is not possible — within RPG and LARP certain character types or alignments (personality orientations), such as rogues or evil priests, have their own goals that might run counter to the group's goals. In LARP, teamwork may reflect cooperation within groups fighting on the same side. LARP games may be quite large. It is not uncommon to have dozens of players "LARPing" over a weekend, with their campaigns taking place at campgrounds or even historical sites that add to the LARP mood. As a social skill, the ability to work cooperatively may be understood as a preferred gaming style in facilitating fun, engrossment and achievement of campaign goals.

Analytical thinking includes respect for "problem solving" ability and "thinking outside of the box." The ability to analyze and solve problems in the game is a skill that may be helped by "real world" experience, but may have little application to the FRPG world. This skill, combined with player creativity, may make for more interesting and far-ranging adventures.

Within the shared fantasy, a sense of humor may apply to how a character is role-played as well as whether the character has a sense of humor. Having a sense of humor also includes any comments referring to "entertaining." Bumbling thieves or drunken bards entertain and keep game play light as well as show the animator's lighter side in not playing at their characters too seriously. We may look back to the teamwork attribute however, if such entertaining character facets serve to endanger the group. In the game structure, a sense of humor makes the social aspect of gaming more rewarding. Comments indicating the game application include "just being with good friends," "fun," and even "mature whimsy."

Listing rules knowledge as an attribute recognizes the complex and freeform nature of FRPG. Despite having handbooks explaining basic system rules, the game-master or group will modify many rules as they see fit. This attribute becomes even more important considering continuous publication of supplemental handbooks, books depicting alternate worlds and histories, and popular gaming-related media. Knowing the rules of game play encompasses basic system rules and requires understanding of the specific rules for a particular campaign. Players who skillfully use and adapt to system rules may gain prestige as well as facilitate gaming action, and this knowledge is a resource in social networks.

Flexibility and adaptability attributes apply to the game structure as game systems differ from one another and rules and styles of play differ across gaming groups and settings. Game-masters have different rules and styles, even when playing the same prefabricated module. Also, a campaign may change abruptly, through diversions from a primary goal, e.g., treasure, saving a wealthy regent's daughter, or running smuggled goods across a border. These diversions are part of the game, not separate from it.

This attribute may also apply to players that can adapt to new characters being played or to playing with new groups. Several respondents desired to play with gamers who could play characters as they were "rolled up," as the dice statistics determined rather than manipulated to create better attributes, flawed avatars who were likely to get killed. Many characters die in-game, especially during long campaigns or in games such as *Call of Cthulhu*, where encounters with monsters render characters increasingly insane. In such worlds, the odds of being killed by a team member may equal the odds of being killed by monsters or demons.

In some cases, players have animated the same characters over years and may grow quite attached. Flexibility and a sense of humor become more important. This attribute may be connected to adaptability of game rules, analytical modes of game play and with characters as mentioned above. Andrew compared his military experience with the necessity of flexibility in the "role-play world":

> In the role-playing sense it's less physically traumatic when your character dies, but no less emotionally painful for a lot of people. And we both in that sense have a very high self-preservation streak. But, it's really surprising how one works off the other. You have to be a mental gymnast to succeed at both counts because if you're flipping back and forth between hard rules that say, "here are the boundaries you operate under." If the dice does not equal X you fail. That's a hard rule, there's no, "maybe it's a seven, or kinda, sorta." Binary. But then you have relatives. Okay, there's a description of the village, what does that village look like? You get some aids, but they're flat, some markings on

a paper ... you have to bring that flatness up to a three-dimensional model through your head [Andrew, personal interview].[6]

Skills and Knowledge Gained in Gaming Used Outside the Game

Survey and interview respondents were asked whether they had used something that they learned from gaming outside of gaming. The responses of fifty-eight gamers fell into twelve general skill attributes (Table 2). As in the above section, responses are connected to particular forms of cultural, social and human capital, with each indicated as it applies in- and out-of-subculture. For much of this section, however, I focus on respondents' indications of how they used these skills themselves.

Table 2: Has There Ever Been an Occasion Where You Used Something That You Learned from Gaming Outside of the Gaming Format?

Attribute	Number	Percent*
Vocabulary/Trivia	27	46.6%
Social Skills	24	41.4%
Mythology	17	29.3%
History	14	24.1%
College Study/Research Skills	13	22.4%
Critical Thinking	13	22.4%
Empathy	12	20.7%
Writing/Reading	12	20.7%
Probability/Statistics/Math	10	17.2%
Leadership	9	15.5%
Acting/Public Speaking	8	13.8%
Martial Arts/Weaponry	8	13.8%
	*N=58	

The majority of responses fell into several general and specific areas of knowledge gained in-game, listed in the table as vocabulary/trivia, mythology, history, and martial arts/weaponry knowledge. Most game systems have extensive handbooks steeped in mythological, historical and military lore. Some FRPG sourcebooks are a hodge-podge of facts taken from various time periods, civilizations and cultures all over the world while others focus on one period, recent military operation or social life aspect, but most are well researched. Gamers tend to be an educated lot and have no compunction about writing to authors to correct "errors." One respondent noted that games gave him "all sorts of Jeopardy answers."

Another revealed that facts were handy for "impressing women at parties"—a particularly coveted social capital application.

Respondents reported gains in weaponry knowledge, primarily aspects of swordplay or martial arts, lore surrounding swordplay and martial arts history. A few responses indicated knowing how to use swords or martial arts as well. One woman wrote, "I knew what each weapon was when I went to the Metropolitan Museum of Art in NYC, along with the armor." I probed this question in one interview with a young man reporting gains in weapons and martial arts knowledge. He recognized that, despite having no specific training as a fighter, he might be better prepared in case of a "real life" attack, reflecting as well on the differences between RPG and LARP styles.

> It's only a sort of tertiary kind of knowledge. If you squared off with any gamer who had a weapon on them, then you put yourself in a combat environment and you start going into rounds ... and you consider every three seconds what's going to happen ... so that when I walk down the street, I think to myself, "hmmm, what weapons do I have on me, what's my first attack if I get mugged out of a corner." In a table-top environment, you have all the time in the world to consider what you're going to do for the next three seconds ... your adrenaline is not running. In a LARP environment ... you've got just as much time to think about what you're going to do as the time that it's happening, it's real time. And if you stand there dumbfounded trying to think, "uh, what are my skills, uh, what can I do, oh crap I'm dead" [Jake, personal interview].

Some listed knowledge application skills, including college study, research and writing/reading skills. Many respondents reported using specific gaming-derived knowledge — mythology, history or character aspects in papers, class discussions or on tests in various subjects. Many reported developing their research skills while reading gaming handbooks, creating more in-depth characters or preparing for game-mastering modules. One woman reported, "after researching a historical period for a character background, I ended up using some of the information later for an essay in a class." Other respondents reported gaming as creative writing fodder and experience in the actual writing process. Handbook familiarization and character research helped a few improve reading skills.

Another knowledge application skill, critical thinking, includes problem-solving skill responses. Most FRPG involves adventures with unsolved mysteries, dangerous traps and protracted battles taking place in other worlds, times or dimensions, requiring the ability to think outside the real-world box. I relate this to the respect skill of analytical thinking. From my own gaming experience, I find it is preferable to encounter the occasional puzzle too hard to solve rather than to engage in endless dungeon door-opening in search of treasure.

Math skill improvement was an unexpected finding. Many RPG systems use dice-generated matrices or probabilities to obtain elements of randomness in determining character attributes, actions, and battle outcomes. Ranging from six- to twenty-sided, each die-type has a particular application; weapon ranges, magic spell or weapon hit success, or levels of character attributes like charisma, beauty or intelligence. Respondents reported improved statistical or probability skills, which "applied in more day to day stuff," or "in other situations involving variables and chance, I can figure the odds better by thinking of it in terms of dice systems." More interesting, one respondent stated, "understanding of dice mechanics allowed me to get a job as a statistician," a human capital skill that literally paid off.

Social skills include more specific comments indicating growth towards extroversion. For one respondent, gaming, "helped me be a bit more outgoing." For another, gaming "increases creativity in general socialization skills." This gain in social skills relates to a survey question about social orientation. Nineteen percent of survey respondents reported social introversion and another fifty-three percent reported being in-between introversion and extroversion. Respondents felt the ability to mediate a social situation was learned over time through role-playing. According to one respondent, "I am normally an introverted person. To game at a Con, you have to be extroverted. I can drop into persona quickly, using voices and mannerisms from past characters." Another claimed gaming helped her "get over a fear of interacting with strangers." Andrew explained that the fantasy environment makes social interaction safer, but still productive, which James Gee (2003:67) called a psychosocial moratorium:[7]

> The gaming world gives you a very safe outlet. Frankly what's the worst that happens, you screw something up, you miss a dice roll and somebody zaps you, go build another character. Heartbreaking, but not that traumatic ... and over time you do gain experience, because whether you like it or not you're still dealing with another human being sitting across the table [Andrew, personal interview].

Empathy attributes include diplomacy, negotiation skills and "taking the role of the other person" responses. This ability to put oneself in another's shoes, to understand how they think and to anticipate how they will act, might actually fit a definition of gaming itself, with fantasy roles replacing real roles. Both RPG and LARP are really nothing more than playing at the roles of imagined or historical characters, albeit ones that animators have a hand in creating. Indeed, according to classical symbolic interaction theorist George Herbert Mead (1934:23), the ability to take the role of the other is gained as children develop from imitation, to play, to game stages.

Skillful gaming is more than simply knowing what the avatar is doing, but anticipating and understanding roles of other players and avatars, putting the situation in perspective. Players may respect successful boundary maintenance; however, building empathy requires some porous boundaries. Empathy skills involve at least five general nodes of interaction that enhance game play and influence cultural and social capital applications: person to persona, player to persona, persona to persona, player to player, and person to person, although it is unclear where in gaming they felt they had learned this skill.

The person to persona empathy loop involves Gee's projective identity, wherein a person's active care and involvement in avatar growth expands critical learning which in turn grows the person. From player to persona, empathy and rules knowledge require active, critical learning and reflection on the avatar within the game structure. Persona to persona empathy, the respected standard, occurs as characters anticipate how other characters act and respond. In-game, players must anticipate other players' actions and responses. Despite sanction toward playing characters as themselves, not all gamers succeed equally. Knowing how much of the player is involved in the character makes empathy more like boundary gymnastics, critical thinking about who is acting where and when. Among persons, gamers spend long periods, hours or even days, at a time at play. Introverted persons may learn to cooperate or come out of their shells in pursuit of amiable, fun gaming. Extroverted gamers may tone things down in order to create a cohesive, satisfying gaming experience.

Blair reflects on person to persona, player to persona and person to person empathy:

> You can kind of see other points of view a little bit better. You're used to saying, "well if this were me, I would do X action, but my character is going to do Y action," and I understand the reasoning behind that. So when someone in a situation in real life takes an action that's not what I would do, I can still see the reasoning and understand why they might have done that ... being able to see it gives me more sympathy for that than I would have had otherwise ... while I still think, "what an idiot, I can't believe he did that," I won't say that out loud as much as I used to 'cause I will stop myself and say "yeah, but, that's why" [Blair, personal interview].

The last attributes relate to certain social and human capital skills. Leadership attributes include decision-making, planning and quick thinking skill responses. The abilities to plan attacks, coordinate and make decisions, and do these things quickly make for more interesting and success-ful campaigns. Acting/public speaking skills are directly related to role-playing skills. FRPG, especially with more experienced players and char-acters, involves skills that public institutions teach. Police forces and emer-gency response agencies also use role-play training to develop these skills. One respondent stated, "It occurred to me that on average, my game char-acters were better prepared for emergencies/the unexpected than I was in real life — they carried bags of supplies 'just in case,' whereas I didn't even have jumper cables in my car. I've tried to be more proactive and 'forward thinking' in real-life." Another respondent, in-between extrovert and intro-vert, noted, "the ability to bullshit on the fly is useful in the business world." An introverted respondent indicated that game-mastering specifically aids these skills: "I believe that I've become a better public speaker from my expe-rience of being a convention GM. It is an environment where I am the cen-ter of attention of a group of strangers and I must be able to communicate effectively with them."

Using Characters Developed In-Game Outside the Game

I asked respondents whether they had used an aspect of a gaming char-acter outside of the gaming format, which was listed by fifty-two respondents, including every interviewee. This was asked as an open-ended question and some general trends emerged that relate to cultural, social and human cap-ital applications, again noted primarily by respondents themselves.

Most reported using characters, gaming stories or anecdotes inside the gaming subculture exclusively and rarely around non-gamers who "would not get it." Lana laughingly talked about sharing gaming stories with her mother, who reminded her, "that it's just a game, just make believe." The shift from real-world to game-world among likeminded friends can be instan-taneous, creating a mood, taking them fantastical places and times in conversations traveling between first and third person, from player anecdotes to stories told in-character. Andrew indicated that his ex-wife thought "I was delusional because she couldn't keep track of which world I was talking about." Some characters become famous within the subculture for their exploits, gaffes or turns of phrase. These aspects constitute forms of social and cultural capital, stories that can last hours. Jake noted the convention's imaginative camaraderie, recognizing the fantasy worlds gamers enter:

> A gamer sitting at a table surrounded by nachos, pizza and sodas, you don't last any more than thirty minutes in that environment unless you're getting into what's happening. Otherwise, people that are hanging out

near a bunch of gamers that aren't playing the game, I walked through the gaming room and I saw familiar environment after familiar environment and I could only imagine where they were. And if you hang around long enough then you have to become involved in that. Or else you know, you say, "well, this seems sorta stupid, a bunch of people sitting around a table, just talking nonsense" [Jake, personal interview].

Twelve respondents reported using character aspects or a gaming frame of mind in social interaction. Responses reflected use outside of the gaming subculture, to meet people or to facilitate conversation, as like "slipping into characters in social settings." An experienced gamer stated that she "used to be shy and reluctant to approach strangers when traveling. When I tried seeing the situation as a (gaming) encounter, I could often negotiate the situation with more ease and confidence. This has eventually internalized itself so that I can now handle these situations with confidence." Several respondents admitted to using characters to meet the opposite sex, one commenting that she used a Vampire LARP character's "uninhibited personality on the dating scene."

There were a few unusual but interesting uses noted by fourteen respondents that have social and human capital application. These anecdotes included a substitute teacher who used character humor to get her students' attention, parents who used character and gaming stories to tell bedtime stories or to give "examples of moral thought," and one respondent who used "aspects of formal characters in job interviews." Stan reported therapist encouragement of gaming to overcome marital difficulties, involving person to persona empathy:

We started out just enjoying ourselves and over time realized that we were hitting on some things in our relationship through the lens of the game. And coming to an understanding of each other better as a result. For example, she's a very black and white kind of person ... and I'm a feeling personality, I'm a squishy guy. We were able to basically have situations happen in the game where things weren't black or white, there was a shade of grey there that she had to deal with. On the other hand, I also acknowledged in-game that people who are squishy don't always make good boundaries and therefore that was bad too. It was a way for us to talk about things in the relationship ... it was for fun first, but then our therapist said, "I don't know what you guys are doing, but just keep it up" [Stan, personal interview].

Conclusion

This research departed from its original intent-understanding how players used in-game-derived characters in out-of-game contexts-to explore the norms and outcomes of the many hours spent engaged in the

FRPG subculture, in the fantasy, game and social frames surrounding game play. The nature of the games, their heart, is the fun that comes of playing with identities in shared adventures-controlled yet imaginative environments. Rather than finding players engaged in a time-wasting curiosity, this sample of FRPG convention participants reported gaming membership and activity as positive contributions to their rest-of-lives.

I have connected the development of cultural capital to the development of social and human capital. Respondents expressed respect for creative role-play among many skills and habits which contribute to in-game enjoyment-skills and styles which may be learned through modeling and mentoring in the game environment. In turn, these gamers found that the development of these experientially learned skills and forms of knowledge in-game engenders social and interpersonal growth as they use them in the subculture as well as out in the "real world." Although this study is limited to a small, convenient sample of FRPG convention participants, it contributes to our understanding of the links between situated cognition in any semiotic domain and contributions to wider personhood.

Acknowledgments

I would like very much to thank Patrick Williams for his time, patience, and guidance, without which this chapter would still be an idea left over from a phone call.

References

Coleman, James S. 1988. "Social Capital in the Creation of Human Capital." *American Journal of Sociology* 94: 95–120.

Coutu, Walter. 1951. "Role-Playing vs. Role-Taking: An Appeal for Clarification." *American Sociological Review* 16: 180–187.

Farkas, George. 1996. *Human Capital or Cultural Capital?* New York: Aldine de Gruyter.

Fine, Gary Alan. 1983. *Shared Fantasy: Role-Playing Games as Social Worlds*. Chicago: University of Chicago Press.

Gee, James Paul. 2003. *What Video Games Have to Teach Us about Learning and Literacy*. New York, NY: Palgrave MacMillan.

Hillis, Ken. 2003. "From Description to Depiction: Free Indirect Discourse and Online Graphical Chat." *Culture, Theory and Critique* 44: 73–89.

Mackay, Daniel. 2001. *The Fantasy Role-Playing Game: A New Performing Art*. Jefferson, NC: McFarland.

Mead, George Herbert. 1934. *Mind, Self, and Society*. Edited by C. Morris. Chicago: University of Chicago Press.

Turkle, Sherry. 1995. *Life on the Screen: Identity in the Age of the Internet*. New York: Simon and Schuster.

Waskul, Dennis, and Lust, Matt. 2004. "Role-Playing and Playing Roles: The Person, Player, and Persona in Fantasy Role-Playing." *Symbolic Interaction* 27:333–356.

Notes

1. Daniel Mackay (2001:4-5) gives a broad yet concise definition of FRPG: "I define the role-playing game as an episodic and participatory story-creation system that includes a set of quantified rules that assist a group of players and a game-master in determining how their fictional characters' spontaneous interactions are resolved. These performed interactions between the players' and game-master's characters take place during the individual sessions that, together, form episodes or adventures in the lives of the fictional characters. A role-playing game varies in durations. It could be anything from a couple hours in length to an all-night gaming marathon. The complexity of the episode or adventure also fluctuates depending on the game, intricacy of the adventure concept, and the temperament or dynamics of the role-playing group. An episode might be contained within the few hours of a single session, or it might be composed of a half dozen or more sessions that take place over weeks or months. Some role-playing groups continue to meet after the conclusion of a single episode, playing the same characters in ongoing role-playing adventures. In this case, the episodes become part of a single grand story that I call the role-playing game narrative. The role-playing game narrative, sometimes called the "campaign" or "chronicle," may barely outlive a single episode, or it may continue to unfold over the course of many years."

2. Mackay (2001) recognized that much borrowing from popular culture for character fodder goes on. This borrowing from the "cultural sphere" stocks the player's repertoire with character types, quotable lines and scenes, "fictive blocks" of information pieced together to form "strips of imaginary behavior." According to Mackay, the larger a player's imaginary store and the more creatively and skillfully combined, the better and more artful the player.

3. Daniel Mackay (2001:182) differentiates between the two forms, "... the table-top role-playing game (FRP) was the first kind of role-playing game. It is distinguished by players performing their characters in a social, face-to-face setting, yet refraining from acting-out their characters' actions to the extent of wearing costumes or walking and moving through space as the character does. The live-action role-playing game (LARP) is distinguished by the players' bodily movement through space and their assumption of costumes and other tools or techniques of naturalistic theater."

4. In borrowing the "constructs of awareness" from Glaser and Strauss's, Fine (1983:187) labels the frames awareness between levels of reality as "open," "closed" and "pretense" awarenesses. In open awareness, persons are aware of others' identities and their own identities as seen by others. In closed awareness, persons are not aware of others' identities, nor are they aware of their own identity as seen by others. Somewhere in between is pretense awareness, where individuals are aware of others' identities, but pretend that they are not. Fine points out that although characters should have closed awareness of their animating players, in fact, this inability to completely limit information flow from personhood and player knowledge acts more like pretense awareness. Other players and the game-master normatively act as monitors of this flow in the social and structural environment. Sanctioning in interest of or redress of believability of character actions serves to discourage open awareness and at least keep pretense awareness intact.

Fine (1983:69) repeatedly notes that although common understanding of gaming is toward playing characters as themselves, the game environment, age and sex of players and preferences of game-master and other players all have a hand in character action. For example, game settings in which any of the players are women usually results in less violent sexual activity among characters and toward nonplayer characters. It is interesting to note that although this is sometimes considered a limitation of game play range for some male gamers in the addressing chapter, it is not considered in the chapter noting frames of awareness. Despite efforts toward pretense awareness, it probably seems insensitive for players to inquire as to why Marghul did not rape the wives remaining at the enemy village as he invariably would if his campaign ally Chrashatt is animated by a woman.

5. In the endnotes to chapter seven, "Role-Playing and Self-Playing," Fine (1983) invites readers to consult a Walter Coutu paper written in 1951 to better understand the intricacies of role interaction. In this note, Fine differentiates between role-taking, "the ability to place oneself in the position of another," and role-playing, "acting as another (real or hypothetical) might" (p. 264). After reading the Coutu paper, I find that Fine himself does not make clear two distinctions that Coutu makes that would better explain some of the frame awareness difficulties that Fine notes. Coutu notes that the term "playing-at" a role involves two processes: (1) role-taking on an elementary level and (2) playing-at, or pretending to play, some well known role. While

under certain conditions adults engage in the latter practice, the sociological term refers almost exclusively to the activity in which a child pretends s/he is, say, a milkman and in which s/he thinks, talks and performs like one. The child can not play this role, since s/he cannot occupy the appropriate position, but s/he can play at it, thus learning both role-taking and role-playing. "Playing-at" thus involves both the "playing" and "taking" concepts in make-believe, playful and fictitious or fantasy form (181).

6. Gary Alan Fine (1983:91-102) devotes an entire twelve pages to dice rolls—cheating with dice, player perception of power over dice rolls, and gamer and game-master negotiation over dice rolls. Although the interviewee uses dice rolls as an example of a hard rule, in actuality, rules regarding dice rolls are more flexible than the rulebooks indicate. This is another demonstration of flexibility within gaming as the hardness of dice rules depends on idiocultural context, game-master preference and gamer interaction. This research took place at a gaming convention, however where dice rules tend to be more uniform. Also, the tendency for gamers and game-masters to negotiate over how to use a dice roll or to permit subsequent, "luckier" dice rolls still does not change the "binary" (to use the interviewee's words) nature of reading a roll correctly.

7. Following Sherry Turkle's (1995:203) work with Erik Erikson's concept of "psychosocial moratorium," Gee (2003:67) writes about how "learners can take risks in a space where real-world consequences are lowered."

10. VICARIOUS EXPERIENCE

Staying There Connected With and Through Our Own and Other Characters

Tim Marsh

Irrespective of technology (e.g. mobile, console, desktop, projected, head-mounted, or others), the display is the window into the illusion of fantasy or the simulated three-dimensional digital gaming environment. Digital games provide opportunities for player activities in scenarios with artifacts and other players. The environments' real-time responses to players' actions induce feelings of acting vicariously[1]— imaginatively experiencing something through another person, being, object or character — within a mediated environment. While much interaction in digital games is performed with and through character, there are limitations in theories and methodologies for their analysis and design from the subject area of human-computer interaction (HCI) and the experiential concept of presence, commonly referred to as a sense of "being there."

In an effort to bridge this gap, my research looks to other study areas, in particular, activity theory, social-cultural studies and film, and is working towards the development of ways to reason about player's sense of connection to characters in interactive mediated environments (IMEs, e.g., virtual reality, virtual environments, digital games). In response to the inadequacy of the concept of presence and limitations of work in HCI, I have developed a framework of experience — i.e. three V's: voyeuristic, visceral, vicarious (Marsh 2001, 2002, 2003a) — informed from filmmaking (Boorstin 1995) that provides a way to reason about experience that is either induced in, evoked in, or witnessed by participants of interactive mediated environments. Recently, key publications in HCI have adapted Boorstin's (1995) three V's framework to inform experiential analysis and design of products and technological devices (e.g., Norman 2004; McCarthy and Wright 2004). However, because of the similarities between the developments of IMEs and film (Marsh 2003a), my work holds closer to Boorstin's (1995) analysis from a filmmaking perspective. Specifically, for the purpose of this chapter, the prevalence of character(s) (e.g., virtual, synthetic, avatar) within IMEs means we can utilize Boorstin's (1995) analysis of character through "vicarious experience." Adapting his analysis to interactive mediated environments, I argue that studying player's vicarious experience enables us:

i.   a way to reason about the connection between player's own and other characters.
ii. a way to reason about a player's sense of connection to a fantasy (or other) social and cultural structure through constraints in behavior.
iii. a way to reason about player engagement (referred to as being "vicariously there") as an alternative to the concept of presence.

As illustrated in Figure 1, vicarious experience from encounters with three-dimensional digital gaming or mediated environments is derived from undertaking various pursuits and is identified as falling into three main categories. First, those that come from navigation and exploration (e.g., transfer of spatial knowledge) and second, from the manipulation of artifacts (mediated, simulated or fantasy). These two categories are identified as primary or fundamental vicarious experiences that can occur with or without the involvement of characters. Further, they share similarities with the concept of "telepresence," the sense of acting vicariously in a remote or hazardous location, such as in outer space or on a deep sea dive. The focus of this chapter, however, is on the third category, vicarious experience through character. With increasing technological and artistic innovations, vicarious experience has become more complex through empathy with character. Vicarious experience has long been associated with other media, such as literature, theatre, television and cinema, through interpretation of and identifying and empathizing with characters such as the protagonist. However, digital games provide players with the unique opportunity to assume the role of anybody or anything they wish, and to interact in scenarios (through either a first or third person perspective) within mediated, simulated, fantasy environments and with other characters in a non-linear narrative manner. Players in digital games can not only identify and empathize with characters through spectatorship as in theatre, television and cinema, but they are also able to identify, empathize and interact with their own and other characters. Hence, vicarious experience can be conceptualized as a link, connection or mediator between a player and gaming environment.

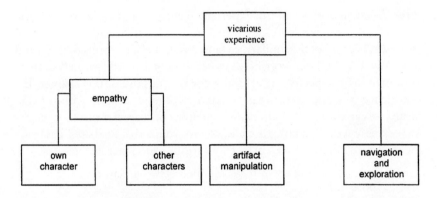

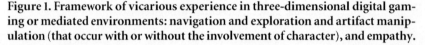

Figure 1. Framework of vicarious experience in three-dimensional digital gaming or mediated environments: navigation and exploration and artifact manipulation (that occur with or without the involvement of character), and empathy.

I identify three kinds of vicarious and empathic experience through character. First, I argue that the greater a player perceives him/herself to be vicariously in character acting in a digital game, the stronger the sense of belonging or connection between player and the gaming environment. Second, other characters' behaviors (actions, gestures, facial and vocal expressions) tell us something about their emotions. The more players recognize and attribute these emotions, the more they have a sense of being connected (vicariously or empathically) with other characters. Third, how other characters respond to a player's character not only acknowledges their existence, but also tells us something about a player's character's emotions and disposition and may reflect the empathy they have for the player's character.

The term "corpsing" or "to corpse," derived from a British acting term to denote falling out of character, has been aptly used to describe this shift in focus of attention (Marsh 2001, 2003b). While much research on experiential interaction with IMEs has been carried out, this has largely focused on a player's sense of connection through the concept of presence — commonly described as a sense of "being there" in a three-dimensional mediated environment. Previously, I have argued that stimulating experience encourages players in "staying there," or continuing to pursue activities in a gaming environment (Marsh 2003a, 2003b). Staying there is a shift away from considering encounters with IMEs as "instant by instant" or "being there" experiences and is a similar concept to those used to hold spectators' attention in film and theatre, concepts which have attracted interest in informing user-interface design. These concepts include, for example, Laurel's (1986; 1993) ideas of engagement, direct agency and mimetic illusion, borrowed from theatre, and ideas borrowed from filmmaking to inform the design of virtual environments (e.g. Laurel, Strickland, and Tow 1994; Marsh and Wright 2000; Pausch et al. 1998). Likewise, stimulating *vicarious* experience encourages players in "staying there." Here I introduce a new term to describe this sense of player engagement as "vicariously there." Unstimulating vicarious experience will not hold players' attention, shifting their focus from the gaming to the real world environment.

In addition, the sense of connection between a player and a character can tell us something about the connection or feeling of belonging that a player has to the virtually-depicted social or cultural environment. However, there is some difficulty in attempting to reason about player-character behavior in a virtually depicted social and cultural structure because digital games can be fantasy or artificial worlds: unlike the real world, digital worlds can be "individualistic" (solitary, single player) and "ahistorical" (having no past) (Engeström 1999:23). Attempting to consider cultural structures shaped by successive generations and successive successful adaptations (that in turn affect activities) in these environments can be problematic. While attempts to overcome these issues and to formulate a methodology to accurately analyze the social and cultural context of digital gaming environments is a complex endeavor, requiring a sustained research effort, an alternative approach is to consider the idea of *constraints* in artifact behavior[2] and player-character behavior. Poortinga (1992) argues that culture is "manifest in shared constraints that limit the behavior repertoire available to members of a certain social and cultural group, in a way different from individuals belonging to some other group" (p. 10). To varying degrees, people tend to restrict their behavior to what is considered appropriate and acceptable depending on which group they participate in. Likewise, players participating in a scenario within a digital gaming environment are likely to adhere to certain social and cultural norms. Players-characters perform, conform, react and respond appropriately within the constraints governed by the situational and episodic events of a scenario. Whether an environment is "individualistic" or highly populated, historical or "ahistorical," appropriate behavior can be judged by the way players-characters act and respond within constraints imposed by a social-cultural structure and the appropriateness of their behavior can be captured and reasoned about through vicarious experience.

From "Being There" to "Vicariously There"

The concept of presence has its roots in "telepresence" (see: Sheridan 1992; Steuer 1995). Telepresence occurs when a user or tele-operator's interactions with, for example, a hand-controlled device (e.g. joystick, glove), are mirrored by a robot or mechanical arm within a mediated environment and viewed on a display screen. As a consequence, users describe a sense of being connected, vicariously acting, navigating/exploring or manipulating artifacts within a remote environment, as illustrated in Figure 1. The adoption of concepts from telepresence in computer-mediated communication provides a convenient way to describe the effects experienced by users interacting within mediated environments. To distinguish telepresence from the more specialized experience of "being there" in an IME, the shortened version, presence, has been adopted.

Many researchers from the presence community see presence as a primary driver for design and analysis of IMEs, and consequently this concept has prompted much research in an attempt to elucidate the underlying determinants of presence and find measures for its assessment. Researchers in the presence community generally argue that a sense of presence occurs in several ways, some of them interrelated: *social, physical and real* (e.g. Lombard and Ditton 1997). Let us consider realism or fidelity of stimuli first. While some argue that fidelity of stimuli (e.g., visual, aural, tactile and force-feedback, etc.) is not necessarily linked to a sense of presence (e.g. Whitelock, Brna and Holland 1996; Brna 1999), a prevailing argument is that increasing the fidelity of stimuli will lead to a sense of presence. If it were possible to replicate/simulate the world in every conceivable detail, the situation might provide users with the ultimate sense of being *physically* situated or present somewhere indistinguishable from the real world. Perhaps this is the closest that we can get to Licklider's (1960) visionary idea of a "man-computer symbiosis." A similar notion is Nozick's (1974) idea of plugging humans directly into an "experience machine," providing a more literal meaning to the term "plug and play":

> Suppose there were an experience machine that would give you any experience you desired. Superduper neuropsychologists could stimulate your brain so that you would think and feel that you were writing a great novel, or making a friend, or reading an interesting book. All the time you would be floating in a tank, with electrodes attached to your brain. Should you plug into this machine for life, preprogramming your life's experiences? If you are worried about missing out on desirable experiences, we can suppose that business enterprises have researched thoroughly the lives of many others. You can pick and choose from their large library or smorgasbord of such experiences, selecting your life's experiences for, say, the next two years. After two years have passed, you will have ten minutes or ten hours out of the tank, to select the experiences of your next two years. Of course, while in the tank you won't know that you're there; you'll think it's all actually happening ... Would you plug in? [Nozick 1974:42-44].

Practical difficulties aside, even if we could replicate/simulate the real world in every detail, would we ever really believe that we were actually there? Apart from a situation in which we were unknowingly taken and placed in an IME (or plugged in), or arguments that assert we may already be there (Bostrom 2003), we would remain aware that we were interacting in an IME because we could remember going from the real to the virtual world. This prompts the question: Does it matter if users don't know whether or not they are in a mediated world?

Phillips (2000) raises similar points in analysis of the film *The Matrix* (Wachowski and Wachowski 1999), in which people are "living" in an illusion that is indistinguishable from the real world of the year 1999. In considering the potential for recreating such a virtual world he suggests that, "if we were not able consciously to locate the virtual experience as being different [from our sense of the real], we would not be able to take pleasure in it as an event" (p. 143). A similar analysis can be applied to *Matrix Reloaded* (Wachowski and Wachowski 2003) and *Matrix Revolutions* (Wachowski and Wachowski 2003). Laurel (1993) elegantly elucidates a similar argument through the description of a child experiencing a simulation ride, "a wild ride combining flight simulator technology with Star Wars content." Pausing momentarily during the simulation, the child shouts, "if this was real, I'd be scared!" (p. 120).

It is precisely the unreal that allows subjects with phobia-related disorders to confront their fears in IMEs developed for therapeutic purposes. It is difficult to imagine them agreeing to spend much time in, or even enter an environment indistinguishable from the real world, where their fear exists. Similarly, it is the unreal that allows trainee pilots to practice takeoffs and landings and games players to fly fighter jets or race formula-one cars. If they had to be as highly trained as a jet fighter pilot or as talented as a racing car driver, games would not be enjoyable or worse, they would be unplayable. People take comfort from knowing that a mediated environment is mediated and that it is an environment in which they can act out situations, confront fears, make mistakes and experience things that would not be possible in the real world without causing untold fear, harm or damage to oneself or others. Support for this can be found in Scheff's (1977) arguments of experiencing emotions and cathartic release from an "aesthetic distance." The ability to identify and distinguish the virtual, mediated or gaming world from the real is a necessity that provides a safe distance enabling users and players to gain experience and pleasure.

Many academics outside the presence community view the idea of presence and the sense of "being there" in an IME to be too contentious and believe the arguments surrounding this concept need to be re-examined. As indicated above, much work in presence has moved away from its original highly specialized focus of "being there" towards a wider arena as captured, for example, in Lombard and Ditton's (1997) definition of "perceptual illusion of non-mediation." Central to this concept is the idea of non-mediation, meaning a user fails to perceive the existence of supporting or mediating technology during an encounter and so experiences an illusion of a non-technologically mediated environment. Furthermore, feelings of being connected with other people in a mediated environment are said to provide feelings of *social* presence. While encapsulating a wider perspective on user experience, the term "perceptual" refers to "continuous (real time) responses of the human sensory, cognitive, and affective processing systems," restricting discussions to experience that occurs "instant by instant" (Lombard 2000). This makes it difficult, if not impossible, to describe unfolding events, episodes of a scenario, or the after-effects and consequences of a mediated encounter with IMEs within the boundaries imposed by definitions of presence (see for example discussions by Heeter 2000).

Previous Work on Vicarious and Empathic Experience

Research on empathy from numerous fields of study is beginning to attract increased attention. For example, work linking cognitive science and phenomenology identify empathy as one of the fundamental aspects of being and self awareness: "[o]ne's consciousness of oneself as an embodied individual in the world is founded on empathy — on one's empathic cognition with others, and other's empathic cognition of oneself" Thompson (2001:2). Increasing support can be found linking empathy to presence. For example, Sas and O'Hare (2003) looked for correlations between presence and empathy. Additionally, in "The Cyborg's Dilemma," Biocca (1997) highlights similar philosophies to those of Thompson (2001) by turning to Zillman (1991) to link embodiment to presence: "observers of the physical or mediated body read emotional states, intentions, and personality traits by an empathic simulation of them" (Biocca 1997).

Past work on empathy and its measures from psychology also inform my work, including Ickles (1993, 1997), Levenson and Ruef (1992), and Zhon, Valiente and Eisenberg (2003; see the last two for informed reviews). According to Levenson and Ruef (1992), empathy comes in three forms. "Cognitive empathy" is to know what someone is feeling, but does not automatically imply kindness. "Compassionate empathy" is responding kindly to someone, for example, by being comforting. "Emotional empathy" is to know what a person is feeling but also, to feel what that person is feeling. Empathy may be transferred through actions, stories/anecdotes or facial expressions, usually from one person to another person. The more one person feels what another is feeling, the higher the degree or accuracy of "emotional information being transmitted" (Levenson and Ruef 1992:234), an idea elsewhere referred to as "empathic accuracy" (Ickles 1993; 1997). These three types of empathy can be found within IMEs. However, because a player controls a character, I argue that they should be considered from a player's perspective. Therefore, slight differences to Levenson and Ruef's (1992) three types of empathy can be identified. For example, compassionate empathy can be demonstrated by player-characters responding kindly to other characters. Cognitive empathy can manifest itself through players knowing how other characters are feeling by observation or spectatorship, or through interacting with other characters. Emotional empathy is similar to cognitive empathy, but in addition to knowing how other characters are feeling, the players feel these emotions as their own.

The general idea of empathy in IMEs is further complicated by the extent to which a player perceives him/herself to be vicariously in character. So in addition, I argue that cognitive empathy in IMEs occurs when players recognize how their own character should feel in certain situations and emotional empathy occurs when players feel these emotions as their own. Moreover, other characters' behavior acknowledges a player-character's existence and may also reflect the empathy those characters have for that player-character.

In the next section I describe a matrix questionnaire I developed and a study I carried out to capture vicarious experience and empathic experience. I then discuss results from the study and briefly relate these results to cognitive and emotional empathy between the player and other characters.

Capturing Vicarious Experience and Empathic Experience

Although there are multiple way to measure empathy (Zhon, Valiente and Eisenberg 2003), I use a self-report, questionnaire-based approach, utilizing a vicarious empathic matrix.[3] The matrix questionnaire builds on the literature review provided by Levenson and Ruef (1992), in which they describe one approach developed for use during marriage guidance counseling sessions. The idea is an attempt to identify couples' relationship and communication difficulties. In it, one half of the couple (the listener) views a video recording of his or her spouse (the talker) and rates the spouse's (the talker's) feelings and emotions. The spouse (the talker) then views the video recording and rates what he or she believes to be his or her own feelings, moods and emotions expressed during the recording, that is, their feelings at the time when the video was shot. The correlation between the partners' ratings (i.e., between talker and listener) then provides an indication of the accuracy of the emotional information being transmitted between the talker and listener. The higher the correlation, the higher the "empathic accuracy" (see Ickles 1993; 1997).

In digital gaming environments however, it is not feasible to ask virtual characters about their own feelings to provide correlation data. One option would be to ask the designer or developer to rate the virtual characters' emotions, moods and traits. However, this is open to bias and inaccuracies as they could see or read things into their artistic creations that others don't. To overcome these drawbacks, I devised a method whereby players were asked to rate their virtual characters' emotions, moods and traits using the empathic matrix questionnaire. They were then asked to rate their own emotions, moods and traits using an identical copy of the aforementioned matrix questionnaire. The correlation between the matrices provides a measure of empathy between a player and his or her character. The higher the correlation between the two matrices, the greater the empathic accuracy. A weak correlation between the two may point to a weak attachment or lack of engagement between the player and player's character.

Table 1. Matrix Questionnaire Adjective Pairings
Used in the Role-playing Study

confident	scared
relaxed	tense
calm	angry
happy	sad
strong	weak
brave	cowardly
cheerful	serious
kind	evil
honest	dishonest

The matrix used in the study consists of nine adjective pairings (see Table 1). Pairings were obtained following observation of and interviews and preliminary studies with digital games players[4]. They were chosen so that a minimal number of pairings would be appropriate to as many game genres as possible. These were designed to illustrate the extent to which emotions, moods and personality traits could be induced in players. The matrix data was obtained by initially posing questions along the lines of: " ... in a moment I'm going to ask you for words to describe your character," then, for each adjective pairing: " ... would you say that your character [*player's identified character inserted here]* was" ..."confident" or "scared," etc. Questioning in this way continued until all emotions, moods or traits were rated. Next, players were asked to rate their own feelings while controlling their character using the second matrix. As mentioned, the correlation between this matrix and the matrix describing their characters' emotions, moods and traits provides a measure of empathy between the two. A number of pilot studies have been undertaken to test the matrix questionnaire-based approach[5].

Case Study: A Role-Playing and Storytelling Educational Digital Game

The study was carried out within a prototype (i.e., largely in an experimental or design phase) role-playing and storytelling environment in which players speak to each other via microphones and headphones. The environment was comprised of rich graphics, music and atmospheric sound effects, incorporated many characters including female, male and sorcerer (female), and was designed to appeal to children. The study was undertaken in a "natural" setting (i.e., school) where the mediated environment was used. The study attempted to answer the following research questions:

1. How effective is the matrix questionnaire at capturing players':
   a. emotions, moods and traits?
   b. empathy with their own character?
   c. empathy with other characters in the digital gaming environment?
2. How effective is the matrix questionnaire method in reasoning about players behaving appropriately in a social and cultural environment depicted virtually?

Data collection was carried out with as little disruption as possible to participants. That is, players were able to experience the mediated environment in its entirety without being prompted or interrupted for a response from me. During study sessions, I made observations and wrote research notes. Following each study session I read aloud and filled out each question of the vicarious matrix. The wording of adjective pairings was made suitable for children (see: Table 1) in an attempt to ensure that the players understood their meanings.

Method

Twenty-four nine to eleven year old school children (fourteen females, ten males) from several classes and grades volunteered to take part in the study. Within each role-playing session, two children were placed back-to-back facing their computer screens. Each student assumed the role

of one of two characters (i.e., female or male). The assignment of character was randomized by getting children to select objects (i.e., toy animals)
that determined which character (female or male) they were to play. Cor-
respondences between toys and characters were intermittently swapped.

Although players were given the impression of complete autonomy
to move around the gaming environment, the game was in fact directed
by a human operator (i.e., actress) responding to players' movements and
steering them in one direction. Hence, the game in this respect was more
akin to a linear rather than non-linear narrative structure. To drive the
game along, instructions and clues were interwoven into a story through
the actress playing the role of several characters, including the sorcerer.
The actress was separated from the children by a partition screen. This is
commonly referred to as the "Wizard of Oz" set-up. This arrangement
attempted to conceal the artificiality of the mediated environment and
give children the impression of autonomously responsive characters within
an automatically responsive environment.

At the beginning of each session, the two children were introduced
to their colleague's and their own characters. During a five to ten minute
practice session (depending on the children's ability, skill and prior experience), students familiarized themselves with keyboard and mouse operations and watched themselves move around as seen on their colleague's
display (from a third-person perspective) and through their own screens
(from a first-person perspective). During the study, children were encouraged to take a first-person perspective by viewing only their own screens.
Following each session, I read aloud the adjective pairings, providing an
opportunity for further explanations where necessary to ensure they all had
the same understanding of the meaning of each adjective pairing. I then
administered the matrix questionnaire and recorded their responses.

Results

Nineteen participants reported playing computer games between one
and five hours per week, four played six to ten hours and one reported not
playing computer games. Participants variously identified their preferred
computer games genres and these were categorized as: action/adventure, simulation, role-playing, point and click, and first-person shooter. While the
test environment's intended future use was educational, it incorporated so
many attractive features (e.g. rich graphics, sound, character interaction)
that the environment was referred to by the children as a role-playing "game."
In response to the question: "what was *your* character" in the game, all
identified their character as being the male or female without any difficulty.

The choice of toy that, unbeknown to the children, determined the sex of the character they would play, was evenly distributed between boys and girls.

Vicarious Matrix: Emotions, Moods and Traits

Players had no difficulty in providing responses for the vicarious matrix while controlling their characters during the game, and there was no apparent difference between ratings for players playing male characters and those playing female. All players rated themselves as feeling *kind* and *honest*. Eighty-three percent said they felt *brave* and the same for *strong*; 70.8% said they were *confident*. Some players said they couldn't choose between the two anchors *happy* and *sad* because they felt "a bit of both" at different points during the encounter. This suggests a limitation with both this adjective pairing and the method, and the need for a continuous assessment method, or more options in an attempt to capture variability.

Empathic Matrix

This was an attempt to match players' emotions and traits with their characters' and hence to provide a measure of the extent to which players adopted their characters' personas. Table 2 shows empathic matches for players with male, female and sorcerer. Players 1 to 12 assumed the role of male and players 13 to 24 the role of female. So for example, reading from left to right, player 1 who took the role of male had empathic accuracy with her or his character for eight out of nine paired adjectives; likewise eight with female and five with sorcerer. The empathic match for both male and female for all players was very similar, ranging between five (56%) and nine (100%). In contrast, the empathic match with sorcerer for all players was comparatively smaller, from one (11%) to six (67%).

Table 2. Empathic Accuracy of Role-playing Characters: Players 1-12 Played Male Characters, Players 13-24 Played Female Characters

Players	Male	Female	Sorcerer
1	8	8	5
2	7	7	4
3	9	9	6
4	8	9	2
5	9	8	6
6	7	7	5
7	6	6	5
8	8	9	2
9	6	4	1
10	6	5	3
11	5	5	2
12	9	8	4

Table 2. Empathic Accuracy of Role-playing Characters: Players 1-12
Played Male Characters, Players 13-24 Played Female Characters

Players	Male	Female	Sorcerer
13	7	7	5
14	9	9	5
15	7	9	6
16	8	7	2
17	7	6	3
18	9	8	2
19	7	6	4
20	9	7	3
21	5	7	4
22	6	7	6
23	7	7	6
24	9	6	1

Discussion

While there was little difference in empathic match between players' characters and their colleagues' characters, as expected, it was higher than empathic match with the sorcerer. So, while data demonstrates that the method can distinguish between protagonist and antagonist, it does not distinguish as well between player and colleague (i.e., protagonists). This may be because of the close proximity of player and colleague throughout the game, or a limitation in the method (i.e., matrix questionnaire). While every attempt was made to block out noise external to the game using headphones, sound or awareness of each other outside of the game may have contributed to the players' empathic-matched pairs. In this situation, players empathized with their colleagues outside the game, rather than with the characters in the game.

Through observation it was apparent that the game engendered excitement and emotions, demonstrated through utterances by most players, and players' focus of attention, which stayed on acting within the unfolding scenario of the role-playing game. This suggests that the game was stimulating for players and so encouraged them in "staying there," continuing to pursue their activities in the gaming environment. Using the matrix questionnaire, we see that no players had an empathic match that was under 50% with their own characters and only one had an empathic match under 50% with a colleague's character. Five players were 100% in agreement with their own characters and seven were 100% in agreement with their colleagues' characters. The high "empathic accuracy" as measured through the matrix questionnaire approach suggests that most players perceived themselves to be strongly connected to their own and their colleagues' characters. In other words, this suggests players had stimulating vicarious encounters; I have termed "vicariously there" to describe this sense of player engagement.

Conversely, using the matrix questionnaire, a lower "empathic accuracy" suggests players had a weaker sense of connection to their own and their colleagues' characters. In this situation, it could be argued that players were less likely to continuously maintain their focus of attention in the role-playing game, so their attention may have shifted from the gaming to the real world environment. Hence, there is the potential that players may fall out of character or "corpse" (Marsh 2003b). While future work requires refinements of the matrix questionnaire method described herein before it can provide an effective way to capture cognitive, emotional and compassionate empathy through interaction among characters, it is a step in this direction. Through analysis of the results we can reason that a high empathic match between a players and their colleagues suggests they know what their colleagues are feeling (i.e., cognitive empathy) and they feel what their colleagues are feeling (i.e., emotional empathy). The lower empathic match between players and the sorcerer might suggest they know what she is feeling but they do not feel what she is feeling.

Reasoning About Players' Behavior in the Social-Cultural Gaming Environment

Questionnaire responses provided an indication of whether players' behavior adhered to social and cultural constraints determined by the IME context. As shown in table 2, of the 24 players, no players had under 50% agreement or empathic match with their own characters and only one player ("9") had under 50% match with a colleague's character. Five players had 100% matches with their own characters and seven had 100% matches with their colleagues' characters. The high agreement or empathic match suggests that players' behavior adhered to constraints imposed by the social and cultural environment. Observation of players' behavior during study sessions was in keeping with the context (scene, setting and scenario) of the game. That is, players tended to restrict their behavior to what was considered appropriate and acceptable depending on the role-playing "group" in which they were participating. For example, players followed behavioral patterns in keeping with the eerie castle environment and scenario, and these were different than behaviors from studies of other digital game genres.

Problems with Questionnaire-Based Approach

This research was exploratory and certain limitations became evident during my analysis. One limitation of the matrix questionnaire is that the results may have been tainted by players providing socially desirable responses. For example, some children are less likely than others to admit to feeling *scared, weak or cowardly*. Another disadvantage was the limited set of questionnaire items that might not have accurately reflected some players' role-playing encounters within the empathic matrix. Future research should work towards identifying an appropriate number of items that can adequately capture empathic experiences. One approach could be to pursue a more inductive method whereby adjective pairings were obtained from players themselves in post study, open-ended interviews. Similarly, another approach and source for future work to overcome this limitation is George Kelly's (1955) Personal Construct Psychology. According to Kelly (1955), because we all have a different repertoire of constructs, it may be more appropriate to let respondents choose their own. I have already carried out some work in this direction and applied it to a study to capture children's experience of role-playing characters within a computer game. Constructs were elicited from the children by asking simple questions like "what words would you use to describe [insert character's name]" and then asking them for the opposites of the words that they had just provided. Using these as bipolars, children were asked to rate each character against each elicited construct while at the same time showing pictures of each character. This may go some way to overcoming children's difficulty of not understanding or misunderstanding some of the items and constructs in the questionnaire.

Probably the most serious limitation of the matrix questionnaire was its inability to detect variations in emotions, moods or experience between adjectives during the unfolding of a mediated encounter. Although continuous assessment methods such as sliders, dials and verbalizations get around this problem, they require players to divide their attention between the mediated experience and the data collection technique being used, thus disrupting what is being measured (i.e., experience). While facial analysis and physiological measures do not require the player to perform any additional operations, some work is still required in order to employ these techniques to accurately measure a range of player experiences. Valuable directions for future work would be to develop these and other continuous techniques. While it could be argued that study subject numbers were small, the results of the questionnaire matrix did provide a way to reason about the extent to which participants empathize or take-on emotions and traits of their character and other characters. Finally, supplementing this quantitative approach with qualitative data may provide a way to better relate what players feel from an encounter with a digital game to cognitive, compassionate and emotional empathy (Levenson and Ruef 1992).

Conclusion

While much interaction in digital games is performed with and through character, there are limitations in theories and methodologies for their analysis and design from the subject areas of human-computer interaction (HCI) and the experiential concept of presence. Building on previous work (Marsh 2002), this chapter has described research that looks to activity theory, social cultural studies and film in an effort to bridge this gap. To this aim, I have proposed a way to capture and reason about the extent to which a player perceives him/herself to be vicariously in character, is able to empathize with other characters-players, and has a sense of being connected to a fantasy or simulated social and cultural mediated environment. The term coined herein to describe this sense of player engagement with character(s) and a digital game/mediated environment is "vicariously there." Results of the study presented here show that using a questionnaire-based matrix approach provides one way to capture and reason about the extent to which players empathize or take on emotions and traits of their character and other characters. Future research should continue to work towards validating player sense of engagement through the idea of "vicariously there" by linking empathy-match ratings and a desire to play the game or pursue activities. In addition, work should identify what causes players to fall out of character, or "to corpse," and shift their focus of attention to the real-world environment. Limitations of a questionnaire-based approach have been identified and recommendations have been made for future work. In particular, a continuous and unobtrusive assessment technique has been argued for to detect variations in players' emotions, moods or experience during an encounter.

Digital games provide the potential for players to assume the role of anyone or anything they choose. Studying the vicarious and empathic connection between players and their own and others' characters is an important step towards understanding and in turn informing the creation or development of more complex characters. The development of more complex characters can help to stimulate players, encouraging them to keep playing and so continue to be "vicariously there."

References

Biocca, F. 1997. "The Cyborg's Dilemma: Progressive Embodiment in Virtual Environments." *Electronic Journal of Computer Mediated Communication,* 3:2. Retrieved February 17, 2005 *(http://www.ascusc.org/jcmc/vol3/issue2/biocca2.html)*

Boorstin, J. 1995. *Making Movies Work: Thinking Like a Filmmaker.* Beverley Hills, CA: Silman-James Press.

Bostrom, N. 2003. "Are You Living in a Computer Simulation?" *Philosophical Quarterly*, 53, 211: 243–255.

Brna, P. 1999. "Collaborative Virtual Learning Environments for Concept Learning." *International Journal of Continuing Engineering Education and Life-Long Learning* 9,3/4:315–327.

Engeström, Y. 1999. "Activity Theory and Individual and Social Transformation." pp. 19–38 in *Perspectives on Activity Theory-Learning in Doing Social, Cognitive and Computational Perspectives, Part 1: Theoretical Issues*, edited by Y. Engeström, R. Miettinen, and P. Punamäki. Cambridge, UK: Cambridge University Press.

Heeter, C. 2000. "Interactivity in the Context of Designed Experiences." *Electronic Journal of* Interactive Advertising, Volume 1, Number 1. Retrieved February 17, 2005 (*http://jiad.org/vol1/no1/heeter/*).

Ickles, W. 1993. "Empathic Accuracy." *Journal of Personality* 61: 587–610.

_____. 1997. *Empathic Accuracy.* editor. New York: Guilford Press.

Kelly, G. 1955. *Principles of Personal Construct Psychology.* New York: Norton.

Laurel B. 1986. "Interfaces as Mimesis." pp. 67–85. in *User Centered System Design: New Perspectives on Human-Computer Interaction*, edited by D. A. Norman and S. W. Draper. Hillsdale, NJ: Lawrence Erlbaum Associates.

_____. 1993. *Computers as Theatre.* Second Edition. Reading, MA: Addison-Wesley.

_____, R. Strickland. and R. Tow. 1994. "Placeholder: Landscape and Narrative in Virtual Environments." ACM SIGGRAPH *Computer Graphics* 28, 2:118–126. Levenson, R.W. and A.M. Ruef. 1992. "Empathy: A Physiological Substrate." American Psychological Association Inc., *Journal of Personality and Social Psychology* 63, 2: 234–246.

Licklider, J.C.R. 1960. "Man-Computer Symbiosis." IRE (now IEEE) *Transactions on Human Factors in Electronics* HFE-1: 4–11.

Lombard, M. 2000. "The Concept of Presence: Explication Statement." Retrieved March 27, 2005. (*http://www.temple.edu/ispr/frame_explicat.htm*).

_____, and T. Ditton. 1997. "At the Heart of It All: The Concept of Presence." *Electronic Journal of Computer-Mediated Communication* 3, 2. Retrieved February 17, 2005. (*http://www.ascusc.org/jcmc/vol3/issue2/lombard.html*).

Marsh,T. 2001. "Presence as Experience: Framework to Assess Virtual Corpsing." paper presentation at *Presence 2001: 4th International Workshop on Presence*, Temple University, Philadelphia, PA.

_____. 2002. "Towards Invisible Style of Computer-Mediated Activity: Transparency and Continuity." PhD. dissertation, Department of Computer Science, University of York, UK.

_____. 2003a. "Presence as Experience: Film Informing Ways of Staying There." *Presence: Teleoperators and Virtual Environments* 12,5:538–549.

_____. 2003b. "Staying There: An Activity-based Approach to Narrative Design and Evaluation as an Antidote to Virtual Corpsing." pp. 85–96 in *Being There: Concepts, Effects and Measurements of User Presence in Synthetic Environments*, edited by G. Riva, F. Davide and W. A. IJsselsteijn. Amsterdam, The Netherlands: IOS Press.

_____, and P. Wright. 2000. "Using Cinematography Conventions to Inform the Design and Evaluation of Virtual Off-Screen Space." pp. 123–127 in *AAAI 2000 Spring Symposium: Smart Graphics*, Stanford University, CA: AAAI Press.

McCarthy, J.C. and P.C. Wright. 2004. *Technology as Experience.* MIT Press.

Merriam-Webster's on-line. Retrieved February 17, 2005 (*http://www.m-w.com/dictionary.htm*).

Norman, D.A. 1988. *"The Psychology of Everyday Things."* New York: Basic Books, Inc.

_____. 1999. "Affordances, Conventions and Design." *ACM Interactions Magazine*, May/June, pp. 38–42.

_____. 2004. *Emotional Design: Why We Love (or Hate) Everyday Things.* New York: Basic Books.

Nozick, R. 1974. *Anarchy, State and Utopia.* New York: Basic Books.

The Oxford English Dictionary. 1989. Second Edition. edited by J. A. Simpson and E. S. C. Weiner. Oxford, UK: Clarendon Press.

Pausch, R., J. Snoddy, R. Taylor, S. Watson and E. Haseltine. 1998. "Disney's Aladdin: First Steps Toward Storytelling in Virtual Reality." pp. 357–372 in *Digital Illusion: Entertaining the Future with High Technology,* edited by C. Dodsworth, Jr. London, UK: Addison-Wesley.

Phillips, P. 2000. *Understanding Film Texts: Meaning and Experience.* London, UK: BFI Publishing.

Poortinga, Y. 1992. "Towards a Conceptualization of Culture for Psychology." pp. 3–17 in *Innovations in Cross-Cultural Psychology,* edited by S. Iwawaki, Y. Kashima, and K. Leung. Amsterdam, The Netherlands: Swets & Zeitlinger.

Sas, C. and G.M.P. O'Hare. 2003. "Presence Equation: An Investigation into Cognitive factors Underlying Presence." *Presence: Teleoperators and Virtual Environments* 12,5:523–537.

Scheff, T.J. 1977. "The Distancing of Emotion in Ritual." *Current Anthropology* 18,3:483–505.

Sheridan, T.B. 1992. "Musings on Telepresence and Virtual Presence." *Presence: Teleoperators and Virtual Environments* 1,1:120–126.

Steuer, J. 1995. "Defining Virtual Reality: Dimensions Determining Telepresence." pp.33–56 in *Communication in the Age of Virtual Reality,* edited by F. Biocca and M.R. Levy. Hillsdale, NJ: Lawrence Erlbaum Associates.

Thompson, E., ed. 2001. "Empathy and Consciousness." in *Between Ourselves: Second-person Issues in the Study of Consciousness.* Charlottesville, VA: Imprint Academic.

Wachowski, Andy and Larry Wachowski. 1999. *The Matrix.* Warner Brothers.

_____. 2003. *The Matrix Reloaded.* Warner Brothers.

_____. 2003. *The Matrix Revolutions.* Warner Brothers.

Whitelock, D., P. Brna, and S. Holland. 1996. "What Is the Value of Virtual Reality for Conceptual Learning? Towards a Theoretical Framework." pp. 136–141 in *Proceedings of the European Conference on Artificial Intelligence in Education.* Lisbon, Portugal: Edicoes Colibri.

Zhon, Q., C. Valiente and N. Eisenberg. 2003. "Empathy and Its Measurement." pp. 269–284 in *Positive Psychological Assessment: A Handbook of Models and Measures,* edited by S. J. Lopez and C. R. Snyder. Washington DC: American Psychological Association.

Zillman, D. 1991. "Empathy: Affect from Bearing Witness to the Emotions of Others." pp. 135–169 in *Responding to the Screen: Reception and Reaction Processes,* edited by J. Bryant, & D. Zillman. Hillsdale, NJ: Lawrence Erlbaum.

Notes

1. *The Oxford English Dictionary* (1989) defines vicarious as: "1a. That takes or supplies the place of another thing or person; substituted instead of the proper thing or person." "4d. Experienced imaginatively through another person or agency." Merriam-Webster's on-line defines vicarious as: "1a: serving instead of someone or something else." "3: experienced or realized through imaginative or sympathetic participation in the experience of another."

2. These discussions share similar arguments with those on affordances borrowed from J. J. Gibson and introduced to HCI by Norman (1988). "The affordances of an object refers to its possible functions: A chair affords support, whether for standing, sitting, or the placement of objects. A pencil affords lifting, grasping, turning, poking, supporting, tapping, and of course, writing" (Norman 1993:105-106). While Norman (1999) acknowledges limitations of earlier discus-

sions (contained in: Norman 1988) that may have lead to some misunderstandings (e.g. arguing that what he was really talking about was "perceived affordances" as opposed to "real" or physical affordances), he adds that the HCI community enthusiastically took-up the idea of affordances (Norman 1999:39) while generally disregarding related concepts of constraints and culture (see: Norman 1988). He asserts that much discussion in HCI on affordances is really about conventions and behavioral constraints, i.e. "physical" (Norman 1988:84), "logical" (p. 86) and "cultural" (p. 85), and the latter two in particular, are shaped by their "shared" practice that "inhibits some activities and encourages others" (Norman 1999:41). However, Norman's (1988; 1999) discussions on concepts of constraints and culture are very brief and need developing if they are to be useful to inform interface analysis and design. Research that has applied activity theory to interactive mediated environments (IME: computer games, virtual reality, virtual environments) (Marsh 2003b) is now being combined with the notion of constraints in an attempt to work towards informing analysis to reason about appropriate artifact behavior defined by the social cultural environment depicted virtually.

3. The four ways identified by Zhon, Valiente and Eisenberg (2003) to measure empathy are firstly, self-report using questionnaires or picture-stories, secondly, other-report from teachers, parents or peers, thirdly, coding of individuals' facial, gestural and vocal indices, and fourthly, physiological measures such as heart rate and skin conductance.

4. Adjective pairings for the matrix were initially derived from investigation of digital games reviews and magazines, interviews with a games design manager and interviews with players in arcades and a on a University campus to identify the language and descriptions. In addition, an investigation of empirical studies, questionnaires and related published work on presence and experiential design and evaluation from the HCI literature applied to interactive mediated environments was conducted. Several amendments to the matrix were made following pilot studies, for example, the study as described in footnote 5.

5. One pilot study was conducted at a computer games club with eight male computer games members (aged thirteen to twenty-two) using a first-person perspective shooter game played on networked desktop computers. All were very experienced games players who spent around seven to twenty-eight hours per week (14.5 mean) playing games. When asked "what character did you control?" and "who were you in the game?" all participants immediately responded "I was a: "terrorist," "counter-terrorist" or "British SAS [Special Air Service]." Eight adjective parings were used for the matrix questionnaire. This earlier version of the matrix was made appropriate for this genre and for young male teenagers and adults, and had slight variations to those listed in table 1.

Following game play, players frankly identified their objectives in the game as: "kill people," "shoot opponents" and "kill other team." Players had no difficulty identifying their own and their characters' emotions, moods and traits except for the anchors "happy"-"sad" in which four players were unsure or didn't feel that it was appropriate to select only one because they or their characters felt both happy and sad, but at different points in the unfolding scenario. Empathic matches between players' emotions, mood and traits and the ratings for their characters varied with only one having an agreement (i.e., empathic match) below 50% and one with 100%. It seemed irrational that players with offensive roles and characters with defensive roles or vise versa would have empathy for each other and so no attempt was made to provide a rating for empathic match between them. In general, the responses suggested that players adhered to the social and cultural context of the game and observation of players' behavior during their encounter seemed to concur with this.

ABOUT THE CONTRIBUTORS

Florence Chee

Florence Chee is a researcher at the Centre for Policy Research on Science and Technology (CPROST) in Vancouver, Canada. She has investigated issues concerning technology and society, such as online fan culture, technological adoption, and mobility as a factor of social change. Completing her M.A in the School of Communication at Simon Fraser University, her thesis research concentrates on ethnographic investigations of the compelling nature of online game communities and cultural perceptions of addiction. She has conducted fieldwork online, offline, and in-between, with correspondingly exotic locations as Norrath, South Korea, and PC game rooms worldwide. Contact: *fchee@shaw.ca*.

Sean Q. Hendricks

Sean Q. Hendricks has been a role-playing gamer for almost 20 years, playing games that range from *Dungeon & Dragons* to *Champions* to *Star Wars*, among others, and he is still active in the gaming community. Dr. Hendricks received his Ph.D. from the University of Arizona in 1999 in the field of linguistics, and has pursued a career in linguistic anthropology and digital technologies. Currently, Dr. Hendricks is a lecturer and research consultant at the University of Georgia at Athens, where he has been for the past four years. He has recently recognized the richness of gaming culture as a site for social and behavioral research, and his paper, "Negotiation of Expertise in Fantasy Role-Playing Gaming," appeared in the proceedings of the eleventh meeting of the Symposium About Language and Society — Austin (SALSA). Contact: *shendric@uga.edu*.

Tim Marsh

Tim Marsh is a Post-Doctoral Research Associate in the Integrated Media Systems Center (IMSC) at the University of Southern California. He received his Ph.D. degree in Computer Science from the Human-Computer Interaction (HCI) Group at the University of York, UK. He has MSc. and BSc. degrees in Computer Graphics and Visualization, and Information Technology respectively. Dr. Marsh's current research interests are in experiential (learning, engaging, emotive and entertaining) design and evaluation of visually mediated environments, including digital games, virtual reality and other virtual environments. Contact: *marsh@imsc.usc. edu.*

Heather L. Mello

Heather Mello holds an A.A. in Intelligence Collection from the Community College of the Air Force, a B.S. in Vietnamese and Russian languages from SUNY Albany and an M.A. in Sociology from Georgia Southern University. She currently teaches sociology in an adjunct capacity at several Pennsylvania universities. Her academic interests include social inequality and sociolinguistics. She was introduced to the world of role-play gaming in ninth grade study hall, quickly falling in with the game's ability to overwhelm reality even with the smell of cafeteria food permeating the dungeon. Heather has gamed in many capacities, including: dramatic and combative role-play; magic-using, thief and fighter characters; and as DM's girlfriend. Contact: *anais67@excite.com.*

Michelle Nephew

Michelle Nephew brings to this project a personal interest in role-playing as an enthusiastic participant in the hobby, an academic background in cultural and literary studies, and years of professional experience in the adventure games industry. Her Ph.D. dissertation, from which her chapter is derived, dealt primarily with authorship as it relates to role-playing games and was informed by her behind-the-scenes perspective as production coordinator and lead developer/editor for Atlas Games, an established publishing company specializing in adventure games. She has been involved with every part of the publication of dozens of RPG sourcebooks, served as a panelist for seminars at both GenCon and at the Game Manufacturer's Association Trade Show, contributed material to several RPG sourcebooks, authored a published d20 System adventure, and met many of the designers who have steered the course of role-playing over the past 30 years. Contact: *michelle@atlas-games.com.*

Kevin Schut

Kevin Schut received his Ph.D. from the University of Iowa in Communication Studies and is currently Assistant Professor of Media Communication in the Department of Communications at Trinity Western University in Langley, British Columbia, Canada. His doctoral thesis was a textual analysis investigating the technology, communication and culture of fantasy role-playing computer games. His research interests include the digital game industry, masculinity and games, textual criticism of games, and religion and games. When he is not researching computer games, he's likely playing them. Contact: *Kevin.Schut@twu.ca.*

Richard Smith

Richard Smith is an Associate Professor in, and the Associate Director of, the School of Communication at Simon Fraser University. He is also a member of the Centre for Policy Research on Science and Technology (CPROST) at SFU. Smith's research focus is new media — as a technology, as a business, and as a factor in and outcome of social change. He has an ongoing interest in online games, new technology for education, privacy and surveillance in public spaces, online communities, and the wireless information society.

Marcelo Vieta

Marcelo Vieta is a Ph.D. candidate in Social and Political Thought at York University in Toronto, Canada. Vieta's work looks into the phenomenological underpinnings of internet-mediated communication (IMC); democracy and technology; and the interplay between our technological condition, notions of subjectivity, and everyday life.

Dennis D. Waskul

Dennis D. Waskul is an assistant professor of sociology at Minnesota State University — Mankato. He is author of *Self-Games and Body Play:Personhood in Online Chat and Cybersex* (Peter Lang, 2003) and editor of *Net.SeXXX: Readings on Sex, Pornography, and the Internet* (Peter Lang 2004). He has published numerous articles in various journals on subjects relating to the internet, sociology of the body, and intersections between fantasy, imagination, and reality. Contact: *dwaskul@hotmail.com.*

Csilla Weninger

Csilla Weninger is a Ph.D Candidate in Linguistics at the University of Georgia. Her main concentration is in the area of Sociolinguistics, with diverse research interests in the relationship between language and the social world. She has done research on code choice among multilingual speakers and explored the relationship among discourse, ideology and academia. Her dissertation research focuses on the role of discourse, particularly of interdiscursivity and recontextualization, in shaping urban spaces. Contact: *weninger@uga.edu*.

J. Patrick Williams

J. Patrick Williams has been playing fantasy games since middle-school, with some of his favorites being *Dungeons & Dragons*, *Magic: The Gathering*, *Diablo 2*, and *Mage Knight*. He received his Ph.D. in Sociology from the University of Tennessee, where he specialized in social psychology and cultural studies, and is a Post-Doctoral Fellow in Sociology at the University of Georgia. He has published empirical research addressing various aspects of (sub)culture, identity and community in various professional journals. His substantive interests focus on youth subcultures, internet cultures and gaming cultures, and the study of identity. Contact: *subcultures@gmail.com*.

W. Keith Winkler

W. Keith Winkler holds a B.A. in English and Anthropology from Emory University (1994), an M.B.A. in International Business from Georgia State University (1999), and is currently working on his M.A. in Linguistics at The University of Georgia. He was introduced to *Dungeons & Dragons* in 1979 and has been a gamer ever since. He remained an avid role-playing gamer throughout high school and college. While still an undergraduate at Emory University, he secured a summer internship at White Wolf Game Studio. He continued working at White Wolf part-time until completion of his B.A., and was subsequently hired to full-time employment in a marketing capacity. He left White Wolf to pursue his M.B.A., noting that formal business training was in short supply in the industry. While earning his business degree, he continued to freelance with various industry manufacturers and does so even to this day, mostly in the areas of marketing, business development and convention support. His clients, friends, and colleagues include White Wolf, Inc., Holistic Design, Inc., and Atomoton, Inc. Contact: *keith.winkler@gmail.com*.

INDEX